THE QUEST FOR SHAKESPEARE

JOSEPH PEARCE

THE QUEST
FOR
SHAKESPEARE

IGNATIUS PRESS   SAN FRANCISCO

Cover art:
Nicholas Hilliard, *Man Holding a Hand from a Cloud* (miniature)—possibly
William Shakespeare, 1588. Victoria and Albert Museum, London

Photo Credit:
Victoria & Albert Museum, London / Art Resource, N.Y.

Cover design by John Herreid

© 2008 Ignatius Press, San Francisco
All rights reserved
ISBN 978-1-58617-224-4
Library of Congress Control Number 2007928877
Printed in the United States of America ∞

For
Albert Arthur Pearce
1930–2005
The Last of England

CONTENTS

PREFACE

The quest pursued in the following pages is designed to show objectively who Shakespeare was, and what his deepest beliefs were. We will be dealing solely with the facts, and I ask the reader to expect that all suppositions be founded upon, be subject to, and be judged from the perspective of the facts presented. If, in any of the proceeding pages, this is not the case, I will consider myself to blame for a failure in scholarship. I will add, however, that the following work also represents a quest in the subjective as well as in the objective sense. It has been, for the author, a true enlightenment. I began as a skeptic, doubting that there was sufficient biographical evidence to know who Shakespeare was, or what he believed, excepting of course what could be adduced from his work. I was particularly skeptical of those who claimed that Shakespeare was a Catholic, dismissing the arguments of those Catholics who made such claims as mere wishful thinking. I was convinced that the only honest position was one of agnosticism because not enough was known about England's greatest poet to come to any definitive conclusions. Such was my position.

It was only slowly that I came to realize that much more was known about Shakespeare than most of us have been led to believe. One fact followed upon another until a point was reached where I decided to embark upon some serious research myself. Doing so, I became convinced that Shakespeare was indeed a Catholic, at a time when Catholics were subject to a great deal of ruthless persecution, and that this fact has radical consequences with regard to the study of his works.

In chapter 1, and in greater depth in appendix A, I have alluded to, or sketched, what might be termed a philosophy of the creative process that is needed to read Shakespeare or indeed any text objectively. It is rightly called a philosophy as opposed to a literary theory because the *ratio* underpinning it is not a theory but a demonstrable truth. I have not succumbed to the radical relativism, in its various theoretical guises, that has possessed the study of literature in the Academy, but have insisted that literary criticism is a discipline, as opposed to an "art", which needs to subject itself to the objective authority of the Author. I have not denied nor belittled the transcendent nature of creativity, though I insist that such transcendence is itself inseparable from, and incarnated in, the personhood of the author and needs to be seen as such. This authorialism, for want of a better label, is necessary for the restoration of sanity in the field of Shakespeare studies and in the wider field of literary criticism itself. Needless to say, I have not been able to elucidate this philosophy at any great length within the confines of this particular study, but intend to return to it at greater length when time and opportunity permit. In the interim, I trust and believe that I have demonstrated the philosophy adequately for the purposes of this work.

I am also painfully aware that the quest is not yet completed.

Although this work assembles the considerable body of biographical and historical evidence that points to Shakespeare's Catholicism, the quest will not be completed successfully until the considerable body of textual evidence for his Catholicism is assembled also. This is a much larger undertaking, since it will necessitate a close reading of the plays and poems, in the light of his known Catholicism. It was, however, necessary to complete the biographical and historical aspects of the quest first. If, instead, we had begun with the text, presuming Shakespeare's Catholicism, we could be accused, justifiably, of reading into the works what we want to see. Establishing Shakespeare's *bona fides* enables the scholar to establish his own *bona fides*, rooted in indisputable fact, and thereby allows him to avoid the pitfalls of relativism into which most Shakespeare criticism has fallen.

I hope to embark on the second part of the quest myself in the near future, writing another book examining the textual evidence for the Bard's Catholicism that can be found in the plays and poems. As a foretaste of this later study, I have included an essay on *King Lear* (appendix B) that shows how our knowledge of the playwright's religious faith and philosophy permits us to read the plays through the eyes of the playwright himself. Reading the plays through Shakespeare's eyes is not merely enlightening, but is an adventure in the presence of genius. The second part of the quest promises to be even more thrilling than the first!

ACKNOWLEDGMENTS

I am deeply indebted to many friends and colleagues for their assistance in manifold ways during the research and writing of this volume. Henry Russell, R. A. Benthall, Aaron Urbanczsyk, Andrew Moran, Travis Curtwright, Peter Milward, S.J., Michael Sugrue, and R. V. Young all offered their help, as did my friends, Al Kresta and Marcus Grodi, both of whom lent me rare tomes from their personal libraries to aid me in my research. Peter Kreeft and Thomas Howard offered me invaluable practical support, and I have no doubt that this volume would have been considerably weaker had it not benefited from their inestimable advice. I am indebted indeed!

Members of the library staff at Ave Maria University have tirelessly buttressed my labors, and I must thank the powers-that-be at Ave Maria University for facilitating the writing of this book. Father Joseph Fessio and his colleagues at Ignatius Press continue to support my work, and I remain grateful for all that they have done and are doing to promote my books. I'm also grateful for the editors at Ediciones Palabra in Spain for their own efforts to make this and others of my work available to the Spanish-speaking world.

It would be somewhat remiss of me to fail to acknowledge the scholarly pioneers who have laid the path along which the present study has trod. As such, I doff my cap in the direction of my illustrious forebears while refraining from listing them by name here. Suffice to say that a perusal of the bibliography at the end of this volume will identify those scholars upon whose shoulders I have stood in order to gain the perspective contained herein.

My wife, Susannah, has read every chapter, as it has been written, and I am grateful for her sagacity and for her efforts, not always successful, to curb the acerbic excesses of my pen. She has sought to steer my robust Muse in the direction of Chestertonian charity and away from Bellocian bellicosity but oft times in vain. And though, indeed, I make no apology for my robust approach, if I have sinned in these pages against charity it will not be the fault of my greatest and dearest critic.

The ultimate acknowledgment belongs to my father, Albert Arthur Pearce, who introduced me to Shakespeare when I was only knee-high and who could recite, by heart, whole soliloquies from the plays. There can have been few greater admirers of England's greatest poet than was my father, and, since his enthusiasm was contagious, I have him to thank for my own passion for the Bard. Of all my books, and he read them all with paternal loyalty, none filled my father with as much excited expectancy as my promised book on Shakespeare. Alas, the promise was not fulfilled before his death but is offered to him posthumously in gratitude for the abundant gifts he has bestowed upon me, not least of which is my love of good literature. It is, therefore, to Albert Arthur Pearce that this book is dedicated.

PROLOGUE
SHAKESPEARE: AN INTRODUCTORY NOTE

Shakespeare is perhaps the greatest writer who ever lived. He is certainly one of only three writers to whom such a claim can be made with any real credibility. The others are Homer and Dante. Taken together, this literary trinity straddles the centuries from pagan antiquity to the present day. Homer looms large over the pagan world, overshadowing his illustrious disciple and imitator, Virgil; Dante towers to the heights of Christendom, the literary fruit of the philosophy and theology of his mentor, St. Thomas Aquinas; and Shakespeare strides like a colossus across the modern age, surpassing all others and surprising each new generation with the wisdom that emerges from his work.

In the following pages we will embark upon the quest for Shakespeare, seeking to make his words flesh by adding factual flesh to the bare bones of his life. It might be helpful, however, to begin with the bare bones. Let's look at the basic facts of Shakespeare's life, those documented events that are beyond dispute and are accepted by all Shakespeare scholars, in order to lay the foundations upon which the rest of what follows will be built. When we have done so, we will be better able to fill in the gaps and to get to know the real Shakespeare, who is the object of our quest.

William Shakespeare was born in April 1664 in Stratford-upon-Avon in the English county of Warwickshire, during the reign of Queen Elizabeth I. His family was relatively wealthy, owning a good deal of land in the local area, and his father was, at the time of William's birth, Chamberlain of the Stratford Corporation. It is likely that he was educated at the local grammar school, probably beginning in 1571 and ending in 1579 or thereabouts. Little is known of Shakespeare's whereabouts from 1579 until his marriage to Anne Hathaway in 1582, and it has been conjectured that this was a period in which he served as a tutor to a wealthy Catholic family in the north of England. Shakespeare's first child, Susanna, was born in 1583, and his twins, Hamnet and Judith, in 1585. The Shakespeares would have no further children, and it seems that Shakespeare left Stratford for London soon after the birth of the twins. The reason for Shakespeare's sudden departure, and the nature of his marriage to Anne, continue to excite the discussion and debate of Shakespeare scholars. It is known, however, that he kept in touch with his family, returning to Stratford regularly, and that he continued to provide financially for their needs.

The period between Shakespeare's departure from Stratford-upon-Avon in the mid-1580s until the time he reemerges as a rising playwright in the early 1590s has become known as the "lost years", because so little is known of his actions or his whereabouts during this time. From the early 1590s onwards, however, he became the most popular and most respected playwright in England, writing more than thirty plays before his retirement twenty or so years later.

Shakespeare spent the last years of his life in his hometown of Stratford, reunited with his wife and family. He died on St. George's Day in 1616 and is buried in the chancel of the local Holy Trinity church.

These, then, are the bare bones. What follows will bring the bones to life and will introduce us to the real William Shakespeare.

I

WILL THE REAL SHAKESPEARE PLEASE STAND UP?

Time shall unfold what plighted cunning hides.

—Cordelia (*King Lear*, 1.1.282)

The quest for the real William Shakespeare is akin to a detective story in which the Shakespearian biographer is cast in the role of a literary sleuth, pursuing his quarry like a latter-day Sherlock Holmes. In fact, since the object of the chase is not to elicit the confession of a crime but the confession of a creed, it could be said that Chesterton's clerical detective, Father Brown, might be better suited to the task than Conan Doyle's coldly logical Holmes. Chesterton certainly believed that the evidence pointed toward Shakespeare's Catholicism, stating that the "convergent common sense" that led to the belief that the Bard was a Catholic was "supported by the few external and political facts we know".[1] One presumes from this assertion that Chesterton was familiar with Henry Sebastian Bowden's *The Religion of Shakespeare*, published in 1899, in which Father Bowden assembled the considerable historical and textual evidence for Shakespeare's Catholicism that had been gathered by the Shakespearian scholar Richard Simpson.

Throughout the twentieth century a good deal of solid historical detective work was done, adding significantly to the "few external and political facts" known by Simpson and Chesterton. In consequence, the claims made by Carol Curt Enos in *Shakespeare and the Catholic Religion*, published almost exactly a century after Bowden's volume, were more self-confidently emphatic: "When many of the extant pieces of the puzzle of Shakespeare's life are assembled, it is very difficult to deny his

---

[1] G. K. Chesterton, *Chaucer* (1932); republished in *G. K. Chesterton: The Collected Works*, vol. 18 (San Francisco: Ignatius Press, 1991), p. 333.

Catholicism." [2] Every piece of the puzzle, placed painstakingly where it belongs, brings us closer to an objectively verifiable picture. As more and more of the facts of Shakespeare's life and times emerge from the fogs of history (to switch metaphors), the more clearly are those fogs lifted and the more clearly does Shakespeare emerge from the centuries-laden gloom that has surrounded him.

Even as the solid work of historians brings the real Shakespeare to life, the vultures of literary criticism continue to pick over the bones of the corpse of their unreal Shakespearian chimera. It is for this reason that Anthony Holden, on the opening page of his biography of Shakespeare, complained that "the long-suffering son of Stratford is ... being picked apart by historicists, feminists, Marxists, new historicists, post-feminists, deconstructionists, anti-deconstructionists, post-modernists, cultural imperialists and post-colonialists". "Perhaps," Holden added, "it is time someone tried putting him back together again." [3]

Whereas the imagery of carrion-critics picking over the bones of a corpse, killed by the poison of their theories, is a powerful one, the implicit allusion to "putting Humpty together again" is less so. Unlike Humpty Dumpty, Shakespeare has never had a great fall and, therefore, unlike Humpty, does not need putting together. It is not Shakespeare who has fallen. He is as he always was. It is all the king's men who have had the fall, and it is they who cannot be put together again. The historicists, new historicists, feminists, postfeminists, deconstructionists, et cetera ad nauseam, are lying broken at the feet of the unbroken Shakespeare, picking over the pieces of their own theories, arguing over the meaning of the monsters of their own monstrous musings, missing the point and impaling themselves on the point of their own pointlessness. This is where we shall leave them, arguing amongst themselves, whilst we begin to look at the real William Shakespeare.

Though Shakespeare is real, he is also elusive, defying our efforts to define him. Try as we might to pin him down, he always seems to get away. We don't even know for certain what he looked like. The various paintings claiming to be portraits of him are most probably of someone else. The painting that seems to have the greatest claim to authenticity,

[2] Carol Curt Enos, *Shakespeare and the Catholic Religion* (Pittsburgh: Dorrance Publishing, 2000), p. 45.

[3] Anthony Holden, *William Shakespeare: The Man Behind the Genius* (Boston: Little, Brown, 1999), p. 1.

the famous Chandos portrait, looks at us with the enigmatic suggestiveness of the Mona Lisa. As with Leonardo's famous portrait, the Chandos Shakespeare seduces us with its aura of mystery, its unanswered questions. Who is this man who looks at us knowingly from the canvas? What secrets does he conceal? The questions are asked, but there's no hint of an answer. Its eyes meet ours, teasing us with evasive promptings of we know not what. It remains silent, keeping its secret.

"We ask and ask: Thou smilest and art still, / Out-topping knowledge." Thus wrote Matthew Arnold in his sonnet to Shakespeare. Today, almost four hundred years after Shakespeare's death and more than a century after Arnold's sonnet, we are still asking. We ask and ask and are still met with the same beguiling silence, the same suggestion of a smile. Perhaps, on one level at least, this is as it should be. On the level of metaphor, the Chandos portrait serves as a representation of Shakespeare himself. The man who looks at us knowingly from the canvas is the man who looks at us knowingly through the plays. He knows us, even if we don't know him. He shows us to ourselves, even if he conceals himself while he does so. As with the picture of Dorian Gray, the portrait is a mirror. And if the mirror shows us ourselves does it really matter that we can't see the mysterious man who is holding it? This seems to have been the question on Matthew Arnold's mind when he composed his sonnet and, as the conclusion of the sonnet testifies, the great Victorian believed that the identity of his elusive Elizabethan forebear was not particularly important.

> And thou, who didst the stars and sunbeams know,
> Self-school'd, self-scanned, self-honour'd, self-secure,
> Didst walk on earth unguess'd at. Better so!
> All pains the immortal spirit must endure,
>   All weakness that impairs, all griefs that bow,
>   Find their sole voice in that victorious brow.

Arnold appears to be saying that since Shakespeare shows us ourselves so well, it doesn't really matter that he fails to show us himself. There is, however, a serious problem with such a conclusion, a problem that is so serious that it amounts to a fatal flaw in the reading of Shakespeare's works and a consequent blindness to the truths that emerge from them. It is this. What if the image of ourselves that we see in the mirror is distorted by our lack of knowledge of the one who holds the mirror? What if our understanding of Shakespeare is essential to our understanding of ourselves as reflected by Shakespeare? What if we misunderstand and misconstrue what he is showing us if we misunderstand and misconstrue what he *means* to show us? What if Shakespeare is not simply holding the mirror? What if he *is* the mirror? What if the plays are, in some mystical or immanent way, an artistic incarnation of the playwright? What if the words only become flesh if we understand the personhood and philosophy of the flesh that gave birth to the words?

Pace Matthew Arnold, it is clear that knowing Shakespeare increases our knowledge of the plays. It is equally clear that a misunderstanding of Shakespeare will invariably lead to a misunderstanding of the plays. Misread the man and you misread the work. This being so, it is evident that the quest for the *real* William Shakespeare is at the heart of Shakespearian literature. The quest for the author of the plays and sonnets is a quest for the authority needed to read them properly.

In some ways the quest for the real Shakespeare can be likened to the quest for the Holy Grail. Some refuse to join the quest on the basis that the Grail is unimportant. These are the postmoderns and deconstructionists who believe that they are as capable of understanding the plays as was the playwright himself, and that they do not need his help to do so, or else they believe that the plays have no meaning anyway and that, therefore, there is nothing to understand. For these hollow men, slaves of the zeitgeist, there is little hope. With a yawn of tedious ennui, and a sigh of slothful hubris, they close the book and wander wearily into the vestibule of the Futile, perhaps en route to somewhere worse. Then there are those critics who join the quest for the Grail but discover that it was not, in fact, holy; it was merely a cup, like any other, or, at any rate, a cup remarkably like a graven image of the critics themselves. For these critics, Shakespeare emerges, in spite of the abundance of evidence for his Catholicism, as a progenitor of modern secularism, as a man who, ahead of his time, turned his back on the faith of his fathers and embraced the agnosticism of the future. "The safest and most likely conclusion", wrote Peter Ackroyd in his life of the Bard, ". . . must be that despite his manifold Catholic connections Shakespeare professed no particular faith. The church bells did not summon him to worship. They reminded him of decay and time past. Just as he was a man without opinions, so he was a man without beliefs. He subdued his nature to whatever in the drama confronted him. He was, in that sense, above faith." [4] One cannot resist a riposte to such arrant nonsense. The fact is that there is no such thing as "a man without opinions" or "a man without beliefs". Indeed, "a man without beliefs" is simply beyond belief. Agnosticism is a belief, atheism is a belief, nihilism is a belief; and these beliefs obviously inform our opinions. Shakespeare may or may not have been a believing Catholic, but he clearly could not have been "without beliefs". Such men do not exist.

Perhaps Ackroyd was trying to say, and saying badly, what the philosopher George Santayana had said much better more than a century earlier. "Shakespeare is remarkable among the poets", Santayana claimed, "for being without a philosophy and without a religion", adding that "the absence of religion in Shakespeare was a sign of his good sense". With unremitting logic, Santayana concluded that the absence of religion in Shakespeare's plays, as he perceived it, led inevitably to the implied triumph of nihilism: "For Shakespeare, in the matter of religion, the choice lay between Christianity and nothing. He chose nothing; he chose to leave his heroes and himself in the presence of life and of death with no other philosophy than that which the profane world can suggest and understand." [5]

Against this "profane" interpretation of Shakespeare's works, there is a long tradition of belief that Shakespeare's plays betray an element of Catholicism. In 1801 the French writer François René de Chateaubriand asserted that "if Shakespeare was anything at all, he was a Catholic". [6] Thomas Carlyle wrote that the "Elizabethan era with its Shakespeare, as the outcome and flowerage of all which had preceded it, is itself attributable to the Catholicism of the Middle Ages". [7] Carlyle's great Victorian contemporary John Henry Newman was even more emphatic about the Catholic dimension, stating that Shakespeare "has so little of a Protestant about him that Catholics have been able, without

---

[4] Peter Ackroyd, *Shakespeare: The Biography* (New York: Nan A. Talese/Doubleday, 2005), p. 474.

[5] George Santayana, "Absence of Religion in Shakespeare"; originally published in 1896, and collected in George Santayana, *Interpretations of Poetry and Religion* (New York: Charles Scribner's Sons, 1922), pp. 152, 161, 163. Although Santayana's words can be taken to imply an element of nihilism in Shakespeare, I am not implying, of course, that Santayana was himself a nihilist in the strict sense of the word.

[6] Quoted in H. Mutschmann and K. Wentersdorf, *Shakespeare and Catholicism* (New York: Sheed and Ward, 1952), p. vi.

[7] Quoted in Ackroyd, *Shakespeare*, p. 472.

extravagance, to claim him as their own".[8] Hilaire Belloc, echoing the verdict of Newman, insisted that "the plays of Shakespeare were written by a man plainly Catholic in habit of mind".[9] G. K. Chesterton stated his own belief in Shakespeare's Catholicism in his book on Chaucer, published in 1932: "That Shakespeare was a Catholic is a thing that every Catholic feels by every sort of convergent common sense to be true."[10] Years earlier, in 1907, Chesterton had compared the chasm that separated Shakespeare the Catholic from Milton the Protestant:

> Nearly all Englishmen are either Shakespearians or Miltonians. I do not mean that they admire one more than the other; because everyone in his senses must admire both of them infinitely. I mean that each represents something in the make-up of England; and that the two things are so antagonistic that it is really impossible not to be secretly on one side or the other.... Shakespeare represents the Catholic, Milton the Protestant.... Whenever Milton speaks of religion, it is Milton's religion: the religion that Milton has made. Whenever Shakespeare speaks of religion (which is only seldom), it is of a religion that has made him.[11]

Not surprisingly perhaps, Chesterton was asked to clarify the rationale behind his assertion of Shakespeare's Catholicism:

> A correspondent has written to me asking me what I meant by saying that Shakespeare was a Catholic and Milton a Protestant. That Milton was a Protestant, I suppose, he will not dispute.... But the point about the religion of Shakespeare is certainly less obvious, though I think not less true.... These impressions are hard to explain.... But here, at least, is one way of putting the difference between the religions of Shakespeare and Milton. Milton is possessed with what is, I suppose, the first and finest idea of Protestantism—the idea of the individual soul actually testing and tasting all the truth there is, and calling that truth which it has not tested or tasted truth of a less valuable and vivid kind. But Shakespeare is possessed through and through with the feeling which is the first and finest idea of Catholicism that truth exists whether we like it or not, and that it is for us to accommodate ourselves to it.... But I really do

---

[8] John Henry Newman, *The Idea of a University* (1873); quoted in Peter Milward, *Shakespeare the Papist* (Naples, Fla.: Sapientia Press, 2005), p. x.

[9] Hilaire Belloc, *Europe and the Faith* (1920); quoted in Velma Richmond, *Shakespeare, Catholicism, and Romance* (New York: Continuum, 2000), p. 16.

[10] G. K. Chesterton, *Chaucer* (1932); republished in *Chesterton: The Collected Works*, vol. 18, p. 333.

[11] G. K. Chesterton, *Illustrated London News* (May 18, 1907).

not know how this indescribable matter can be better described than by simply saying this; that Milton's religion was Milton's religion, and that Shakespeare's religion was not Shakespeare's.[12]

Chesterton's comparison of Shakespeare with Milton is intriguing, indicating that, in Chesterton's judgment, the former belonged to the old England of Catholicism whereas the latter belonged to the new England of Protestantism. He is saying that Shakespeare, living during the crucible of religious change, was rooted in the Old Faith, whereas Milton, as a genuine modern, had embraced post-Catholicism, with the implicit relativism of a custom-built or personalized faith, in much the same way as his successors would embrace "post-Christianity", with the explicit relativism of faithless individualism. Milton is the missing-link between the Christian past and the "post-Christian" future; Shakespeare, on the other hand, is a remnant of the Christian past in defiance of the very same emergent and embryonic "post-Christianity". Milton is "early modern" in the sense that he was the herald of much that was to follow; Shakespeare is only "early modern" in the sense that he was responding to, and reacting against, the emergence of the modern "enlightened" mind.

The fact that Shakespeare has much more in common with the mediaeval past than with the postmodern present has been stressed by modern Shakespearian scholars, such as Gene Fendt, who states that the "Renaissance and medieval are arguably closer to each other than, for example, we (post)moderns are to either of them". As such, he continues, "it is more licit to read Shakespeare next to Aquinas than next to Freud, Jung, Lacan, Foucault, et al."[13] Taken to its logical conclusion this means that all (post)modern readings of Shakespeare are inevitably, and by definition, awry.

Heinrich Mutschmann and Karl Wentersdorf, in their comprehensive study *Shakespeare and Catholicism*, documented the numerous "references to Catholic dogmas, ideas and customs" in Shakespeare's works and concluded that "we are in every respect justified in accepting these as irrefutable testimony of the poet's personal views, views which are quite clearly pro-Catholic."[14] Take, for example, Shakespeare's condemnation of each

---

[12] Ibid. (June 8, 1907).

[13] Gene Fendt, *Is Hamlet a Religious Drama? An Essay on a Question in Kierkegaard* (Milwaukee: Marquette University Press, 1998), p. 93. Fendt is referring specifically to notions of "ecstasy" in *Hamlet*, but his conclusions are nonetheless applicable in a much wider sense.

[14] Mutschmann and Wentersdorf, *Shakespeare and Catholicism*, p. 212.

of the seven deadly sins. Pride: "Sin of self-love possesseth all mine eye." [15] Envy: "I sin in envying his nobility." [16] Sloth: "Hereditary sloth instructs me." [17] Gluttony: "Let him be damned like the glutton." [18] Avarice or covetousness: "My desire of having is the sin of covetousness." [19] Anger: "It hath pleased the devil of drunkenness to give place to the devil of wrath." [20] Lust: "My blood is mingled with the crime of lust". [21]

Shakespeare did not merely condemn each of the seven deadly sins; he ordered them in conformity to the teaching of the Catholic Church, as reflected in the work of St. Thomas Aquinas and as echoed by Dante in his Thomistic masterpiece, *The Divine Comedy*. In league with his great mediaeval forebears, Shakespeare condemns the sin of pride, i.e., the sin of Satan and the sin of Adam, as the most grievous of all the sins: "Self-love, which is the most inhibited sin in the canon." [22] And he describes lust or "unchastity" as the least grievous: "Of the deadly seven it is the least." [23] Yet even the "least deadly" of the mortal sins is still deadly, a fact that Shakespeare is at pains to illustrate. When, for example, Claudio, in *Measure for Measure*, makes the crucial error of suggesting that unchastity, as the least grievous of the deadly sins, is perhaps not a sin at all, Shakespeare exposes his flawed logic. He does so in the wisdom of the profoundly orthodox words of Claudio's sister, Isabella, uttered in the previous act:

> Better it were a brother died at once
> Than that a sister, by redeeming him,
> Should die for ever. [24]

The virtuous Isabella knows that actions have eternal consequences and that it would be better for her brother to lose his earthly life than that she should suffer eternal punishment for committing a mortal sin, i.e., a sin that kills the soul and condemns the sinner to "die for ever". She

---

[15] Sonnet 62.
[16] *Coriolanus*, 1.1.230.
[17] *The Tempest*, 2.1.223.
[18] *2 Henry IV*, 1.2.34.
[19] *Twelfth Night*, 5.1.47.
[20] *Othello*, 2.3.296–97.
[21] *Comedy of Errors*, 2.2.141.
[22] *All's Well That Ends Well*, 1.1.144–45.
[23] *Measure for Measure*, 3.1.110.
[24] Ibid., 2.4.107.

knows that it would be wrong to "redeem" her brother temporarily, i.e., to save him from the sentence of death with which he is condemned, if, by doing so, she was condemning her own soul to eternal punishment.

Mutschmann and Wentersdorf are very insightful and lucid in their balanced analysis of the invocation of the saints in Shakespeare's plays:

> What traces of the Catholic veneration of saints, condemned in Elizabethan England, are nevertheless to be found in Shakespeare's works? It would not be wise to attach too much importance to the exclamations such as "by Saint Paul", "by Saint Anne", "by'r Lady", etc., which the poet often puts into the mouths of his characters. The same applies to such expressions as "by the holy rood" or "by the mass". It must be borne in mind that such and similar asseverations, although Catholic in origin, remained in popular use in England after the schism; it cannot be assumed that they were used in a religious sense, much less that the speakers were aware of their dogmatic significance. And yet it is noticeable that asseverations of this kind are hardly ever used by Protestant writers in their works; where exclamatory phrases are introduced, they are mostly of a neutral character such as "by heaven", "by God", or "by the cross". Furthermore, it is noteworthy that expressions such as "by'r Lady" and "by the mass", which occur in the old Quartos, i.e., the editions nearest to Shakespeare's manuscript, were almost entirely expunged in the First Folio edition, which quite clearly demonstrates that they were regarded as "offensive" or even unlawful.[25]

Mutschmann and Wentersdorf also stress "the highly significant fact that Shakespeare . . . reveals a very exact and detailed knowledge of Catholicism", and they quote Father Sebastian Bowden's conclusion that the repeated allusions to Catholic rites and practices "are introduced with a delicacy and fitness possible only for a mind habituated to the Church's tone of thought".[26] The accuracy of Shakespeare's depiction of Catholic practices contrasts with the proliferation of errors that emerge in the plays of his contemporaries, such as in the anonymously authored *The Troublesome Raigne of King John* (printed in 1591) or in John Webster's *The White Devil* (1612). This woefully inaccurate depiction of Catholicism by non-Catholic writers has continued to plague literature down the centuries, from Schiller's *Maria Stuart* (1800) and Mary Shelley's

---

[25] Mutschmann and Wentersdorf, *Shakespeare and Catholicism*, p. 252.
[26] Ibid., p. 263.

Frankenstein (1818) to Dan Brown's inanely ubiquitous *Da Vinci Code*. In contrast, Shakespeare's depictions of, and allusions to, Catholicism are invariably accurate, proving his experience and knowledge of the Catholic Faith. Such textual evidence would suffice to illustrate that Shakespeare had been a practicing Catholic at some stage in his life, if not necessarily that he had always remained one. As we shall see in the following chapters, there is an abundance of solid historical evidence to prove, beyond all reasonable doubt, that Shakespeare was raised a Catholic and that he probably remained a Catholic throughout his life.

Perhaps at this juncture, however, it might be prudent to consider, albeit briefly, those who claim that Shakespeare was not really Shakespeare but that he was really someone else. Nobody denies that the real William Shakespeare existed, but many have claimed that the plays ascribed to him are not really his. These "anti-Stratfordians" have erected fabulously imaginative theories to prove that someone other than Shakespeare wrote the plays. Some have claimed that Francis Bacon was the real author of the plays, others that they were written by the Earl of Oxford, and some even believe that Queen Elizabeth was William Shakespeare! It is difficult to take any of these rival claims very seriously. Edward de Vere, the Earl of Oxford, died in 1604, a year after the death of Queen Elizabeth, and about eight years before the last of Shakespeare's plays was written and performed! Needless to say, the Oxfordians, as they are known, have gone to great lengths, stretching the bounds of credulity to the very limit (and beyond), to explain why the plays were not performed until after their "Shakespeare's" death.

The claims of the Oxfordians might be bizarre, but they are positively pedestrian compared to some of the wackier "Shakespeare" theorists. Other aristocrats who are alleged by some to have been the real Shakespeare include King James I, and the Earls of Derby, Rutland, Essex, and Southampton. Others have claimed that Mr. Shakespeare was really Mrs. Shakespeare, in the sense that the plays were really written by Shakespeare's wife, Anne Hathaway, using her husband's name as a *nom de plume*.

The difficulties that the Oxfordians face in trying to explain (or explain away) why many of Shakespeare's finest plays were not performed until after the Earl of Oxford's death are as nothing compared to the difficulties faced by another group of "Shakespeare" theorists. The "Marlovians", as the members of this particular anti-Stratfordian sect are known, are convinced that all of Shakespeare's plays were really written by

Shakespeare's contemporary Christopher Marlowe. The fact that Marlowe was murdered in 1593, when most of Shakespeare's plays had still not been written, does not trouble the ingenious Marlovians. They claim that Marlowe's "murder" was a sham, and that Marlowe had been spirited away to France and Italy by his powerful patron Thomas Walsingham, returning secretly to England where, in hiding, he wrote plays under the pseudonym "William Shakespeare". Faced with such ludicrous conspiracy theories one is reminded of present-day theories about the allegedly staged death of Elvis Presley, as exemplified in the reports in the lower-brow tabloids of Elvis sightings alongside the sightings of UFOs. Yet even the resurrection of the dead, whether it be Marlowe, the Earl of Oxford, or Elvis, seems uncontroversial beside the claims of another bizarre anti-Stratfordian theory that the plays were written by Daniel Defoe, the author of *Robinson Crusoe*. Since Defoe was not born until 1660, almost half a century after the last of Shakespeare's plays had been performed, it seems that we are dealing not only with the raising of the dead but with the raising of the unborn!

It would, of course, be a little unfair to suggest that the relatively sober scholarship of the Baconians or the Oxfordians is as ridiculous as the evident lack of scholarship of those who favor Daniel Defoe as the real Shakespeare. Ultimately, however, all the rival theories can be disproved through the application of solid historical evidence, combined with common sense. Take, for example, the central premise of the Oxfordian or Baconian case that the plays must have been written by an aristocrat or, at least, by one with a university education, on the assumption that Shakespeare, as a commoner without a university education, must have been illiterate, or, at any rate, incapable of writing literature of such sublime quality.

Let's look at the facts.[27] Shakespeare's father was not poor but, on the contrary, was relatively wealthy. He was, furthermore, a highly respected and influential member of the Stratford-upon-Avon community. With regard to Shakespeare's education, the historian Michael Wood has shown that the sort of education that Shakespeare would have received at the Stratford Grammar School would have been of exceptionally good quality. On the other hand, the plays and sonnets do not display the great knowledge of classical languages that one might have expected if

---

[27] Full details of the sources for the assertions made in this brief summary are given in subsequent chapters where these summarized facts are treated more fully.

Shakespeare had been an aristocrat or if, like Bacon, he had been to Oxford or Cambridge. Francis Bacon did much of his writing in Latin, whereas Shakespeare, to quote his good friend Ben Jonson, had "little Latin and less Greek" and wrote entirely in the vernacular. The evidence illustrates, therefore, that William Shakespeare would have had a good education but that he might not have been as comfortable with classical languages as he would have been had he been to Oxford or Cambridge. This excellent but non-classical education is reflected in the content of his plays. It should also be noted that Francis Bacon was vehemently anti-Catholic. His mother was a zealous Calvinist and his father an outspoken enemy of the Catholic Church. Such an upbringing would have precluded him from being able to write the profoundly Catholic plays attributed to Shakespeare.

As for the presumption of the Oxfordians and Baconians that Shakespeare's "humble origins" would have precluded him from being able to write the plays, one need only remind these proponents of supercilious elitism that great literature is not the preserve of the rich or the privileged. Christopher Marlowe was a shoemaker's son, and Ben Jonson's stepfather was a bricklayer. Poverty prevented Jonson from pursuing a university education. Since Marlowe and Jonson, along with Shakespeare, are the most important dramatists of the Elizabethan and Jacobean period, it is clear that having humble origins did not disqualify a writer from producing great literature; on the contrary, it could be argued from the evidence that such origins were an important ingredient of literary greatness in Shakespeare's day. Furthermore, the importance of humble origins to the pursuit of literary greatness is not confined to Shakespeare's contemporaries. Later generations have also produced an abundance of "humble" greats. Daniel Defoe was the son of a butcher, and Samuel Johnson, arguably the greatest wit and literary figure of the eighteenth century, was also born of poor parents. Poverty would force Johnson to abandon his university education. Charles Dickens, the greatest novelist of the Victorian era, experienced grinding poverty as a child and, when his father was sent to prison for debt, the ten-year-old Dickens was forced to work in a factory. Moving into the twentieth century, G. K. Chesterton, the "Dr. Johnson of his age", was born of middle-class parents and never received a university education. And these are but some of the brightest lights in the humble firmament of literary greatness. Many others could be added to the illustrious list. Perhaps the most applicable parallel to Shakespeare's situation is, however, the appropriately named Alexander Pope, the son of a draper, who was denied a formal education because his parents were Catholic. Pope's humble origins helped him become perhaps the finest poet of the eighteenth century.

So much for the weakness of the Oxfordian argument about Shakespeare's "humble origins". The other argument often employed by the Oxfordians is that Shakespeare was too young to have written the sonnets and the early plays. Shakespeare was only in his midtwenties when the earliest of the plays was written and was in his late twenties when he wrote the sonnets. There is no way that such a young man could have written such work, whereas the Earl of Oxford, being born in 1550 and therefore fourteen years Shakespeare's senior, would have been sufficiently mature to have written these masterpieces. So the argument runs. Whether the Earl of Oxford, a most violent and volatile individual, was ever "sufficiently mature" to have written the works of Shakespeare is itself highly questionable. Nonetheless, let's look at the crux of the matter, namely, whether a young man is able to write great literature.

Christopher Marlowe, who was born in the same year as Shakespeare, wrote the first of his produced plays in around 1587, when he was only twenty-three, two or three years younger than Shakespeare is thought to have been when the first of his plays was produced. The first of Marlowe's plays, *Tamburlaine the Great*, is generally considered to be the first of the great Elizabethan tragedies. Since Marlowe was murdered when he was still in his late twenties, the whole of his considerable literary legacy rests on his formidably young shoulders. Ben Jonson's first play, *Every Man in his Humour*, was performed in 1598, with Shakespeare in the cast, when Jonson was only twenty-six years old. Thomas Dekker published the first of his comedies in 1600, when he is thought to have been around thirty years old. Thomas Middleton's first printed plays were published in 1602, when the playwright was about thirty-two, but they were probably first performed a year or two earlier. John Webster published his first plays in 1607, when he was twenty-seven years old, but is known to have made additions to John Marston's *The Malcontent* three years earlier. As for Marston himself he wrote all his plays between 1602 and 1607, between the ages of twenty-six and thirty-one. Looking at his contemporaries, Shakespeare was at exactly the age one would expect him to be when he first started writing plays. The Earl of Oxford, on the other hand, would have been around forty when the first of the plays was performed, making him a positive geriatric by comparison.

So much for the youthfulness of Shakespeare the playwright, but what about the Oxfordian argument that he would have been too young to write the sonnets? Again, let's begin with Shakespeare's contemporaries. Michael Drayton published his first volume of poetry, *The Harmony of the Church*, in 1591, when he was twenty-eight years old, exactly the same age as Shakespeare is thought to have been when he wrote the sonnets. Many of John Donne's finest sonnets were written in the early 1600s when the poet was in his late twenties or early thirties. Many other great Elizabethan poets died at a young age, having already bequeathed a considerable body of work to posterity. Sir Philip Sidney was thirty-two when he died; Robert Southwell was thirty-three; Marlowe, as already noted, was twenty-nine; and Thomas Nashe was thirty-four.

Moving forward in time to the eighteenth century it is worth noting that Samuel Johnson was twenty-eight when he finished his play *Irene* and was only a year older when his poem *London* was published, the latter of which, according to Boswell, was greeted with adulation and the judgment of his contemporaries that "here is an unknown poet, greater even than Pope".[28] And as for Pope, he published his first poems at the tender age of twenty-one.

Should these examples fail to convince us that the art of the sonnet is not beyond the reach of the young, we need look no further than the example of Byron, Shelley, and Keats. Byron had reached the ripe old age of thirty-six when he died, Shelley was thirty, and Keats a mere twenty-six years old. As for the precocious talent of the youngest of this youthful trio, Keats is said to have written some of his finest sonnets in as little as fifteen minutes! And Keats never even lived to the age at which Shakespeare is thought to have written his own sonnets.

Before we leave the anti-Stratfordians behind, we should at least address the few remaining remnants of their arguments against "the Stratford man". The fact that Shakespeare's signature is described as being shaky or untidy is used as evidence of his "illiteracy". Although some Oxfordians admit grudgingly that most of the surviving signatures date from the period of Shakespeare's retirement when the infirmity that would eventually lead to his relatively early death might account for the infirmity of the signature, there is still the implicit suggestion that the untidy signature is evidence that Shakespeare could not have written the plays.

---

[28] James Boswell, *The Life of Samuel Johnson* (London: Macmillan, 1912), p. 83.

Perhaps it is necessary to remind these "scholars" that there is absolutely no connection between calligraphy and literature, or that beautiful writing and beautiful handwriting do not necessarily go hand in hand. Many of the greatest writers had bad handwriting, and, no doubt, many of the greatest calligraphers were incapable of putting two literary sentences together. The temptation to produce a further list of great writers, this time itemizing those who had illegible handwriting, will be resisted. Let it suffice to say that any scholar who has pored over the mercilessly illegible handwriting of great writers will know that there is absolutely no connection between legibility and literacy.

In similar vein, anti-Stratfordians point a scornful finger at the lack of literary flourish in Shakespeare's will or the questionable literary merit of the poetic epitaph on his grave. Why, one wonders, should Shakespeare feel inspired to turn his will into a work of literary art? Why, one wonders, should he bother to write his will at all? Why shouldn't he get his lawyer to do it? And why, one wonders, would Shakespeare be the least concerned with writing verse for his own gravestone? How common is it for self-penned epitaphs to adorn the tombs of the dead? Isn't it far more likely that someone else wrote the lines? At any rate, these pieces of "evidence" hardly warrant any serious doubt as to the authorship of the plays.

In the final analysis, there is no convincing argument against Shakespeare's authorship of the plays and, in consequence, no convincing evidence that someone else wrote them. If the very foundations upon which the anti-Stratfordian edifice is built are shown to be fallacious, the rest of the ingenious, if far-fetched, historical arguments for other "Shakespeares" fall to the ground ignominiously. After the dust has settled on the fallen edifices of false scholarship, what is left standing among the ruins? There is no Earl of Oxford, no Francis Bacon, no Queen Elizabeth nor King James, no Christopher Marlowe, no Daniel Defoe, no Elvis. We are left with the reliable, if mundane, reality that William Shakespeare was, in fact, William Shakespeare. We are also left with the equally reliable, if paradoxical, observation of G. K. Chesterton that "Shakespeare is quite himself; it is only some of his critics who have discovered that he was somebody else." [29]

---

[29] G. K. Chesterton, *Orthodoxy* (London: Sheed and Ward, 1939), p. 15.

2

HIS FATHER'S WILL

Let's begin our investigation into Shakespeare's life by looking at the overwhelming evidence that the faith of his family was Catholic. Let's begin, in fact, with the conclusion of Mutschmann and Wentersdorf that the new evidence emerging throughout the twentieth century has led inexorably to the acceptance of his parents' Catholicism:

> There can be no doubt that Shakespeare was born and reared in a strictly Catholic home: his father was a stubborn "papistical" recusant, his mother came from a family which likewise strictly adhered to the old faith. There was at one time widespread skepticism concerning Bowden's downright conclusion (1899) that the poet's parents were Roman Catholics. The progress of time and intensive research, however, have revealed much more fresh evidence, which now makes any other conclusion impossible.[1]

Much of the historical scholarship centered on the spiritual will of John Shakespeare, the poet's father, which had been discovered in 1757. In 1930, the Shakespearian scholar E. K. Chambers published *William Shakespeare: A Study of Facts and Problems*, in which he affirmed the genuineness of John Shakespeare's spiritual will in the face of earlier suggestions that it had been a forgery.[2] Four years later, G. B. Harrison, another eminent Elizabethan and Jacobean scholar, best known for his edition of Shakespeare's works (1952), concluded cautiously that "Shakespeare's family was apparently Catholic" and that, therefore, "it follows that

---

[1] H. Mutschmann and K. Wentersdorf, *Shakespeare and Catholicism* (New York: Sheed and Ward, 1952), p. 73.

[2] The evidence for the genuine nature of the spiritual will is utterly convincing, but a full examination of all the facts is beyond the scope of this study. Those wishing to pursue the matter further are referred to John Henry de Groot's masterful treatment of the whole issue in his scholarly magnum opus, *The Shakespeares and "The Old Faith"* (Fraser, Mich: Real-View Books, 1995); originally published in 1946.

Shakespeare was brought up in the old faith".[3] Then, in 1946, John Henry de Groot, in his work of groundbreaking scholarship *The Shakespeares and "The Old Faith"* asserted that the spiritual will "offers strong evidence that John Shakespeare was a Catholic throughout his life, and that his household was infused with the spirit of the old Faith".[4] It is worth noting that de Groot, who was professor of English at Brooklyn College from 1946 until 1967, had originally trained for the Presbyterian ministry and is not, therefore, prejudiced in favor of the conclusion he reached in his study but, on the contrary, would have been predisposed, presumably, to a prejudice against such a conclusion. Nonetheless, as a good scholar placing himself at the service of objectivity, he continues: "It makes reasonable the conclusion that when John and Mary Shakespeare sought to instill religious sentiments and foster religious values in the minds and hearts of their children, those sentiments and values were of the Catholic tradition. It is now more certain that William Shakespeare was brought up in a Catholic home." [5]

Let's look in more detail at the spiritual will of John Shakespeare, which is believed to have been written in 1581 or thereabouts, when William was seventeen years old. It was discovered in 1757, as we have said, during renovation of the house in which Shakespeare had been born almost two hundred years earlier. During the retiling of the roof, the builder, Joseph Mosely, noticed a small, handwritten booklet wedged between the tiling and the rafters. Mosely kept the curious document for many years, but eventually on June 8, 1784, he passed it to Edmond Malone, the most prominent Shakespearian scholar of the time. "I have taken some pains to ascertain the authenticity of this manuscript," wrote Malone, "and after a very careful inquiry am perfectly satisfied that it is genuine." [6] He continues:

> The writer, John Shakespeare, calls it his *Will*; but it is rather a declaration of his faith and pious resolutions. . . . It is proper to observe that the finder of this relique bore the character of a very honest, sober, and industrious man, and that he neither asked nor received any price for it;

---

[3] G. B. Harrison, "The National Background", in H. Granville-Barker, ed., *A Companion to Shakespeare Studies* (Cambridge: Cambridge University Press, 1934; cited in Mutschmann and Wentersdorf, *Shakespeare and Catholicism*, p. 73.

[4] De Groot, *The Shakespeares*, p. 110.

[5] Ibid.

[6] Ibid., p. 65.

and I may also add that its contents are such as no one could have thought of inventing with a view to literary imposition.[7]

As for the spiritual will itself, it demonstrates John Shakespeare's Catholic *bona fides* and itemizes his earnest desire to die a Catholic, in good faith and conscience. Item 4 is particularly striking for its enunciation of his desire that he should receive the last rites of the Church, and his hope that the *desire* for the last rites should suffice should there be no priest to administer the sacrament at his moment of death. In the time of persecution in which John Shakespeare was living it was a crime, punishable by death, to harbor a priest in one's home. It was, therefore, very possible that no priest would be available for the Catholic *in extremis*. It is in the spirit of this gloom of persecution, with the cloud of unknowing looming overhead, that John Shakespeare's defiant desire for the last rites should be read:

> I John Shakspear do protest that I will also pass out of this life, armed with the last sacrament of extreme unction: the which if through any let or hindrance I should not then be able to have, I do now also for that time demand and crave the same; beseeching his divine majesty that he will be pleased to anoint my senses both internal and external with the sacred oil of his infinite mercy, and to pardon me all my sins committed by seeing, speaking, feeling, smelling, hearing, touching, or by any other way whatsoever.[8]

In item 7, John Shakespeare laments his sins of "murmuration against god, or the catholic faith" and his giving "any sign of bad example", renouncing "all the evil whatsoever, which I might have then done or said". These words resonate powerfully in the light of John Shakespeare's evidently reluctant involvement, in 1564, the year of his son William's birth, in the desecration of the Guild Chapel in Stratford.

From 1561 until 1565, John Shakespeare was the Chamberlain of the Stratford Corporation and must have been party to the decision to break the altar, pull down the rood loft with its cross, and whitewash over mediaeval paintings. This act of vandalism has often been seen as evidence that John Shakespeare was a Protestant, even though a closer scrutiny of the facts indicates otherwise.

---

[7] Ibid.

[8] All citations from the will of John Shakespeare are taken from de Groot, *The Shakespeares*.

The desecration of the chapel was probably carried out after a visitation to Stratford by the Anglican Bishop of Worcester, who would have ordered the Stratford authorities, of which John Shakespeare was an official, to carry out the act of destruction. Such destruction was demanded by the anti-Catholic injunctions originally introduced by Thomas Cranmer in 1547, during the reign of Edward VI, which had condemned relics, pilgrimages, and the Rosary and had ordered the destruction of all images in churches, even those in windows. This injunction had been repealed during the brief reign of Mary Tudor but had been reinstated in 1559, upon Queen Elizabeth's ascension to the throne, with the added stipulation that all clergy must "take away, utterly extinct and destroy all shrines, covering of shrines, all tables and candlesticks, trundles or rolls of ware, pictures, paintings and all other monuments of feigned miracles, pilgrimages, idolatry and superstition, so that there remain no memory of the same in walls, glasses, windows or elsewhere within their churches or houses". It is clear, therefore, that the political authorities would have had no choice but to have obeyed the law once specifically ordered to do so following the Bishop of Worcester's visitation. The only alternative would have been open defiance of the law and imprisonment, or worse.

There is, in fact, much circumstantial evidence to suggest that John Shakespeare and his colleagues on the town council were not in favor of the law and were only reluctantly carrying it out. It is curious, for instance, that the authorities in Stratford took so long to carry out the order and only did so after a visitation from the bishop. In other areas the destruction of altars and religious images in churches had been carried out in 1560, within months of the reinstatement of the injunction. The delay in Stratford suggests a reluctance to carry out the law, presumably because the Stratford authorities disagreed with it. It is also curious that the religious paintings were not mutilated, as was the case in militantly Protestant areas, but were whitewashed over. The significance of such an action should not be overlooked. Protestants believed that religious images were idolatrous, and therefore blasphemous, and, as such, they believed that they could destroy and mutilate religious art with a feeling of righteous justification, and a belief that they were doing God's will and therefore acting virtuously. Catholics, on the other hand, believed that the destruction of religious images was a grievous sin and would not do so, in conscience, if they could possibly avoid it. Thus, whitewashing over mediaeval paintings could be seen as a lesser sin, necessitating only a covering of the images, or a concealing of them, and not their defilement or desecration. In the case of the Guild Chapel in Stratford, the mediaeval paintings that were whitewashed over, at the apparently reluctant behest of John Shakespeare and his colleagues on the town council, were representations of St. Helen and the Finding of the Cross, St. George and the Dragon, the Murder of St. Thomas Becket, and the Day of Judgment. From a Catholic perspective the destruction of such images must have struck John Shakespeare as being evocatively symbolic of the fate of Catholic England in his day. As the beautiful paintings were whitewashed over, he would have seen the losing of the Cross, the triumph of the Dragon, the vindication of Becket's murder (Catholics saw a parallel between Becket's martyrdom in 1170 and the martyrdom of John Fisher and Thomas More in 1535), and, last but not least, a turning away from the Day of Judgment.

Returning to John Shakespeare's spiritual will, one can imagine, as he was repenting any "fall into impatience and temptation of blasphemy, or murmuration against god, or the catholic faith", or the giving of "any sign of bad example", even though such sin was carried out under fear of the "violence of pain and agony, or by subtlety of the devil", that his actions seventeen years earlier in acting as the agent of the Protestant state in the desecration of the Guild Chapel was at the forefront of his mind and conscience.

Item 9 of the spiritual will renders "infinite thanks" to God for all the benefits he has received, including "vocation to the holy knowledge of him and his true Catholic faith", and item 10 invokes the Communion of Saints with the Blessed Virgin named as the "chief Executress" of the will:

> I John Shakspear do protest, that I am willing, yea, I do infinitely desire and humbly crave, that of this my last will and testament the glorious and ever Virgin mary, mother of god, refuge and advocate of sinners, (whom I honour specially above all other saints,) may be the chief Executress, together with these other saints, my patrons, (saint Winefride) all whom I invoke and beseech to be present at the hour of my death, that she and they may comfort me with their desired presence, and crave of sweet Jesus that he will receive my soul into peace.

It need not be stressed that such veneration of the saints had been rendered unlawful in the England in which John Shakespeare found himself, as had a belief in Purgatory, the subject of item 12:

I John Shakspear do in like manner pray and beseech all my dear friends, parents, and kinsfolk, by the bowels of our Saviour jesus Christ, that since it is uncertain what lot will befall me, for fear notwithstanding least by reason of my sins I be or pass and stay a long while in purgatory, they will vouchsafe to assist and succour me with their holy prayers and satisfactory works, especially with the holy sacrifice of the mass, as being the most effectual means to deliver souls from their torments and pains; from the which, if I shall by gods gracious goodness and by their virtuous works be delivered, I do promise that I will not be ungrateful unto them, for so great a benefit.

It's not possible to read John Shakespeare's exhortation to his family to pray for him, after his death, nor his promise to pray for them, without imagining the impact that such an exhortation would have had on his son. As a Catholic, William would have been very much aware that the filial duty to his parents extended beyond death, beyond the grave. Such awareness of the eternal bonds that exist between father and son conjures to our minds the ghost of Hamlet's father, who now looms larger than ever in our imagination as the ghostly presence of Shakespeare's own father.

The mystery surrounding John Shakespeare's spiritual will, and many of the questions connected to its authenticity or otherwise, were solved by an extraordinary stroke of luck, or providence, in 1923, when Herbert Thurston, S.J., found, in the British Museum, a Spanish version of a spiritual testament which corresponded, phrase for phrase, from the middle of Item III to the end, with the spiritual will of John Shakespeare. Printed in Mexico City in 1661 it was entitled "The Testament or Last Will of the Soul" and was ascribed to St. Charles Borromeo. Father Thurston subsequently discovered another Spanish version of the "Testament", dating before 1690, and a version in the Romansch language that had been printed in Switzerland in 1741, both of which also ascribe authorship to St. Charles Borromeo, the cardinal archbishop of Milan who died in 1584.

How does this trail of manuscripts, stretching across two centuries and three thousand miles, connect with Shakespeare's father? The connection, as we shall see, is St. Charles Borromeo himself, via the Jesuit missionaries to England, Edmund Campion and Robert Persons.

It seems likely that St. Charles Borromeo wrote the devotional formula some time between 1576 and 1578 when the plague struck Milan, killing an estimated seventeen thousand people. In such circumstances it would have been impossible for priests to hear the confessions and give the last rites to all the dying. The "Testament" would, therefore, have been written as a "spiritual insurance policy", asserting the person's desire for the sacrament of extreme unction, and serving as a "confession of desire" in the absence of a priest. The saintly shepherd Charles Borromeo was supplying his sickly sheep with a standard formula by which they could prepare themselves for a holy death in difficult circumstances.

Although the reason that the penitent soul might die in the absence of a priest was very different in the plague years in Milan than in the penal times in England, the need for the "Testament" was the same in both places. It seems, therefore, that the Jesuits brought copies of the "Testament" with them when they arrived in England in 1580. We know that Edmund Campion and Robert Persons stayed with Charles Borromeo on their way to England from Rome, stopping with the cardinal in Milan in May 1580.

> St Charles Borromeo received our pilgrims into his house, and kept them there for eight days. He made Sherwin preach before him, and he made Campion discourse every day after dinner. "He had," says Persons, "sundry learned and most godly speeches with us, tending to the contempt of this world, and perfect zeal of Christ's service, whereof we saw so rare an example in himself and his austere and laborious life; being nothing in effect but skin and bone, through continual pains, fasting, and penance: so that without saying a word, he preached to us sufficiently, and we departed from him greatly edified and exceedingly animated.[9]

We know that Edmund Campion stayed in the vicinity of Stratford-upon-Avon en route to Lancashire, shortly after his arrival in England, and this has led to conjecture that the Shakespeares, including sixteen-year-old William, might have met him in person. Either way, it seems entirely reasonable to assume that Campion left copies of the Borromeo "Testament" for the use and consolation of the Catholic faithful as he passed through Warwickshire. Although this seems the most likely means by which John Shakespeare received the copy that he used as the template for his own "spiritual will", it would not have been the only means by which he could have received a copy. Other priests from the English College in Rome also stayed in Milan with Charles Borromeo en route to England, and we know specifically that he entertained another

---

[9] Richard Simpson, *Edmund Campion: A Biography* (Edinburgh: Williams and Norgate, 1867), pp. 111–12; cited in de Groot, *The Shakespeares*, p. 86.

group of England-bound priests in September 1580, only four months after Campion and Persons had stayed with him.[10]

Further evidence for the dissemination of the Borromeo "Testament" is supplied in a letter from William Allen, the rector of the English College in Rheims, to Father Alphonsus Agazzari, rector of the English College in Rome, on June 23, 1581, in which Allen wrote that "Father Robert [Persons] wants three or four thousand or more of the Testaments, for many persons desire to have them."[11] It has been suggested that the "Testaments" mentioned by Father Persons were copies of the New Testament in the Rheims translation. This is unlikely. First, the translation of the Vulgate New Testament into English would not be completed until March of the following year and would not, presumably, have been published until a month or two later. The title page reads: "Printed at Rhemes by John Fogny, 1582". Second, "three or four thousand or more" of such a costly and bulky volume would have created a major logistical problem for the Jesuit mission. How would one smuggle thousands of copies of an expensive eight hundred-page quarto volume past the wary officers at the English ports? And assuming that one managed to smuggle the shipment into England, how would one transport such a bulky cargo around the country? In the very same letter in which Allen wrote of Persons' desire for the "Testaments", he reported that "the persecution still rages with the same fury, the Catholics being haled away to prison and otherwise vexed, and the Fathers of the Society being most diligently looked for". Is it likely that fugitive priests, traveling incognito from one secret Catholic household to another, would be able to transport such a heavy cargo with them? Surely it is much more likely that the "Testaments" being referred to were the Borromeo "Testaments", which, when printed, would be a booklet of not more than six pages.

Since John Shakespeare's spiritual will is quite clearly an English translation of St. Charles Borromeo's "Testament", the only question remaining is, why is it handwritten and not printed? The answer is obvious. It is clear from William Allen's letter that Father Persons had exhausted his original supplies of the printed version, hence the desire for several thousand more, and it is equally clear that demand was outstripping supply, "for many persons desire to have them". It seems that John

---

[10] De Groot, *The Shakespeares*, p. 86.
[11] Ibid., pp. 87–88.

Shakespeare was one of these "many persons" and that he had signed a hand-copied version in the absence of supplies of the printed originals.

The strength of the evidence that John Shakespeare remained a defiant Catholic, in the midst of widespread anti-Catholic persecution by the Elizabethan state, has forced most modern scholars to accept that William Shakespeare was brought up as a believing Catholic. Such evidence is strengthened, as we shall see, by the fact that John Shakespeare would later fall foul of the law for his continued commitment to the Catholic resistance.

3

THE FAITH OF HIS FATHERS

The exact date of John Shakespeare's birth is not known. Earliest estimates put it at "about 1528", although others have assumed that he was born as late as 1536.[1] It is known that he was born in the village of Snitterfield, about four miles to the north of Stratford-upon-Avon, the son of Richard Shakespeare. He had at least one sibling, a (probably older) brother, Henry. The spelling of Richard Shakespeare's name is recorded, in court documents dating from 1530 to 1550, as being, variously, Shakspere, Shakespere, Shakkespere, and Shaxpere. More curiously, in a document in 1533, he had used the name Shakstaff; and on another occasion, in 1541 or 1542, he had employed the name Shakeshafte.[2] The last of these names is particularly intriguing because, as we shall see, some scholars have suggested that his grandson used the name "William Shakeshafte" during a period in which he is believed to have lived in Lancashire.

Many of the facts about Shakespeare's family remain shrouded in mist, not least the suggestion that he had an aunt or great aunt, presumably a sister of Richard or John Shakespeare who was a nun at Wroxall Priory, thirteen miles north of Stratford and nine miles from Snitterfield. The Comtesse de Chambrun, in *Shakespeare Rediscovered*, emerges as the greatest advocate of the connection between the poet and the nun at Wroxall:

> John Shakespeare's sister had been a nun at Wroxall until the forced dissolution of the Convent, after which the inmates were sent back to their families or thrown upon the world, the sole exception being the prioress

---

[1] See John Henry de Groot, *The Shakespeares and the "Old Faith"* (Fraser, Mich.: Real-View Books, 1995), p. 7, for details of the conflicting evidence for the date of his birth.

[2] Douglas Hamer, "Was William Shakespeare William Shakeshafte?" *The Review of English Studies*, n.s., 21, no. 81 (February 1970): 41–48; also Anthony Holden, *William Shakespeare: The Man Behind the Genius* (Boston: Little, Brown, 1999), p. 11.

who was allowed a slender indemnity from the Crown. Domina Shakespeare who died in Stratford when her nephew was fourteen certainly
must have influenced his childhood.[3]

The source for Madame de Chambrun's statement was presumably a
document, dated 1525, which mentions a "Domina Jane Shakspere" as
the subprioress of Wroxall Priory, a Benedictine convent. There is no
other known documentary record of "Domina Jane" until the register
of her death, in 1571, at Hatton, only three miles from Wroxall. There
are, however, considerable difficulties in making any solid connection
between Domina Jane Shakespeare and her alleged nephew, William.
The first obvious discrepancy is the fact that William would have been
only seven when his "aunt" died, not fourteen as Madame de Chambrun states.

The other discrepancy is the disparity in age between Domina Jane
Shakespeare and her "brother", John, the poet's father. As we have seen,
the earliest estimate for the date of John Shakespeare's birth is 1528,
three years after Domina Jane is listed as being a nun at Wroxall Priory.
Indeed, she is not only a nun but is subprioress and, therefore, one
would presume, already fairly mature in age. If we assume that she was
around twenty-five years old at the time, and surely she could not have
been much younger, she would have been at least twenty-eight when
John Shakespeare was born; and if he was born as late as 1536, as some
scholars believe, his "sister" would have been thirty-six years old when
he was born. If not perhaps physically impossible, it is surely implausible that Domina Jane and John Shakespeare were siblings.

At this point, it is possible to retreat to a second hypothesis and to
assume that the subprioress was not John's sister but Richard's, i.e., John
Shakespeare's aunt and William's great aunt. Either way, the claim that
Domina Jane "must have influenced" her [great?] nephew's childhood,
as Madame de Chambrun claims, is beginning to look a little tenuous.
It becomes even more tenuous once the serious scholarship into Shakespeare genealogy is taken into account.

Charles Isaac Elton, in his posthumously published book, *William
Shakespeare, His Family and Friends* (1904), concluded that, "so far as the
inquiries have as yet proceeded, it cannot be said that there is any evidence

---

[3] Clara Longworth, Comtesse de Chambrun, *Shakespeare Rediscovered* (New York: Charles
Scribner's Sons, 1938); quoted in de Groot, *The Shakespeares*, p. 103.

of the poet's ancestors having come from Wroxall." [4] Sir Edmund K. Chambers was even more emphatic in his rejection of a connection between the Wroxall and Stratford Shakespeares:

> Shakespeares were thick on the ground in sixteenth-century Warwick-shire, particularly in the Woodland about Wroxall and Rowington to the north of Stratford. A Richard Shakespeare was in fact bailiff of Wroxall manor in 1534, but his after-history is known, and excludes a suggested identity with Richard of Snitterfield. [5]

B. Roland Lewis, writing in 1940, came to the same conclusion: "Try as one will, in the light of the present evidence, one is unable to demonstrate that John Shakespeare's ancestral connections were with the Wroxall family of the same name." [6]

There is certainly no doubting that Shakespeares were "thick on the ground" in Warwickshire, especially at Wroxall Priory and in a religious community called the Guild of St. Anne. With regard to the former, we have already seen that Domina Jane Shakespeare was the subprioress in 1525, but earlier, in 1457, Isabella Shakespeare was listed as being the prioress (she died in 1504) and, in the same year, Jane Shakespeare was listed as one of the nuns. Meanwhile, in the register of the Guild of St. Anne there are no fewer than sixteen Shakespeares listed.

In spite of the absence of evidence for a direct connection between the Wroxall Shakespeares and their Stratford neighbors, it is surely not too fanciful to believe that William Shakespeare was related to at least some of these neighboring Shakespeares. After all, the absence of historical documentation only indicates that a fact cannot be affirmed, it does not, strictly or logically speaking, mean that it can be denied. If pieces of an incomplete jigsaw puzzle cannot be found it means they are lost; it does not mean that they don't exist. It is, moreover, bad history to assume that missing parts of the picture are not important to an understanding of those parts that we can see. Since it is impossible

---

[4] Charles I. Elton, *William Shakespeare: His Family and Friends* (New York: E. P. Dutton, 1904), p. 112.

[5] E. K. Chambers, *William Shakespeare: A Study of Facts and Problems* (Oxford: Clarendon Press, 1930); quoted in de Groot, *The Shakespeares*, p. 104.

[6] B. Roland Lewis, *The Shakespeare Documents: Facsimiles, Transliterations, Translations, & Commentary* (Stanford: Stanford University Press, 1940); quoted in de Groot, *The Shakespeares*, p. 104.

to know the full genealogies of all the Shakespeares in Warwickshire, we only have some of the pieces of the jigsaw puzzle with which to work. Therefore, in order to see the whole picture in perspective, we can only make honest and educated guesses, based on probability and common sense, with regard to the missing pieces. Since Wroxall and Snitterfield, where Shakespeare's father was born, are only nine miles apart, and considering that Shakespearian scholars at Boston College have suggested that Richard Shakespeare, the poet's grandfather, might have originated in Rowington, a village only two miles from Wroxall, which had the largest concentration of Shakespeares in Warwickshire, it is not only possible, but is surely probable, that William Shakespeare counted several of these other Shakespeares as his kinsfolk.[7] Furthermore, Michael Wood, an historian of considerable repute, reports that oral tradition in Warwickshire has always embraced the legend that Shakespeare's heart is buried in the grounds of Wroxall Priory, now known as Wroxall Abbey, "his ancestral grounds".[8] It is also curious that Shakespeare's most overtly Catholic heroine, Isabella in *Measure for Measure*, is not only a novice religious sister but that she has the same name as Isabella Shakespeare, the prioress of Wroxall Abbey. Perhaps this is merely a coincidence, but, if so, it is a singularly curious one.

Some time between the end of 1556 and the middle of 1558 John Shakespeare married Mary Arden, the youngest daughter of his father's landlord, Robert Arden of Wilmcote. We know that they were not married before November 24, 1556, because that is the date of Robert Arden's will, in which Mary Arden is referred to in terms that make it clear that she was not married at the time. The Stratford Parish Register records the date of the baptism of "Jone Shakspere daughter to John Shakspere" as September 15, 1558, indicating, obviously, that John Shakespeare had married Mary Arden in the interim.

The Catholicism of Mary Arden's father is clear from the wording of the will, in which he bequeathed his soul "to Almighty God and to our blessed Lady Saint Mary and to all the holy company of heaven". It is also clear that Mary was a favorite daughter because he made her,

---

[7] See the "Shakespeare and Religion Chronology", *Religion and the Arts*, http://www.bc.edu/publications/relarts/supplements/shakespeare/chronology.html; published by Boston College.

[8] The legend is mentioned in Richard Wilson, *Secret Shakespeare: Studies in Theatre, Religion, and Resistance* (Manchester: Manchester University Press, 2004), p. 179, in which Wilson attributes Michael Wood as his source in the footnote, p. 185.

with her sister Alice, co-executor of his will, and bequeathed to her his most valuable possession, "all my land in Wilmcote", i.e., the family estate. Further circumstantial evidence of Mary Arden's Catholic faith is implicit from the very fact that she *was* a favorite of her Catholic father and that she was entrusted to be an executor of his will, as distinct from another sister, Margaret, who had married a Protestant and who was evidently not so highly favored or trusted. Although it cannot be stated with certainty that there is a connection between the faith of Robert Arden's daughters and the settlement of his will it seems the most likely explanation for the discrepancy in the way they were dealt with, especially in light of the religious divisions in England during the final years of Queen Mary's reign.

Aside from the religious issue, John Shakespeare had certainly married well; one might even say that he had married above his station in life. He had not merely married the daughter of his father's landlord, he had married the daughter who had become the chief beneficiary of his father's landlord's will. Economically and socially speaking, it could be said that he had effectively married his father's landlady. This should be borne in mind when we consider the sort of family from which William Shakespeare emerged. True, he was not an aristocrat, but neither was he a pauper—far from it. In modern terms we could say that he was born into the prosperous upper middle class.

It is also necessary to quash the widely held belief of many Shakespeare scholars that John Shakespeare later fell into debt, regardless of how financially comfortable he might have been at the time of his marriage. Recent research has revealed that John Shakespeare remained prosperous until the end of his life, not merely as a humble glover, the trade normally ascribed to him, but as a large-scale trader in wool and even as a banker.[9]

The Catholicism of William Shakespeare's extended family, on his mother's side, is beyond doubt, and, moreover, is marked with controversy. The head of the Arden family in Warwickshire, Edward Arden of

[9] For in-depth historical research into John Shakespeare's personal finances, see D. L. Thomas and N. E. Evans, "John Shakespeare in the Exchequer", *Shakespeare Quarterly* 15 (1984): 315–18. The whole issue is discussed at considerable length by John de Groot in his *The Shakespeares*, pp. 31–41, in which the whole "Poverty Theory", as de Groot calls it, is painstakingly demolished. There is also a good summary of the considerable extent of John Shakespeare's large-scale trading in wool in Ian Wilson, *Shakespeare: The Evidence* (New York: St. Martin's Griffin, 1999), pp. 51–52.

Park Hall, near Birmingham, was executed in 1583 for his alleged involvement in the Somerville Plot. Nothing was proved against him, and it
seems likely that he was the victim of a trumped-up charge, initiated
by his powerful enemy, the Earl of Leicester. John Somerville, the
ringleader of the so-called "plot", was Edward Arden's son-in-law, but
there appears to be no evidence that any of Somerville's relatives approved
of his threats to kill the queen. Nonetheless, protesting his innocence
and insisting that he was dying for his Catholic faith, Edward Arden
was executed for high treason, being hanged, disemboweled, beheaded,
and quartered; his head being placed on a spike at London Bridge as a
warning to other would-be "papist conspirators". Shakespeare would
have been nineteen at the time that his distant cousin suffered such a
horrific fate, and one can only imagine the psychological impact that
Edward Arden's "martyrdom" would have had on the poet's mind and
imagination.

The Arden family was also implicated in other "Catholic plots" against
the Crown, including the Throckmorton Plot of 1583, the Parry Plot
of 1585, the Essex Rebellion of 1601, and the Gunpowder Plot of 1605.
Shakespeare's relatives were, it seems, living on the very edge of danger
in a period of political tension and religious persecution.[10] The life and
times of England's greatest poet and playwright were charged with such
danger, contributing no doubt to what Chesterton referred to as Shakespeare's "delirium", and contributing also no doubt to the tension-
charged nature of his own "plots".

Closer to home, there is ample evidence to show that William Shakespeare was raised in a Catholic household, in spite of, and in defiance
of, the increasing persecution of Catholics in Elizabethan England. Mary
and John Shakespeare's first child, Joan, was baptized, as we have already
noted, in September 1558, by Father Roger Dyos, a Catholic priest
who was driven from his post a few months later after the Protestant
Queen Elizabeth succeeded her half sister, the Catholic Mary, to the
throne. During the final years of Mary's reign, and the first years of his
marriage, John Shakespeare's civic career had flourished. In September
1557 he was appointed a chief burgess of the town of Stratford-upon-
Avon, and, in the following year, while Queen Mary was still on the

---

[10] For detailed genealogies of Shakespeare's familial connections with many of the leading
"plotters" of the Elizabethan period, see the whole section of "Genealogical Tables" in H.
Mutschmann and K. Wentersdorf, *Shakespeare and Catholicism* (New York: Sheed and Ward,
1952).

throne, he was appointed one of the four constables of the town. The fact that John Shakespeare had prospered under the rigorously Catholic regime of Queen Mary is taken by Father Henry Bowden as strong evidence for his Catholicism and is employed by him as a rebuttal of Thomas Carter's claim in *Shakespeare: Puritan and Recusant* (1897) that John Shakespeare was a Puritan:

> This tenure of municipal office by him [John Shakespeare] in 1557–59, when the laws against heretics were rigidly enforced, is our first direct evidence of his Catholicism. Mr Carter, in fact, says, speaking of Robert Perrot, then High Bailiff of Stratford, that none but "an ardent and pronounced Roman Catholic" could have accepted so high an office in times of bitter persecution under a most bigoted king and queen. He, however, entirely overlooks the fact that the same reasoning must apply proportionately to the other members of the corporation at this date, among whom we find, besides John Shakespeare, John Wheeler, his constant associate in his various vicissitudes.[11]

The situation is complicated, however, by the fact that John Shakespeare's civic career continued to prosper during the reign of Elizabeth, at least for a time. After serving eight years as a burgess, he was elected to the office of alderman of the corporation in July 1565. His son William had been born the previous year. By 1567 he is being referred to, in official documents, as "Mr Shakespeyr", a title denoting a degree of dignity, and in the following year he is elected high bailiff, or mayor. As high bailiff, John Shakespeare became justice of the peace, the queen's chief officer, and judge of the Court of Record. Doesn't this indicate that Shakespeare's father was a conformist who had accepted the Protestant ascendancy under Elizabeth? Advocates of the alleged Protestantism of John Shakespeare clearly think so. On the assumption that he would have been obliged to take the Oath of Supremacy required by the Act of Supremacy of 1559, swearing in conscience "that the queen's highness is the only supreme governor of this realm ... in all spiritual or ecclesiastical things or causes", Protestant scholars have concluded that his election to the office of high bailiff in 1568 "is incontrovertible evidence that John Shakespeare was then a loyal member of the Church of England".[12] Such a conclusion is disputed by Catholic scholars, such

---

[11] Quoted in de Groot, *The Shakespeares*, p. 16.
[12] Cumberland Clark, *Shakespeare and the Supernatural* (London: Williams and Norgate, 1931); quoted in ibid., p. 22.

as Father Bowden, who argue that it is extremely unlikely that John Shakespeare would have been required to take the Oath of Supremacy upon his election in 1568:

> At first the lay peers were exempt from taking the oath, which was aimed specially at the bishops and clergy, and it was not till 1579 that it was required of the justices; and in Warwickshire, out of thirty magistrates, Sir John Throckmorton, Simon Arden, and eight others refused to be thus sworn. Up to 1579, then, one third of the magistrates of Warwickshire were Catholics. There is no proof whatever that John Shakespeare ever had the oath of supremacy tendered to him as a qualification for his municipal office. On the contrary, it is in the highest degree improbable that the Sheriff of the County (1568–69), Robert Middlemore, himself a recusant, should have administered to him an oath which he refused to take himself. As regards the oath of supremacy, then, there is no valid argument for John Shakespeare's Protestantism during these years.[13]

One of the underlying reasons for the presumption of many earlier scholars that Shakespeare and his family were Protestants was the related presumption that most people in Elizabethan England were Protestants, and that Catholics were a small and shrinking part of the population, who were generally despised and ostracized by their Protestant neighbors. In fact, as historians such as Eamon Duffy have demonstrated with monumental and meticulous scholarship, most of the population in sixteenth-century England were devout Catholics who resented and resisted the new religion being forced and foisted upon them by first, the king (Henry VIII), and later, the queen (Elizabeth I).[14] What was true of England in general was true of Stratford-upon-Avon in particular. The historian Wood concludes, from the ominous silence of the Stratford Corporation during the period of John Shakespeare's tenure of municipal office, that the people of Stratford were opposed to the Act of Supremacy and the religious changes that it was designed to force upon the people:

> The corporation records from the time of Shakespeare's childhood reveal most by what they *don't* say. They offer none of the tell-tale signs of

---

[13] Quoted in de Groot, *The Shakespeares*, p. 23.

[14] See Eamon Duffy's two books, *The Stripping of the Altars: Traditional Religion in England 1400–1580* (New Haven / London: Yale University Press, 1992) and *The Voices of Morebath: Reformation and Rebellion in an English Village* (New Haven / London: Yale University Press, 2001).

precocious Protestant enthusiasm found in East Anglian towns, or even in neighbouring Coventry. There are no accounts of official hospitality towards visiting Protestant preachers, of anxious debates about church attendance or Sabbath-breaking, or of wheedling investigations of newcomers and strangers. This makes sense in a community in which many aldermen and their wives were avowed Catholics. The Wheelers were firm adherents, who, in 1592, would be accused of being recusants ("refusers of Protestant communion") along with John Shakespeare; as late as 1606 Hamnet and Judith Sadler, godparents of William Shakespeare's twins, were arraigned in the church courts for their Catholicism; the Debdales of Shottery, who also appeared in the 1592 list of recusants, had a son who died on the scaffold as a Jesuit martyr.[15]

In other words, to put the matter simply, Wood is saying that the silence is palpably deafening and that it implies a resolute Catholic resistance to the new religion, the very absence of any evidence of conformity implying the veritable presence of nonconformity. It is the sullen silence of the outlaw, a silence that paints a thousand (unspoken) words.

In his recent biography of Shakespeare, Ackroyd asserts that "any conservative reckoning" would identify thirty avowedly, i.e., defiantly, Catholic families within Stratford, "and of course the available records are by their nature incomplete and inconclusive". "There would have been many more papists, who concealed their private beliefs.... They became, in the language of the day, 'church papists' whose attendance at the Protestant churches masked their true faith. It has been speculated that the majority of churchgoers in Stratford were of this sort." [16]

Further evidence that Stratford had become, tacitly at least, a town of "papist" outlaws can be gleaned from the attitude of Anglican church dignitaries toward it. Hugh Latimer, the bishop of Worcester and a leading reformer, confessed that Stratford lay at "the blind end" of his diocese, and one of his colleagues lamented that in Warwickshire "great Parishes and market Townes [are] utterly destitute of God's word", i.e., the reformed religion had failed to make any inroads with its Protestant gospel.[17] One of Latimer's successors as bishop of Worcester, John Whitgift, who would become a great favorite of Queen Elizabeth and would be made archbishop of Canterbury by her in 1583, complained in 1577

---

[15] Michael Wood, *Shakespeare* (New York: Basic Books / Perseus Books Group, 2003), p. 37.
[16] Peter Ackroyd, *Shakespeare: The Biography* (New York: Nan A. Talese / Doubleday, 2005), p. 39.
[17] Quoted in ibid., pp. 39–40.

that he could obtain no information on recusants in the area around Stratford. This is particularly significant because it suggests that the people of Stratford were a tightknit and largely Catholic community who would not divulge information about recusant activity to the authorities. Once again the silence speaks a thousand words. It is also worth noting that, when Whitgift made this complaint, William Shakespeare was thirteen years old. It seems, therefore, that England's greatest poet was growing up, apparently, in the midst of a clandestine Catholic community, which was resolute about keeping its secrets from the powers-that-be.

The reason that Bishop Whitgift was complaining, in 1577, about the difficulty of obtaining information about recusants is that a witch hunt against recusants had been launched the previous year. In April 1576, after a period in which the 1559 statutes of supremacy had been largely ignored in many parts of the country, including, it would seem, in Stratford, the queen had appointed a Grand Commission to ensure that the laws were enforced more rigidly. The commission's aim was to "order, correct, reform and punish any persons willfully and obstinately absenting themselves from church and service". Fines against Catholics were to be levied by the churchwardens of each parish, and, most significant to the position of John Shakespeare, those in civic office would be made to take the Oath of Supremacy. The investigations were carried out in the latter half of 1576, which coincides exactly with John Shakespeare's mysterious withdrawal from civic life. Having missed only one meeting of the borough council in the previous thirteen years, he failed to appear at the meeting on January 23, 1577, and, thereafter, with one exception, never appeared at a council meeting again. Yet, in spite of his persistent nonattendance, the borough council continued to treat him with deference and respect, and it was only after ten years of nonattendance that his name was finally removed from the list of aldermen. Such tolerance, wrote the Protestant scholar E.I. Fripp, was without parallel in the history of the borough.[18] The obvious conclusion is that John Shakespeare withdrew from civic life to avoid taking the Oath of Supremacy and that the majority of his colleagues on the borough council sympathized with his decision to do so, even if they were not prepared to follow his defiant example. "His decision to retire

---

[18] Mutschmann and Wentersdorf, *Shakespeare and Catholicism*, p. 44.

presupposes great courage and firm faith", wrote Mutschmann and Wentersdorf.[19]

In 1577, a year after the appointment of the Grand Commission, an order was sent to all bishops to "certify the names of all persons in his diocese who refused to come to church, together with the value of their lands and goods", no doubt prompting Whitgift's complaint, as he tried to obey the directive, that there was a distinct lack of cooperation in obtaining information about recusants in the area around Stratford.[20] In the event, Whitgift's list only contained the most well-known Catholics, such as Sir Robert Throckmorton, a friend of Father Dyos, the deposed Catholic priest who had baptized the first of the Shakespeares' children.

On January 29, 1578, a levy was made in Stratford for the strengthening of the militia, which had been formed to enforce the government's anti-Catholic measures and to prevent possible uprisings, such as the major Catholic uprising in the north that had been crushed in 1569. John Shakespeare was assessed at three shillings and four pence, but, in conscience, he refused to pay. He was not alone. Among those who were reported to the authorities for nonpayment of the levy were, in addition to John Shakespeare: George Badger, one of the staunchest Catholics in Stratford who had recently married another well-known local Catholic; Thomas Reynolds, another Catholic who was the father of William Shakespeare's much persecuted Catholic friend William Reynolds; and Thomas Nash, father of Shakespeare's friends John and Anthony Nash. Again, it is patently clear that, for the young William Shakespeare, still only thirteen years old, the persecution of Catholics in Elizabethan England was literally very close to home.

The persecution continued unabated in the following months, and it has been conjectured that the selling of property by John Shakespeare in 1578 and 1579 was connected with his efforts to cope with the prospect of being fined for his recusancy. "These transactions throw a significant light on John Shakespeare's character", wrote Mutschmann and Wentersdorf. "It is clear from the incident of the militia levy and from [his] subsequent financial arrangements that he had not only come out into the open as an opponent of the 'new religion', but that he was

[19] Ibid.
[20] Ibid., p. 45; Wood, *Shakespeare*, p. 69.

attempting to insure himself against the inevitable consequences of the grave step he was taking." [21]

On March 16, 1580, the government appointed another commission, this time charged with forming musters throughout England in "defense of her Majesty, Crown, realm and good Subjects against all attempts both inward and outward", i.e., rebellion from within or invasion from without. The commissioners sent to Stratford were Sir Thomas Lucy, a committed Protestant and indefatigable persecutor of Catholics, and Sir William Catesby, a staunch Catholic who would be arrested the following year for his adherence to the old faith and whose son would later play a leading role in the Gunpowder Plot. The appointment of Sir Thomas Lucy as a commissioner charged with forming militias to defend England from "papist plots" or "papist invaders" seems obvious enough, but the appointment of Sir William Catesby remains a mystery. One can only assume that he had been appointed as a means of testing his loyalty to the queen, since refusal to accept the office could have been considered "treasonable". It might be assumed, therefore, that one of the two commissioners went about his work with zeal whilst the other did so with a bitter mixture of resentment and reluctance. Either way, they did as they were instructed and, in April 1580, drew up a list of "Gentlemen and Freeholders" in Stratford, the wealthiest and most worthy men in town, of which John Shakespeare's name appeared near the top. These men were no doubt "expected" to join the muster or support it financially. As with the position of Sir William Catesby, the Catholics of Stratford were being placed in an awkward position. Should they offer to fight in or finance a militia designed to quash any signs of Catholic rebellion against the new coercive religion being forced upon them? Or should they refuse to support the muster and face the punitive consequences? To be a conformist, or not to be a conformist: that was the question.

Although we don't know for certain how John Shakespeare responded to this latest levy, his earlier refusal to pay suggests that he might have refused again on this occasion. Such a supposition appears to be strengthened by the fact that he is one of 220 Catholics from all over England who were charged with committing a "breach of the Queen's peace" at around this time. John Shakespeare was summoned to appear at the Queen's Bench in Westminster in June 1580 to answer the charges against

---

[21] Mutschmann and Wentersdorf, *Shakespeare and Catholicism*, p. 47.

him. It seems, however, that he was part of a preconceived plan by those charged to boycott the whole proceedings, since he and most of his codefendants from around the country opted not to attend. John Shakespeare was fined £20, a huge sum,[22] for nonappearance in court, and a further £20 for failing to bring John Audley, a Nottingham hatmaker, into court. Audley, in turn, who was also facing the charge of "breaching the Queen's peace", was fined £60 for nonattendance, and a further £10 for not bringing John Shakespeare into court. Furthermore, Thomas Cooley of Stoke in Staffordshire was fined £10 for failure to produce John Shakespeare in court, and a further £20 for not producing John Audley. Two others, both from Worcestershire, were fined £10 each for not bringing John Audley to court.[23]

It is curious that the defendants should not only be forced to pay their own fines for nonattendance, but be held responsible for the nonattendance of codefendants and fined for failing to bring them to court. It certainly begs some interesting questions. Did the government know that the defendants were planning to boycott the proceedings, and, if so, was this the government's way of punishing them for doing so and, perhaps, an effort to break the boycott itself? If so, it illustrates the resilience of the recusants and their determination not to conform to the "new religion". It would also seem to indicate that the recusant network was widespread and that individuals from disparate areas, many miles apart, knew each other fairly well. Nottingham is seventy miles from Stratford; Stoke is nearly eighty.

Having examined the evidence for John Shakespeare's recusancy during the period that his son was living with him in Stratford, it is now time to turn to the most unequivocal evidence of his recusancy, which emerges in 1592, after his son had left Stratford and was already making a name for himself in London.

In November 1591 the Privy Council appointed commissions around the country to clamp down on "papist" recusants. The commission for Warwickshire was charged

---

[22] The Snitterfield property, which John and Mary Shakespeare had inherited from Robert Arden, was sold for £40 in October of the previous year, illustrating the considerable sum that £20 represented. It is estimated that John Shakespeare's total property in 1576 was valued at between £250 and £300; and the price paid by William Shakespeare in 1597 for the second largest house in Stratford was £60.

[23] Mutschmann and Wentersdorf, *Shakespeare and Catholicism*, p. 50.

to enquire what persons ... that do reside in any parte of the County of Warwick ... that probably by their behaviour and manner of life or otherwise may be suspected to have come from beyond the seas in the quality and vocation of Seminaries, Priests, Jesuits or Fugitives ... &c. And in like manner shall cause inquisition and examination to be made of all persons that have heretofore given or shall hereafter give assistance, succour or relief in diet, lodging, pension, reward or in any other sort to any of the aforesaid malefactors [24]

The Warwickshire Commission made its first report at Easter 1592, in which John Shakespeare was included in a list of "all such persons, as either have been presented to them; Or have been otherwise found out by the Endeavour of the said Commissioners, To be Jesuits, Seminary priests, fugitives, Or Recusants ... Or vehemently suspected to be such." [25] This seemingly irrefutable evidence for the militant Catholicism of Shakespeare's father has caused consternation for many scholars who have done what they can to deny it. The most common ploy is to refer to the fact that there was another John Shakespeare in Stratford at the time, a shoemaker, and to suggest that it was he and not the poet's father who was the person listed in the Recusancy Report. Apart from the other evidence suggesting that the poet's father had been a recusant for many years, and the distinct absence of evidence with regard to the other John Shakespeare, the final proof that it was the one and not the other lies in the fact that the Shakespeare in the Recusancy Report is listed as "*Mr* John Shakespeare", denoting that he had been a person of distinction in the town. For John Henry de Groot this serves as definitive evidence that the recusant was Shakespeare's father:

> In the case of John Shakespeare, the poet's father, the title of "Mr" automatically devolved upon him when he was chosen high bailiff in 1568, and it is exactly because a distinction is thenceforth consistently made in the Corporation records between "Mr John Shakespeare" and "John Shakespeare" that the two men can be kept apart. It seems hard to avoid the conclusion that the Mr John Shakespeare of the recusancy returns was the father of the dramatist. [26]

---

[24] Quoted in de Groot, *The Shakespeares*, p. 52.

[25] Public Record Office, SP/12/243, no. 76; quoted in F.W. Brownlow, "John Shakespeare's Recusancy: New Light on an Old Document", *Shakespeare Quarterly* 40, no. 2 (Summer 1989): 186–91.

[26] Ibid., p. 53.

Apart from the solid documentary evidence for John Shakespeare's recusancy, there is strong circumstantial evidence that he might have known or been acquainted with some of the most notorious recusant Catholics of his day. It has been suggested that he might have known William Allen, founder of the first Catholic seminary at Douai in 1568, because Allen had been the schoolmaster in Stratford in 1563, when John Shakespeare was a civic official. It is also very likely, considering that the population of Stratford was only around fifteen hundred,[27] that he would have known Robert Dibdale, a martyred priest who has since been beatified by the Catholic Church. Dibdale was born around 1558 at Shottery, a village less than two miles to the west of Stratford. As such, it is likely not only that John Shakespeare knew the future martyr, who would be hanged, drawn, and quartered at Tyburn in London in 1586, aged about twenty-eight, but that his son William knew him too, being only six years younger than Dibdale and being eleven years old when Dibdale left Stratford to pursue his vocation to the priesthood on the continent. Nor, as we shall see, was Dibdale the only Catholic martyr with whom England's greatest writer seems to have been acquainted.

Although much is known about John Shakespeare's recusant activities, little is known of the activities of his wife. Yet, as Michael Wood asserts, writing of community life in Stratford, "the women were perhaps especially important in terms of holding on to the old beliefs and customs".[28] Such a view appears to be borne out by the concerns of Queen Elizabeth's privy council, which, in 1580, was alarmed by reports that "women in their ordinary meetings among themselves very irreverently speak of the religion now established in this realm".[29] An example of such irreverence was given most memorably by the Shakespeares' friend and neighbor Elizabeth Wheeler, when she told the Puritans on the church court in 1592 exactly what she thought of them and their newfangled religion: "Godes woondes, a plague of God on you all, a fart of ons ars for you!" (God's wounds ... a fart of one's arse for you!) There's no evidence of such an outburst from Mary Shakespeare, the poet's mother, but we can be reasonably certain that she was as resolute in her Catholic beliefs as was her husband, belonging as she did to the

---

[27] This figure is based upon the number of baptisms and burials recorded in the Stratford parish register, as compared with similar population statistics in other places. See James Walter, *Shakespeare's True Life*, 2nd ed. (London: Longmans, Green, 1896), p. 42.

[28] Wood, *Shakespeare*, p. 37.

[29] Ibid.

resolutely Catholic Arden family, and it might be presumed safely that her influence in the home, on her children, and on their faith, was at least as important as Wood's appraisal of the importance of women in general to the wider community. Even as her husband was taking his costly public stand for the faith, Mary Shakespeare remained "perhaps especially important in terms of holding on to the old beliefs and customs". She was perhaps to her husband and children what Chesterton said that William Cobbett's wife was to her own notorious husband. She was "the powerful silence", unheard in public, but, in private, the hidden pillar of fortitude conveying strength to her family, encouraging her husband and children to cling to the faith doggedly and dogmatically. She, perhaps, is the unsung heroine whose praises her son would sing vicariously through the words and actions of his most formidably virtuous heroines.

Once all the evidence for the militant Catholicism of Shakespeare's family is considered objectively, it seems inescapable that England's greatest writer grew up in a staunchly papist home. This is the view of an increasing number of scholars of whom F. W. Brownlow is typical: "[T]he conclusion that John Shakespeare was a Catholic is the economical one, requiring no forcing of the evidence. If that is so, then of course it means that William Shakespeare as a boy and young man experienced the curious, underground world of Elizabethan Catholic loyalism." [30]

The evidence is clear, and many scholars have come to accept it, that the young William Shakespeare spent the most formative years of his life living as part of a family of outlaws.

---

[30] Brownlow, "John Shakespeare's Recusancy", p. 189.

4

LIVING WITH OUTLAWS

As with so much surrounding the life of William Shakespeare, the date of his birth is shrouded in mystery. We know that he died on St. George's Day (April 23), and popular belief has proclaimed that he was also born on St. George's Day, thereby uniting England's greatest son with her patron saint in both his life and his death. It is one of those facts that we feel *should* be true, even if we can't prove that it is true.

The evidence for a St. George's Day birth is rooted in the one piece of solid evidence about his birth that we do know, namely, that he was baptized on April 26, 1564. Since it has been assumed that baptisms in the sixteenth century took place three days after the birth of the child, the date of April 23 as his birthday would seem the most likely.

There are, however, some who have sought to dispel the "myth" that Shakespeare was born on St. George's Day. Anthony Holden declared, with killjoy certainty, that the "myth must be dispelled at the outset". The problem is that his efforts to dispel it are utterly unconvincing. He cites the instruction given to parents in the 1559 Prayer Book that baptism should be performed before the first Sunday or holy day following the birth "unless upon a great and reasonable cause declared to the curate and by him approved". This is cited to show that there was nothing sacrosanct about the baptism being three days after birth. Yet the evidence shows, in fact, that there was nothing sacrosanct, in the eyes of Shakespeare's parents, about the instructions in the Prayer Book. If John and Mary Shakespeare had followed the instructions, their son would have been baptized *before* the feast of St. Mark (April 25), not on the day after. Clearly, therefore, Shakespeare's parents paid no heed to the instruction, which is hardly surprising since the Prayer Book had been introduced to replace the Mass, the latter being formally "abolished" following the accession to the throne of Elizabeth. The Prayer Book, originally introduced in the reign of the ultra-Protestant Edward VI and reintroduced by Elizabeth, was loathed by Catholics who saw it as the New Religion's anti-Catholic "Bible". The date of William's baptism, in apparent defiance of the instructions of the state religion, can be seen, therefore, as further evidence of his parents' recusancy.

In the end, Holden is forced to grasp at very unconvincing straws to "dispel the myth" of the St. George's Day birthday. He reminds us that "the contemporary inscription on Shakespeare's tomb ... reads that he died in his fifty-third year (*'obit anno ... aetatis 53'*)". Since we know that he died on St. George's Day, "this would seem to imply that he was born before it, however marginally".[1] Actually, it could imply equally that he was born *on* St. George's Day itself. The next day begins upon the stroke of midnight; the next year begins on the stroke of one's birthday! The other piece of evidence offered by Holden is even more unconvincingly tendentious:

> There are few more satisfactory resolutions of this problem than that of the poet Thomas de Quincey, who suggested that Shakespeare's granddaughter Elizabeth Hall married on 22 April 1626 "in honour of her famous relation"—choosing the sixty-second anniversary of his birth, in other words, rather than the tenth of his death.[2]

Since de Quincey was writing two hundred years after Shakespeare's death, his view on the subject is of negligible importance. In essence, the evidence we are being offered is that a poet, writing two centuries after the event, happens to opine that the date of Elizabeth Hall's marriage might have been in honor of her grandfather. Note that de Quincy doesn't say that it is in honor of her grandfather's *birthday*, which is merely an unsubstantiated assumption on Holden's part. *If* Elizabeth Hall selected this particular date for this particular reason, and it's a big *if*, might it not have been the nearest Saturday to St. George's Day? The fact is that the date of the wedding, April 22, 1626, *was* a Saturday. Since weddings are not customarily held on Sundays, this would have been the nearest date that the wedding could have been held to Shakespeare's birthday, if his birthday was on St. George's Day. As such, the evidence offered by Holden to suggest that Shakespeare was not born on St. George's Day actually suggests that he might have been! *Pace* Holden, and in the absence of any convincing evidence to the contrary,

---

[1] Anthony Holden, *William Shakespeare: The Man Behind the Genius* (Boston: Little, Brown, 1999), p. 10.

[2] Ibid., p. 11.

it might be safest to trust the voice of tradition on the subject of the Bard's birthday and to assume that he was probably born on the Feast Day of England's patron saint, especially as the voice of tradition is supported by the presence of a good deal of solid circumstantial evidence.

Moving from the circumstantial to the documentary evidence, we know that Shakespeare was baptized in Holy Trinity, the local parish church, on April 26, 1564. Since the church was technically Anglican, it has been suggested that Shakespeare's parents must have been conformists. This is not the case. Catholic parents knew that, if the matter and form were duly applied, the sacrament of baptism was valid, whether it was administered by a layman or a cleric, or whether by a heretic or a Catholic. Furthermore, if they wanted to have their child's birth and baptism officially recorded, or legitimized, they had no choice in law but to have their children baptized in the local parish church. Not only did the law enforce the baptism of all children in the parish church, it severely penalized those parents who failed to comply: "Catholics, even the parents of the child, were subjected to severe penalties for conferring that sacrament."[3] Lord Montague, grandfather of Shakespeare's patron, the Earl of Southampton, and one of the country's most notorious recusants, was discovered to have baptized his son and was forced, in consequence, to dismiss all his servants. In the face of such persecution, and in the knowledge that the baptisms carried out in the parish church were valid and were not explicitly forbidden by the Catholic Church, few Catholics felt the need to defy the law. In Stratford itself, there are many instances of the children of avowedly Catholic parents being baptized in the parish church.[4] It was common practice even amongst the most militant of recusants.

The young William Shakespeare was born into dangerous and turbulent times, the plague claiming the lives of 7 percent of Stratford's population in the year of his birth. His father was listed amongst those who gave money for the relief of the plague victims and, as we have seen, was also a reluctant party, in the same year, to the desecration of the town's guild chapel. In 1568, when William was four years old, Mary, Queen of Scots, fled to England, raising hopes of an eventual Catholic succession, which were seemingly dashed by her imprisonment on the

---

[3] Bowden, cited in H. Mutschmann and K. Wentersdorf, *Shakespeare and Catholicism* (New York: Sheed and Ward, 1952), p. 377.

[4] See chapter 8 of Mutschmann and Wentersdorf, *Shakespeare and Catholicism*.

orders of Elizabeth. In the following year the Northern Rebellion, led by the Duke of Norfolk and the Earl of Northumberland, in support of Mary, was crushed ruthlessly. More than eight hundred mainly Catholic rebels were executed. It has been suggested by several scholars that the two parts of Shakespeare's *Henry IV* were inspired by the Northern Rebellion, enabling him to draw parallels between his own time and the past. On February 25, 1570, Pope Pius V responded to the ruthless crushing of the Rebellion by finally excommunicating Queen Elizabeth. The Bull of Excommunication stated that:

> peers, subjects and people of the said kingdom, and all others upon what terms soever bound unto her; are freed from their oath and all manner of duty, fidelity and obedience ... commanding moreover and enjoining all and every, the nobles, subjects, people and others whatsoever that they shall not once dare to obey her or any of her laws, directions or commands, binding under the same curse those who do anything to the contrary.

The Papal Bull had the effect of polarizing religious opinion in England, intensifying the enmity between Protestants and Catholics and serving to alienate the latter still further from the government. Prior to 1570 "the Church of England largely proved a tolerable substitute for, if an inferior version of, its medieval predecessor", but following the issue of the Bull there was a significant increase in recusancy. Conformity became "gradually less attractive to committed Catholics as religious positions polarized, the Calvinist temper of the Elizabethan Church stiffened, and its puritan vanguard resolved itself into a political movement agitating for progressive liturgical reform and ecclesiastical reconstruction on presbyterian lines".[5] Throughout the 1570s, in spite of "a sudden upsurge in legislative and administrative activity against 'popery'" on the part of the Elizabethan government, increasing numbers of Catholics ceased being "church papists" (who attended Anglican services albeit reluctantly, registering their dissent by abstaining from communion) and became outright recusants (refusing even to attend Anglican services and thereby openly defying the law).[6] This militant tendency amongst England's Catholics was noted by the Calvinist preacher Per-

[5] Alexandra Walsham, *Church Papists: Catholicism, Conformity and Confessional Polemic in Early Modern England* (Woodbridge, Suffolk: Royal Historical Society/Boydell Press, 1993), p. 20.

[6] Ibid., pp. 20–21.

ceval Wilburn, who observed in 1581 that recusancy was but a recent phenomenon, charging the "papists" that it was "but a late taken up scrupulosity among the moste of you".[7] This same tendency was also noted by an observer from the opposing theological perspective, the Jesuit Robert Persons. Writing in 1590 to Claude Aquaviva, general of the Jesuit order in Rome, Father Persons lamented the "days of darkness" at the beginning of the queen's reign, the 1560s, when "[m]ultitudes nominally Catholics [were] in fact traitors to their holy religion and deserters from it" through their attendance at Anglican services.[8] All of this corresponds with the apparent hardening of John Shakespeare's position at this time and is, of course, hugely significant to our efforts to understand the religious background of William Shakespeare's childhood. It means that he was growing up in a family that was becoming increasingly alienated from the government and the state religion, a family of outcasts and outlaws.

Whether his father was an avowed recusant or merely a church papist, there is little doubt that the young William Shakespeare would have been brought up in a traditional Catholic home. His mother would have schooled her children in the Faith, teaching them the Church's doctrine, and the prayers, rituals, and beliefs of the "old religion". This, according to Michael Wood, "is borne out by the numerous references to such things in William's plays and by his palpable affection for the medieval English Christian past".[9]

As for his formal education, there is little doubt that William would have been educated at the local grammar school, which was financed by the Stratford Corporation, over which his father, as bailiff, presided. By the time that boys started school, at the age of seven, they were already expected to have basic skills in reading and writing English, and to have basic reading skills in Latin. It is safe to assume, therefore, that his Latin and English tuition began when he was about five years old, possibly earlier, either at home or at petty school, the most elementary level of Elizabethan education for boys aged five to seven. He progressed to the grammar school, probably in 1571, and would have been

---

[7] Perceval Wiburn, *A checke or reproofe of M. Howlets untimely shreeching in her Majesties eares* (London: At the three Cranes in the Vintree, by Thomas Dawson, for Toby Smith, 1581); cited in ibid., p. 21.

[8] Quoted from papers in the Jesuit Archives in Rome by Philip Caraman, S.J., *Henry Garnet 1555–1606 and the Gunpowder Plot* (London: Longmans, Green, 1964), p. 110.

[9] Michael Wood, *Shakespeare* (New York: Basic Books/Perseus Books Group, 2003), p. 37.

educated there for the next seven years. Although the early records of the school have not survived, Michael Wood emphasizes the strong circumstantial evidence that this was the school that Shakespeare attended. Wood stresses that "the patterns of his quotations and his remembered reading betray the fact that the author [of the plays] was steeped in the Tudor grammar school curriculum".[10] This evidence, coupled with the fact that John Shakespeare was entitled to send his son to the school, makes it "as good as certain that this was the school that William attended".[11]

Since Wood has done exhaustive research into the nature of education in Tudor grammar schools, and since this is almost certainly the education that Shakespeare received, it is worth dwelling on the details of the curriculum. Referring to Ben Jonson's famous "back-handed compliment" that Shakespeare had "small Latin and less Greek", Wood warns us that such comments must be seen in perspective:

> Jonson himself was a very good Latin scholar. What would be "small Latin" in his day was much more than is mastered by many a classics graduate now. Even in country grammar schools from Devon to Cumbria, boys were expected to "speak Latin purely and readily". The quotes in Shakespeare's plays show that he started with the nationally prescribed text Lily's Latin Grammar (which he sends up in *The Merry Wives of Windsor*), then books of "Sentences", before moving on to Dialogues and, at eight or nine, to full texts of writers such as Ovid.[12]

In order to illustrate Shakespeare's knowledge of Latin, Wood highlights the fact that, in *The Tempest*, the playwright gives the correct translation of a word in Ovid that was omitted in Arthur Golding's English translation, proving that Shakespeare did not rely solely on translations for his Latin sources.

Greek was also part of the curriculum, and Wood cites a school in Bangor in Wales, in 1568, that declared that "nothing shall be taught in the said school but only grammar and authors on the Latin and Greek tongues". At Harrow in Shakespeare's day the boys started Greek grammar in the fourth year. Wood conjectures that, if the curriculum at the Stratford grammar school was similar, Shakespeare might have been able to follow, with a crib, a Greek text such as *Aesop's Fables*.

[10] Ibid., p. 49.
[11] Ibid., p. 50.
[12] Ibid.

"If all this is a surprise," Wood remarks, "remember that Tudor England was probably the most literate society that had yet existed in history." Thomas More, in his *Apologye*, estimated that 60 percent of the population were basically literate, the fruits of a tradition of literacy stretching back three hundred years. As far back as the thirteenth century, basic literacy had reached the peasantry, for simple mortgages, legal cases, and prayers, and land documents from mediaeval England, show that it was common for the ancestors of the Tudor yeoman class to employ limited literacy with a personal seal. In the decades after More wrote his *Apologye* literacy continued to increase. Numerous grammar schools had sprung up in the Tudor period, many of which were direct descendants of the mediaeval guild schools, and 160 new schools would open during the reign of Elizabeth alone. In the 1560s and 1570s "literacy figures shot up", prompting Wood to conclude that Shakespeare, as "a child of the English Renaissance", was "lucky to be born in a privileged generation".[13]

If Shakespeare was fortunate to enjoy an education on the cusp of the new literacy he would also receive an education rooted in the old faith. Many of his teachers at the Stratford Grammar School were Catholics who had been consciously hired by the corporation for their "learning and godliness" at a time when John Shakespeare was deputy bailiff and therefore presumably involved in the hiring process.

If William had started school as early as his fifth birthday, in 1569, he would have had John Acton as his first schoolmaster. He would not have had him for long, however, because Acton left Stratford suddenly, and in mysterious circumstances, at the end of the year. It has been suggested that his departure was forced upon him as a consequence of his support for the Northern Rebellion, signifying his strong Catholic sympathies.[14] There is strong evidence that Acton's successor, Walter Roche, was a Protestant, but he, in turn, was succeeded in 1571 by Simon Hunt, another Catholic, who is perhaps remembered in the schoolroom scene in act 4 of *The Merry Wives of Windsor*. If, as is likely, Shakespeare did not begin his schooling at the grammar school until he was seven years old, Hunt would have arrived at around the time that he started. It is assumed, therefore, that he was probably Shakespeare's

---

[13] Ibid., pp. 50–51.
[14] Edgar Innes Fripp, *Shakespeare: Man and Artist*, vol. 1 (London: Oxford University Press, 1938), p. 48.

first schoolmaster. Since Hunt would remain at the school until 1575 he was probably the most important of the young William's teachers with regard to the influence he wielded. It is, therefore, significant that Hunt left Stratford-upon-Avon in order to take a student, Robert Dibdale, to the Catholic college in Douai, in Flanders, which had been established in 1568 to offer a traditional Catholic university education now that such an education was impossible at Oxford or Cambridge and also to serve as a base for Catholic missionary activity in England aimed at the nation's reconversion. Having left Dibdale at Douai, Hunt proceeded to Rome, where he would be ordained as a Jesuit priest. Dibdale would also be ordained to the priesthood and, as mentioned in the last chapter, would be hanged, drawn, and quartered at Tyburn in London. It is hard to imagine the effect that his master's departure to Rome, to become a Jesuit, would have had on the eleven-year-old William, nor the impact that the brutal execution of his school companion Dibdale would have had upon him many years later.

Following Hunt's departure, William was taught by another master whose name is lost to posterity. We know, however, that he remained until 1578, whereupon Thomas Jenkins, a Protestant, assumed the mastership. Jenkins only stayed a year, and he arrived at the time that Shakespeare might have been ending his schooling. It is, therefore, curious that several biographers have laid great claim to Jenkins' influence, in spite of the absence of any real evidence to support such a claim. It seems that the only evidence is the assumption that the character of Sir Hugh Evans in *The Merry Wives of Windsor* is modeled on Jenkins, and the only evidence for this, apart from the schoolroom scene in act 4, which could apply to any of the playwright's masters, is the fact that Evans and Jenkins both have Welsh surnames. Yet Jenkins does not seem to have been Welsh, being the "son of an old apprentice to Sir Thomas White, the founder of St John's College, Oxford" and possibly "a kinsman of Thomas Jenkins (Jenks) of Warwick, who was bailiff there in 1572–3".[15] If this is so, he would not have had a Welsh brogue, and, in consequence, the only tenuous link between him and Sir Hugh is broken. In any event, it seems that Jenkins was unpopular or incompetent, or at any rate unsatisfactory, because he was bought out on July 9, 1579, by his successor, John Cottam.

---

[15] Ibid., pp. 91–92.

It is possible, perhaps likely, that Jenkins' sudden departure was connected to the volatile religious politics in England at the time, and those in Stratford in particular. It was at this time that Shakespeare's father was being forced to sell property in an effort to cope with the prospect of being fined for his recusancy, and in the previous year he had refused, in conscience, to pay the levy imposed by the state to raise an anti-Catholic militia. Tensions were running high, and one can only imagine the anger caused amongst the Catholics in Stratford when Jenkins became active in the musters being raised to crush Catholic dissent. On June 8, 1579, only a month before his sudden departure from Stratford grammar school, he was paid ten shillings for the carriage of the soldiers' implements to Warwick.[16] It seems likely that the two events were connected, and that Jenkins found his position at a largely Catholic school increasingly untenable in the light of his active support for the militia. It should be noted that Shakespeare was now fifteen years old and must have become embroiled in the anger and anxiety surrounding the political situation and the divisions it was causing.

John Cottam, who took over from Jenkins, seems to have been an avowed Catholic. He may have been a friend and fellow student of Simon Hunt at Oxford because they graduated in the same year. He was also an older brother of Thomas Cottam, who graduated from Brasenose College (Oxford) in 1569 and would later be executed as a priest in May 1582.[17] When Thomas Cottam was arrested in 1581 he had been found in possession of a letter home by Robert Dibdale, who, on returning to England the previous year, had been arrested and was languishing in the Gatehouse prison in London. A month after his brother's arraignment, John Cottam left Stratford after serving as schoolmaster for two years.

Whether Shakespeare finished his schooling under the tutorage of the unknown master who succeeded Hunt, or whether under Jenkins or Cottam, we can safely assume that, sometime between 1578 and 1579, he moved on to pastures new. The problem for the Shakespearian detective is that the next period of his life is even more shrouded in mist and mystery than the rest. As Shakespeare leaves school he seems to leave the stage completely, disappearing into the seemingly impenetrable fog of the so-called lost years.

[16] Ibid., p. 92.
[17] Ibid.

5

A ROSE BY ANY OTHER NAME

O, be some other name!
What's in a name? That which we call a rose
By any other word would smell as sweet.

—Juliet (*Romeo and Juliet*, 2.2.42–44)

Very little is known of Shakespeare's life during the "lost years" from 1579 until 1592, from the time that he finished his schooling in Stratford until the earliest known reference to his being a playwright in London. The only documentary evidence during this period relates to his marriage in 1582, and to the births of his children in 1583 and 1585. The rest is silence.

In order to piece together a picture of what he might have done in these years we are forced into the realm of circumstantial evidence, with all the dangers that accompany it. It is all too easy, in the absence of solid and irrefutable documentary evidence, to follow flights of fancy, or to be misguided by one's own preconceptions. It is, in fact, all too easy to confuse the line between the possible and the plausible, on the one hand, and the impossible and the implausible, on the other. This is the danger, and the good historical and literary sleuth must be on his guard against falling into the trap of allowing himself to be fooled by his own prejudice or by the prejudice of others. If we are dealing with fragments of evidence we must be sure that they are not merely figments of our imagination.

It has been suggested by a number of Shakespearian scholars, notably by Father Peter Milward and Clare Asquith, that Shakespeare, like his schoolfellow Robert Dibdale, might have continued his studies abroad after he finished school in Stratford. If so, he would presumably have gone to the English College in Rheims (its having moved from Douai in 1578) or to the new English College in Rome, which was opened in

64

1579. "The evidence for either place is indeed scanty", Father Milward admits. Yet, he continues, "it is interesting that Douai is situated in the Forest of Arden (or Ardennes), which provides the remarkably Catholic setting for most of *As You Like It*, and which may indiscriminately refer to the Warwickshire Arden of Shakespeare's forebears and to the French Ardennes".[1] Milward also reminds us that Rheims is explicitly mentioned as the university of Lucentio in *The Taming of the Shrew*, though this only means that Shakespeare knew of the college's existence and hardly constitutes evidence that he went there himself.

Clare Asquith conjectures that Shakespeare may have attended one of the halls at Oxford still sympathetic to the old religion, "either by taking an alias or without registering at the university at all", thereby avoiding having to take the Oath of Supremacy. Alternatively she agrees with Milward that he might have gone abroad: "Two biographical details support this possibility: for unknown reasons, his father began to lose money in the late 1570s, perhaps as a result of this expensive course of education [in Rheims or Rome]. And Shakespeare reappears in the Stratford records in 1582, a year after the government had recalled all those studying abroad on pain of ruinous fines."[2] Since, as we have shown, Shakespeare's father lost money through his being fined for his recusancy, the argument that the money was used for his son's education seems a little tenuous. Equally, Shakespeare only reappears in the Stratford records in 1582 because he got married in that year. There is no evidence that it had anything to do with the threat of government fines for his studying abroad.

Stronger arguments for the theory that Shakespeare may have studied at Rheims or Rome appear in the textual evidence from his plays, which illustrates that he seems to have known the Spiritual Exercises of St. Ignatius Loyola, the founder of the Jesuits, and that he seems to have been familiar with Gregorian chant.

Father Milward, as a lifelong scholar of Shakespeare and as a Jesuit priest for almost half a century, is uniquely placed to study the influence of the Spiritual Exercises on Shakespeare's works and has done so

---

[1] Peter Milward, *The Plays and Exercises: A Hidden Source of Shakespeare's Inspiration?* (Tokyo: The Renaissance Institute / Sophia University, 2002), p. 78. Milward expands upon this thesis in greater detail in an article in the Winter 2001 issue of *Shakespeare Survey*.

[2] Clare Asquith, *Shadowplay: The Hidden Beliefs and Coded Politics of William Shakespeare* (New York: Public Affairs / Perseus Books Group, 2005), p. 28.

at considerable length.[3] Yet Shakespeare could have read the Exercises without having to go to Europe to do so. Although they were not published in an English translation at this time, he was presumably capable of reading them in Latin. Furthermore, the main themes of the Exercises were published in English by the Jesuit Robert Persons in 1582, as the *Book of Christian Exercise*, better known as the "Book of Resolution". Two years later this was published in a revised form by a Protestant minister, Edmund Bunny, and was described by its publisher as "one of the most vendible books ever issued in this country".[4] Since there is also good evidence that Shakespeare may have known and befriended a number of Jesuit priests, including the martyrs Edmund Campion and Robert Southwell, it is evident that he could have become thoroughly *au fait* with the Ignatian Exercises without ever setting foot outside the country.

In similar vein, the historian Thomas Merriam has shown that there is ample evidence of the influence of Gregorian chant in a number of Shakespeare's plays, ranging from *Henry VI*, part 2, and *Richard III* to *Othello*, *Pericles*, and *Henry VIII*.[5] Again, however, it would hardly have been necessary for Shakespeare to go abroad to attain such knowledge. One of the beauties of Gregorian chant is that it does not require a large choir or a lavish liturgy but can be incorporated into a liturgy at which only a handful of people are present. As such, Shakespeare could have acquired the knowledge of chant from his attendance at illegal Masses in England, and would not have needed to have attended Mass in Rheims or Rome.

When all the evidence, or lack thereof, is weighed, it could be said that, whilst it is possible and plausible that Shakespeare could have studied abroad, there is virtually no evidence to suggest that he did so. It is, therefore, safest and most prudent to presume that he did not do so, in which case what *was* he doing from the time he finished his schooling, in around 1578 or 1579, and the time he married Anne Hathaway in 1582?

The theory that has caused most debate and controversy in recent years is that he spent some time as a tutor at Hoghton Tower, a recusant household in Lancashire. Although the evidence for such a theory seems persuasive, we shall see that it is not without its problems.

[3] See Milward, *The Plays and Exercises*.
[4] Ibid., p. 67.
[5] Thomas Merriam, "Shakespeare and the Good Friday *Reproaches*", *Saint Austin Review* 2, no. 4 (April 2002): 13–17.

According to John Aubrey, one of the earliest sources available, Shakespeare spent some time as a schoolmaster in his youth. Referring to Ben Jonson's famous claim that Shakespeare "had but little Latin and less Greek", Aubrey responded that Shakespeare "understood Latin pretty well, for he had been in his younger years a schoolmaster in the country".[6] Although Aubrey's evidence was gathered within decades of Shakespeare's death it is not always reliable. He also claimed, for instance, that Shakespeare's father was a butcher, which is known to be untrue, and even waxed lyrical about the way that the young Shakespeare had himself plied his father's trade, killing calves "in a high style" and making a speech while he did so! Faced with such high-spirited nonsense it is tempting to simply discredit Aubrey as a witness. Yet to do so is dangerous. Although the stories about Shakespeare's butchering calves in Stratford-upon-Avon are accredited by Aubrey to "some of the neighbours", clearly reducing the status of the report to that of mere gossip, the source for his claim that Shakespeare had been a schoolmaster in his youth is attributed to William Beeston (c. 1606–1682), the son of Shakespeare's former colleague in the Lord Chamberlain's company, Christopher Beeston (died 1638). The latter evidence, the source of which is someone who knew Shakespeare personally, carries considerable weight.

If we can fairly safely assume that the young Shakespeare was indeed "a schoolmaster in the country", we are left with the mystery surrounding where, exactly, "in the country" he spent his time as a tutor. It is possible that the mystery was solved by Chambers, in a paper entitled "William Shakeshafte", published in his *Shakespearean Gleanings* (1944). This paper centered on the contents of the will of Alexander Hoghton, dated August 3, 1581, in which Hoghton bequeathed his stock of costumes and all his musical instruments to his brother Thomas, or, if he did not choose to keep players, to Sir Thomas Hesketh, adding: "And I most heartily require the said Sir Thomas to be friendly unto Fulk Gyllome and William Shakeshafte now dwelling with me and either to take them into his service or else to help them to some good master, as

---

[6] John Aubrey (1626–1697) gathered a good deal of information about Shakespeare and other celebrities, much of which was included in Anthony á Wood's *Athenae Oxonienses* (1692) and was later published as *Aubrey's Brief Lives* (1813). Aubrey's account of Shakespeare, from which this quote is taken, is published *in extenso* in Oscar James Campbell and Edward G. Quinn, eds., *The Reader's Encyclopedia of Shakespeare* (New York: MJF Books, 1966), p. 49.

my trust is he will." [7] Like Alexander Hoghton, Sir Thomas Hesketh, of nearby Rufford Hall, appears to have maintained a small company of players and musicians, leading Chambers to conclude, reasonably enough, that the linking of Fulk Gyllome and William Shakeshafte with Hesketh "seems to make it at least highly probable" that Gyllome and Shakeshafte were players. [8] Believing that William Shakeshafte might actually be William Shakespeare, Chambers reminds us that Shakespeare's grandfather Richard "seems to be both Shakstaff and Shakeschafte, as well as Shakspere ... in the Snitterfield manor records", adding that "it is at least conceivable that William might have adopted the variant as a player". Chambers went on to make connections between Sir Thomas Hesketh and Lord Strange, who kept a well-known company of players, and concludes, tentatively, that Shakespeare might have passed from Hesketh's employment into that of Lord Strange, "and so later into the London theatrical world". [9]

Chambers' "Shakeshafte theory" has been a major bone of contention amongst Shakespeare scholars ever since it was first published. It provides a seemingly feasible explanation for Shakespeare's progress from being an unknown actor in Lancashire to his arrival in London with Lord Strange's Men, and, as such, it could provide the missing link connecting the recusant's son from Warwickshire with the famous playwright in London. And yet, if this is so, how did the recusant's son from Warwickshire find his way to Hoghton Tower in Lancashire? This particular mystery has been the source of much recent conjecture on the part of scholars.

It should be noted, in the first instance, that it was not unusual for recusant families to send their sons away when they reached the age of sixteen, as the historian Antonia Fraser explains: "Catholic parents often voluntarily dispatched their children at sixteen to a distant neighbourhood; this was the age at which these children would incur fines of their own for not attending church, thus increasing the family burden." [10] This being so, we should not be surprised to learn that Shakespeare left home in around 1579 or 1580. Where, however, did he go?

[7] Cited in E. A. J. Honigmann, *Shakespeare: The "Lost Years"* (Totowa, N.J.: Barnes and Noble Books, 1986), p. 3.

[8] Ibid.

[9] Ibid., p. 4.

[10] Antonia Fraser, *The Gunpowder Plot: Terror and Faith in 1605* (London: Weidenfeld and Nicholson, 1996), p. 21.

Peter Milward stressed that "recent investigations have disclosed a remarkable number of connections between Stratford and the part of Lancashire round Preston", near Hoghton Tower.[11] Shakespeare's own extended family, through the Park Hall Ardens on his mother's side, had married into several of the leading Catholic families in northern England.[12] Thomas Hoghton, who had rebuilt Hoghton Tower, was a leading Lancashire recusant who had been forced into exile following the Northern Rebellion in 1569. His son Thomas became a Catholic priest, and his other son, Alexander, succeeded his exiled father as head of the family at Hoghton Tower. It was he, as we have seen, who mentioned William Shakeshafte in his will in 1581. Alexander's half brother, Richard, who was distantly related to Shakespeare as one of the Ardens of Park Hall, was also forced into exile after the Northern Rebellion.

Thomas Hoghton bequeathed to posterity a poignant poem, "The Blessed Conscience", depicting the dilemma facing England's beleaguered Catholics and highlighting the heartbreak of those forced into exile:

> To lovelie Lea then I mee hied,
>   And Hoghton bade fayrwell:
> Ytt was more tyme for mee to ryde,
>   Than longer ther to dwel.
> I durst not trust my dearest frende,
>   Butt secretlie stole hence,
> To take ye fortune God shulde sende,
>   And kepe my conscyènce.
>
>   *   *   *
>
> Thus took I ther my leave, alas!
>   And rode to ye sea-syde;
> Ynto ye shippe I hied apace,
>   Wich dyd for mee abyde.
> With syghs I sail'd from merrie Englande,
>   I asked of none lycènce:

[11] Peter Milward, *Shakespeare's Religious Background* (Bloomington: Indiana University Press, 1973), p. 41.

[12] Charlotte Stopes, *Shakespeare's Warwickshire Contemporaries* (Stratford: Shakespeare Head, 1908), pp. 123–25.

Wherfor my estate fell from my hande,
And was forfeit to my Prynce.[13]

These lines, written by Thomas Hoghton during his exile, would presumably have been known to his son Alexander, who had inherited his
father's land by default, and it is easy to imagine that they would also
have been known to William Shakeshafte, especially as he was living at
Hoghton Tower in 1580, when news of Thomas Hoghton's death reached
the family. Perhaps the best way of conveying the profundity of feeling
that the plight of England's exiled Catholics invoked in the hearts of
their fellow Catholics at home is to quote the epitaph, in the Church
of San Gregorio in Rome, of another English exile, Robert Peckham,
who had died in 1564, the year of Shakespeare's birth: "Here lies Robert Peckham, Englishman and Catholic, who, after England's break with
the Church, left England, not being able to live without the Faith, and
who, coming to Rome, died, not being able to live without his
country." [14]

Even if William Shakespeare and William Shakeshafte are not the
same person, the former would have been well acquainted with the
heartbreaking reality of exile. His schoolmaster Simon Hunt and his
schoolfellow Robert Dibdale were both exiles by this time, and it is
easy to see how the tragedy and the romance of their experience would
have been grist to the dramatic mill of his fertile imagination, even if
he had never set foot in the recusant heartland of Lancashire. There is,
however, ample evidence to suggest that Shakespeare was well connected with the area round Hoghton Tower, apart from the family connections already mentioned. John Cottam, schoolmaster in Stratford from
1579 to 1581, was from Tarnacre, near Hoghton, and is presumed to be
the "John Cotham" who, along with "William Shakeshafte", was a beneficiary of Alexander Hoghton's will. Considering this connection
between "Cotham" and "Shakeshafte" in the will, and therefore the
connection of both men to Hoghton Tower, it has been suggested that
Cottam may have been the person who directed the young Shakespeare
to Lancashire. It should be noted, however, that many of the other
Stratford schoolmasters were also from Lancashire, itself suggestive of
many connections between Stratford and the northern heartland of

[13] These two stanzas of a ballad containing twenty-three stanzas in total are cited in A. C.
Southern, *Elizabethan Recusant Prose 1559–1582* (London: Sands, 1950), p. 17.
[14] This is an English translation of the Latin epitaph.

Catholicism. These include Walter Roche, who was at Stratford Grammar School from 1569 to 1571, and Simon Hunt (1571–1575), both of whom were from Lancaster, about twenty miles from Hoghton, and both of whom had taught the young Shakespeare. Alexander Aspinall, who became a master of the Stratford grammar school in 1582, after Shakespeare had left, was also from Lancaster.

There is also evidence that recusant households, such as the Hoghtons, were in the habit of keeping Catholic schoolmasters to teach their children the Faith in the absence of such teaching at the grammar schools, where it was now illegal. This Elizabethan form of homeschooling was against the law and, in consequence, secretive, but it is clear that some branches of the Hoghton family were willing to break the law in this regard, as was shown by Honigmann in *Shakespeare: The Lost Years*:

> An apostate priest informed Lord Burghley in 1592 that Richard Hoghton of Park Hall "hath kept a recusant schoolmaster I think this twenty years. He hath had one after another; the name of one was Scholes, of the other Fawcett, as I remember, but I stand in doubt of the names." The same informer claimed that Mrs. Anne Hoghton, the widow of Thomas II, kept at her house in Lea Richard Blundell, brother to William Blundell, of Crosbie, gent., "an obstinate papist," to teach her children to sing and play on the virginals; and that Mr. Bartholemew Hesketh (the brother of Alexander Hoghton's widow) "hath kept for sundry years a certain Gabriel Shaw to be his schoolmaster;" and that William Hulton of Hulton, Esq., a close friend of the Hoghtons, had kept a recusant school-master "many years." [15]

It is, therefore, plausible to suggest that Shakeshafte could indeed be an alias for Shakespeare. There were plenty of connections between recusant Stratford and recusant Lancashire, and it seems that recusant households kept recusant tutors, making it feasible that Shakespeare "had been in his younger years a schoolmaster in the country", as was reported by his friend and contemporary Christopher Beeston. Adding further weight to the evidence for the Shakeshafte theory, Honigmann notes "a folk tradition of long standing at Rufford which links Shakespeare with the Hall".[16] This tradition appears to predate the scholarly discussion of Alexander Hoghton's will and serves to corroborate the circumstantial

[15] Honigmann, *Shakespeare*, p. 20.
[16] Ibid., p. 34.

evidence for Shakeshafte's connection to the Heskeths of Rufford Hall implied in the latter.

Another intriguing possibility, if Shakespeare is Shakeshafte, is that he may well have been present when his schoolmaster's younger brother, Thomas Cottam, visited Hoghton Tower "between Easter and Whit-suntide" 1581.[17] Cottam, who at various times was a seminary priest and a Jesuit, was a friend and associate of Edmund Campion, the most famous of England's Jesuit martyrs, and it is at least possible that, like Cottam, Campion had also visited Hoghton Tower during the period that Shakeshafte was there. We know that Campion had visited and preached at one of the Hoghton family residences in 1580, prompting a raid of the house during the following year. We know also that Campion had stayed with Richard Hoghton because it was reported follow-ing his arrest that "the Jesuit had stayed with leading Catholics in Lancashire, whose houses were searched by order of the Privy Council—and especially the house of Richard Hoghton, where it is said the said Campion left his books".[18]

Cottam and Campion were both arrested in June 1581, when Shake-shafte was probably still in Lancashire, and they were arraigned on Novem-ber 14, by which time he had returned to Stratford. After being tortured on the rack, Cottam and Campion were executed as "traitors". Per-haps, in order to reveal the barbarism of the deaths meted out to Cath-olic priests in Elizabeth's reign, and in order to glean some idea of the horror and anger felt by recusants such as Shakespeare, it is decorous to repeat the words that the queen's Lord Chief Justice pronounced to Cottam and Campion: "You shall be taken to the place from whence you came, there to remain until ye shall be drawn through the open city of London upon hurdles to the place of execution, and there hanged and let down alive, and your privy parts cut off and your entrails taken out and burnt in your sight; then your heads to be cut off and your bodies divided into four parts, to be disposed of at Her Majesty's Pleasure."

Although there is a frustrating lack of documentary evidence that Shakespeare knew Campion, there is a great deal of good circumstantial evidence that he may have. Campion landed at Dover in June 1580, and, along with his fellow Jesuit Robert Persons and several others,

[17] Anthony Holden, *William Shakespeare: The Man Behind the Genius* (Boston: Little, Brown, 1999), p. 56.

[18] Honigmann, *Shakespeare*, p. 11.

sought to establish a Jesuit mission to England, determined, as Campion put it in his famous *"brag"* addressed to the queen's privy council, "never to give you over, but either to win you heaven, or to die upon your pikes [and] cheerfully to carry the cross you shall lay upon us, and never to despair your recovery, while we have a man left to enjoy your Tyburn, or to be racked with your torments, or consumed with your prisons".[19]

In the following month, Campion headed for Northamptonshire, Oxfordshire, and East Anglia; Persons to Warwickshire, Worcestershire, and Gloucestershire. Persons stayed with the Grants, business partners of John Shakespeare, at Northbrook, not far from the Shakespeare family farm in Snitterfield, and also with the Skinners at Rowington, about ten miles north of Stratford. Campion would also visit the same area, staying with local recusant families, en route to Lancashire. Government informers reported that Campion had stayed twenty miles north of Stratford, at Park Hall, home of Shakespeare's mother's kinsman Edward Arden, and, although this was never proved, we know from the Jesuit Robert Southwell that Edward Arden was "a friend of Father Persons, in whose house he generally used to hide".[20] It's also reported that Campion stayed with William Catesby at Lapworth, twelve miles from Stratford, in 1580. Some have deduced that this was probably the occasion on which John Shakespeare received a copy of his "spiritual will". De Groot, normally the most sober and conscientious of scholars, surmises that "John Shakespeare was among those reached by the Jesuits early in their mission, before the arrival of the printed testaments from Rome", whereas Milward suggests that the will "must have come into the hands of Shakespeare's father when Persons or Campion passed through the Midlands".[21] Milward goes even further, conjecturing that "John Shakespeare received his copy from Campion at the house of William Catesby".[22] Although it is certainly an attractively romantic conjecture that John Shakespeare received his copy of the will from the hands of Campion in person, and even more so if we imagine that the

---

[19] The full text of Campion's Brag is published as an appendix in Evelyn Waugh's *Edmund Campion: Jesuit and Martyr in the Reign of Queen Elizabeth* (London: Longmans, Green, 1935), pp. 219–23.

[20] Michael Wood, *Shakespeare* (New York: Basic Books / Perseus Books Group, 2003), p. 74.

[21] John Henry de Groot, *The Shakespeares and "The Old Faith"* (Fraser, Mich.: Real-View Books, 1995), p. 89; Milward, *Shakespeare's Religious Background*, p. 44.

[22] Milward, *Shakespeare's Religious Background*, p. 21.

sixteen-year-old William was with his father at the time, it is surely more likely that bulk supplies of the will were left by Campion or Persons, or by others unknown, with their hosts as they were passing through the midlands en route to the north or wherever. As prosaically disappointing as it may seem, it is far more likely that John Shakespeare received his copy of the will from Catesby or Edward Arden, or from the Grants or the Skinners, or from other persons unknown with whom they came into contact, or, even more prosaically, from agents of any of the aforementioned. Nor is de Groot's surmisal very tenable, namely, that John Shakespeare's handwritten copy of the will suggests that he was "among those reached by the Jesuits early in their mission, before the arrival of the printed testaments from Rome". Isn't it likely that those reached early in the mission would have been given copies of the original printed version, prior to supplies running out and new supplies being requested?

Having made the prosaic rebuttal of this romantic guesswork (or wishwork) by various Shakespeare scholars, we should say that it is nonetheless possible that John Shakespeare *could* have met Campion or Persons, and it is possible that his son could have been with him when he did so (on the assumption that the latter was not in Lancashire at the time). The Shakespeares were clearly well connected with their recusant co-religionists, and they *might* have been amongst the select and secretive company who met the Jesuit missionaries during their passage through Warwickshire. It is possible, indeed plausible, to suppose that they *might* have met Campion or Persons, but it is simply not possible or plausible to employ John Shakespeare's spiritual will as convincing evidence to support such a supposition.

Others have sought to show by convoluted and unconvincing leaps of logic that the young William Shakespeare may even have traveled to Lancashire to take up residence at Hoghton Tower in the presence of Campion himself, suggesting that the sixteen-year-old William was even the future martyr's guide. Such arguments stretch credulity to the limit (and beyond). When all the evidence is weighed, it seems that the most likely occasion for a meeting between Shakespeare and England's most famous Jesuit would have been during his sojourn in Lancashire, and that depends on whether William Shakespeare was indeed William Shakeshafte, itself not certain, though perhaps likely. On the other hand, if Shakespeare is Shakeshafte it is possible that the young poet could have met Campion on many occasions, since the latter seems to have hidden himself amongst the recusant families of Lancashire for much of the time he was at liberty. "If Shakespeare was Shakeshafte," wrote Richard Wilson in *Secret Shakespeare*, "he was a member of a household which was for six months, it seems, nothing less than the secret headquarters of the English Counter-Reformation."[23] Such a scenario even conjures up the possibility that Campion, arguably the most brilliant man of his generation, could have been something of a mentor to the budding poet. If so, one scarcely knows how to address the magnitude and the import of such a momentous meeting of minds; the forty-year-old master of rhetoric and the sixteen-year-old genius-in-waiting. Perhaps one can do no better than to repeat the words of another great writer, Evelyn Waugh, in his description of what it must have been like to have attended a secret predawn Mass at which Campion was the celebrant and preacher:

> It needs little fancy to reconstruct the scene; the audience hushed and intent, every member of whom was risking liberty and fortune, perhaps his life, by attendance. The dusk lightened and the candles paled on the improvised altar, the tree tops outside the window took fire, as Campion spoke. The thrilling tones, the profusion of imagery, the polish and precision, the balanced, pointed argument, the whole structure and rich ornament of rhetoric which had stirred the lecture halls and collegiate chapels of Oxford and Douai, Rome, Prague and Rheims, inspired now with more than human artistry, rang through the summer dawn.[24]

Fired with imaginative enthusiasm, Stephen Greenblatt waxes almost as lyrical as Waugh in his excitement at the prospect of Shakespeare and Campion living under the same roof:

> Let us imagine the two of them sitting together then, the sixteen-year-old fledgling poet and actor and the forty-year-old Jesuit. Shakespeare would have found Campion fascinating—even his mortal enemies conceded that he had charisma—and might even have recognized in him something of a kindred spirit . . . Witty, imaginative, and brilliantly adept at improvisation, he managed to combine meditative seriousness with a

[23] Richard Wilson, *Secret Shakespeare: Studies in Theatre, Religion, and Resistance* (Manchester: Manchester University Press, 2004), p. 56.

[24] Waugh, *Edmund Campion*, p. 136.

strong theatrical streak. If the adolescent knelt down before Campion, he would have been looking at a distorted image of himself.[25]

The Shakespearian Jesuit Peter Milward also enthused at the prospect of Shakespeare and the Jesuit actually meeting in the flesh:

> We know ... that Campion confessed (under torture) not only to having spent the spring of 1581 in Lancashire, but also to having stayed part of the time at the home of Alexander's half-brother Richard. ... In that case, we have the interesting situation of both the young William Shakespeare and the mature Jesuit Edmund Campion dwelling at the same time under the same family auspices in the same region of Lancashire. ... Then, what would have been more natural than for William, with his passion for drama, to have asked Campion about the Latin plays which the other had composed for his students at the Jesuit college at Prague, before being sent on the English mission? Thus Campion would have enjoyed the dignity of being Shakespeare's first tutor in the art of dramaturgy. Then on his side, it would have been no less natural for Campion to invite William to make the *Spiritual Exercises* of St. Ignatius Loyola, which Jesuits such as Campion aimed at giving to promising young men such as William. For here and there in the plays one comes upon interesting echoes of various places in these Exercises, such as the dramatist could have heard only from the lips of a Jesuit.[26]

We have already seen that the "interesting echoes" of the Ignatian Exercises in Shakespeare's plays could be attributable to Shakespeare's becoming familiar with them through his reading, without the necessity of his ever having met a Jesuit, and yet it is possible that Campion could have met Shakeshafte during the spring of 1581, when they were both moving in the close-knit recusant world within a few miles of each other, and perhaps sometimes staying under the very same roof. If so, it is possible that the learned Jesuit would have detected in the drama-loving teenage schoolmaster, not merely a kindred spirit but a mind and heart kindled with youthful genius. Why would he not take such a youth under his wing? For all his evident enthusiasm, Milward's scenario is not all that far-fetched. It could have been as he imagines it. The players were in place. The scene was set. And they could have met.

[25] Stephen Greenblatt, *Will in the World: How Shakespeare Became Shakespeare* (New York: W.W. Norton, 2004), pp. 108–9.
[26] Peter Milward, *Shakespeare the Papist* (Naples, Fla.: Sapientia Press, 2005), pp. 12–13.

All of this presupposes, of course, that Shakespeare was Shakeshafte. There are many who have failed to be convinced. Douglas Hamer, in 1970, and Robert Bearman, in 2002, point to the fact that there were several families with the surname Shakeshafte in the vicinity of Hoghton Tower, signifying that it was far more likely that William Shakeshafte came from one of these local families.[27] This seems to be a reasonable enough assumption, all other factors being equal, and it was enough for Michael Wood to assert, in response to Bearman's research, that "the Shakeshafte theory has not survived closer scrutiny".[28] On the other hand, Anthony Holden seems to take the existence of local Shakeshaftes in his stride, even suggesting that they might have contributed to Shakespeare's decision to employ this particular variant of his own name upon his arrival in Lancashire:

> Given the status of sixteenth-century surnames—infinitely flexible, as we have seen—there is scant cause for surprise in the change in name from Shakespeare to Shakeshafte. It can scarcely be called an alias, to cover a young Warwickshire Catholic's tentative tracks amid the network of informers then riddling boldly recusant Lancashire; but it perhaps had its uses as a variant. Shakespeare's grandfather Richard appears as Shakstaff and Shakeschafte as well as Shakspere in the Snitterfield records; in Lancashire, at the time, the familiar local variant was Shakeshafte—a natural enough name for an out-of-county man to assimilate, or an equally natural lapse on the part of the scrivener drawing up Hoghton's will.[29]

So was William Shakeshafte really William Shakespeare? Let's take one last look at the facts before moving on. If the Shakeshafte mentioned in the will was merely one of the local Shakeshaftes, he must also, from the evidence we know, have been an actor and a recusant Catholic. The former is clear from the wording of the will; the latter is clear because the Elizabethan spy network made it perilous, indeed suicidal, for recusant families to employ anyone other than fellow recusants. It is possible that the local Shakeshaftes might have been recusants, but it would certainly be a little surprising to discover that the local Shakeshafte, like his distant cousin in Stratford, was an actor. It is, however,

---

[27] Douglas Hamer, "Was William Shakespeare William Shakeshafte?" *The Review of English Studies*, n.s. 21, no. 81 (February 1970): 41–48; Robert Bearman, "'Was William Shakespeare William Shakeshafte?' Revisited", *Shakespeare Quarterly* 53, no. 1 (2002): 83–94.

[28] Wood, *Shakespeare*, p. 346.

[29] Holden, *William Shakespeare*, p. 54.

possible, and we should certainly not rule out the prosaic possibility that the whole Shakeshafte theory is a huge red herring. If so, we must return to Stratford in order to find him. Once there, we would find him as we had left him. We would find him to be the son of a recusant Catholic, and presumably a recusant Catholic himself, since there is absolutely no evidence to suggest that he was anything else.

Was Shakeshafte Shakespeare? Perhaps, in spite of the huge weight of seemingly convincing circumstantial evidence suggesting that he was, we cannot know, for certain, one way or the other. Perhaps, in the wider scheme of things, it doesn't really matter. In the quest for William Shakespeare we know that he was raised in a militantly Catholic home, whether or not he ever stayed in that other militantly Catholic home in Lancashire. Shakespeare or Shakeshafte? What's in a name? This particular rose, by any other word, would smell as papist.

6

LOVE'S LABORS

In April 1580, as William celebrated his sixteenth birthday, his parents had another son. He was named Edmund, and it is tempting to suggest that he was named after Edmund Campion, soon to emerge as the buccaneering hero of the recusant movement. Since, however, Campion did not arrive in England until several weeks after the baby's birth, and since his fame and notoriety followed the publication of his famous "challenge" or "brag" in the following year, it seems far more probable that the new Shakespeare son was named after Edmund Lambert, John Shakespeare's brother-in-law. On the other hand, if the Shakespeares were following Catholic tradition and had named their son after a favorite or significant saint who would serve as the newborn's patron, it is perhaps significant that St. Edmund had been martyred seven hundred years earlier for refusing to deny his Catholic faith following the invasion of East Anglia by the pagan Vikings. Such a possibility seems more likely once we realize that the child was born at a time in which John Shakespeare was himself suffering major persecution for his faith. In the very month that baby Edmund was born, John Shakespeare's name had been on the list of the wealthy members of the town who were being pressured by a government commission to support the anti-Catholic musters being formed up and down the country. It was also around this time, as has been noted, that he was charged with committing a "breach of the Queen's peace", perhaps as a direct result of refusing to finance or otherwise support the muster, an offense for which he was fined the huge sum of £20. It is surely possible, in the context of the dark days of persecution in which the Shakespeare family found itself, that the choice of an English martyr as their new son's patron seemed singularly appropriate. Again, however, it is necessary to temper such conjectures with other possibilities. It is possible that the new baby was not named after St. Edmund, king and martyr, but after St. Edmund of Abingdon, a thirteenth-century archbishop of Canterbury. Although the latter saint is

less well known, he was particularly venerated in Oxfordshire, immediately to the south of Stratford, and also at Catesby in Northamptonshire,
less than twenty miles to the east of Stratford, where the saint's sisters had
been nuns. As we have seen already, rash conclusions need to be avoided
in our efforts to unravel the mysteries surrounding England's greatest poet.

As for the poet himself, he reemerges in November 1582 from the
fog that had enshrouded him since his schooldays. It was then that he
married Anne Hathaway, a woman eight years his senior. As with almost
everything else touching his life, Shakespeare's marriage is a conundrum
that courts controversy. Since their first child, Susanna, was born in the
following May, it is evident that Anne was already several months pregnant at the time of the wedding. This would seem to be sufficient explanation for the apparently frantic haste to obtain a special license to marry
in November, since Church law forbade marriage during the seasons of
Advent and Christmas and, by mid-January, Anne's pregnancy would
be all the more physically evident. And yet there is another mystery
surrounding the marriage license that is not so easily explained. The
law dictated that the bride and groom must marry in one or other of
their home parishes. Since both parties resided within the boundaries
of the Stratford parish, this meant that their marriage should have taken
place in the Stratford parish church. It is, therefore, intriguing that the
license stipulated that they were to be permitted to marry in a different
parish, that of Temple Grafton, about five miles to the west of Stratford. Why was a different parish requested, and why the parish of Temple Grafton in particular?

The most obvious reason, perhaps, is that Anne's pregnancy neces-
sitated a discreet ceremony away from the hub of their home parish.
Such a conclusion is reinforced by a later memorandum by Bishop Whitgift, under whose authority Shakespeare's marriage license was issued,
in which it was stipulated that marriages could be solemnized in a different parish on the grounds of "reasonable secrecy".[1] Clearly the pregnancy of the bride-to-be might constitute such grounds. So far, so good.
But why Temple Grafton? The answer seems to lie in the person of the
parish priest, John Frith, who, unlike the staunchly Protestant vicar of
Stratford, was sympathetic to the old faith. In fact, since he was an old
man who had been ordained in the reign of Queen Mary, he was actually
a Catholic priest, one of the few and rapidly shrinking number of

---

[1]Michael Wood, *Shakespeare* (New York: Basic Books/Perseus Books Group, 2003), p. 85.

Marian priests who had managed to survive the Elizabethan reformation. It is surely significant that four years after he had officiated at the
marriage of William Shakespeare and Anne Hathaway, Father Frith is
referred to scathingly in an official survey of Warwickshire clergy as
being "unsound in religion", that is, a papist.[2]

"On the face of it," wrote Wood, "Anne and William seem to have
gone to some length to avoid marrying in Stratford, where the vicar at
that time, Henry Haycroft, was a strong Protestant." By contrast, John
Frith "was an old priest from Queen Mary's time, a man who had been
a vicar in the days of Catholic England nearly thirty years before": "Still
accused by informers of papistry, he was typical of the rural Warwickshire clergy we have already encountered: men who stayed loyal to their
flock, baptizing, marrying and burying them according to the old rituals
if so desired; taking some elements of the Protestant Church on board
but still holding on to tradition." [3]

Mutschmann and Wentersdorf make the obvious inferences regarding
the significance of the lengths to which Shakespeare and Anne Hathaway
had gone in order to be married by a validly ordained Catholic priest:

> If Shakespeare was married in Temple Grafton ... then he must have been
> married by Father Frith. And if he went to the trouble of obtaining a license
> to be married by a Roman Catholic priest, he can only have been induced
> to do so by religious considerations. Having entered into a "pre-contract"
> with Anne Hathaway, he wished to legalize his marriage without submit-
> ting to the heretical wedding ceremony. A conforming Anglican would hardly
> have wanted to be married by a "Romish" priest, and for a Puritan the very
> idea would have been abhorrent. The most natural interpretation of the
> evidence is, therefore, that Shakespeare obtained the license expressly for
> the purpose of making it possible to wed according to Catholic rites, so
> that the circumstances of his marriage may be regarded as affording con-
> tributory confirmation of the theory that he was a Catholic.[4]

Although the conclusion of Mutschmann and Wentersdorf seems logical
enough, their presumption that Shakespeare had entered a "pre-contract"
with Anne Hathaway may perhaps be a trifle presumptuous. It is not,
however, particularly far-fetched. It is entirely possible that William and

[2] Ibid.
[3] Ibid.
[4] H. Mutschmann and K. Wentersdorf, *Shakespeare and Catholicism* (New York: Sheed and
Ward, 1952), pp. 94–95.

Anne were married in a secret nuptial Mass celebrated by one of the many missionary priests who had begun to enter the country at this time, in which case, of course, no records would have survived for posterity. It is, therefore, possible that their first child was not conceived out of wedlock, as has been commonly believed, for obvious reasons, and without question, down the ages.

Perhaps, in order to illustrate the possibility of a "pre-contract", we should look at contemporary evidence of such "unofficial marriages" amongst England's recusants. An Anglican church report of around 1590, only eight years after Shakespeare's marriage, shows that such weddings were widespread. In a review, published in the *Athenaeum* in 1876, the reviewer comments on the contents of the sixteenth-century Anglican report from the perspective of a Victorian historian. From a strictly historical perspective the reviewer is far more concerned by the absence of documentary records of marriages and baptisms, the result of the secrecy necessary amongst persecuted recusants, than he is about the religious controversy of the time:

> Secret marriages and baptisms are complained of, though the memorialists do not seem to have felt the evil of them so bitterly as they did many other things of less consequence. To us, for whom all these things are but matters of history, these unregistered marriages and baptisms are of far more import than the ceremonial which gave so much pain to the compilers of the Memorial. It is well known that throughout the whole of the north of England in the sixteenth and seventeenth centuries the more devout among the Roman Catholics were wont to have these rites performed by their own priests. One consequence is that now they are, in many cases, entirely incapable of proof. The Bodleian list of Yorkshire Roman Catholics in 1604 furnishes numerous examples of these secret marriages, and is in some instances the only evidence we have that such marriages were ever contracted. They usually took place far from home, before a few chosen and faithful witnesses only. Here is an instance, notable as relating to one of the higher gentry of the county of York: "Secret marriage. Richard Cholmley, Esquire, married with Mary Hungate, in the presence of John Wilson, William Martin, Hugh Hope, and Christopher Danyell, in a fell with a Popish priest." The lady and her lover dare not be wedded at home, for fear of spies; so they met by appointment at some wild place on the moorlands, where a priest, at the risk of his life, was found ready to perform the marriage rite.[5]

---

[5] Ibid.

It is very easy to share the Victorian historian's frustration that the persecution of Catholics in Elizabethan England has resulted in a secret history that is almost entirely undocumented, for obvious reasons, with the result "that now they [the secret marriages and baptisms] are, in many cases, entirely incapable of proof". This is the same frustration that is inevitably experienced by those on the quest for Shakespeare. The world in which the young Shakespeare and his family moved was a hidden world, even to the eyes of many of their contemporaries, requiring the scholar to piece together the picture of his life in the knowledge that many of the most important pieces will never be found.

Ultimately, and to reiterate the words of the frustrated Victorian, the possibility that Shakespeare and Anne Hathaway were married at a secret nuptial Mass, conducted by one of the increasing number of missionary priests who had entered England illegally to minister to the growing number of recusant Catholics, is "entirely incapable of proof". It may have happened, and considering what we know about Shakespeare's family, it could even be surmised that it is even likely that it happened. It can't, however, be proved. What is without doubt, however, is that Shakespeare and his bride-to-be went to considerable lengths to avoid being married by the Protestant vicar of their local parish. Instead, they were at great pains to ensure that they were married by an ordained Catholic priest, albeit one who had outwardly conformed to the Anglican establishment, though with apparent and occasionally recalcitrant reluctance. We shall never know whether the marriage in late November 1582 in Temple Grafton was the "real thing" or merely a legal formality to ensure that their child would not be a bastard in the eyes of the state, her parents having been married secretly and "unofficially" earlier. Either way, we know that Shakespeare was married by a Catholic priest.

On May 26, 1583, the daughter of William and Anne Shakespeare was baptized in the Stratford parish church by the Reverend Henry Haycroft, as demanded by law. Rather bizarrely, Holden deduced that, since Shakespeare had christened his daughter "with the uncommon and resoundingly Puritan name of Susanna", it was evidence, perhaps, that his "religious beliefs were already on the wane".[6] There is, of course, nothing about Susanna, as a name, that is in the least bit Puritan,

---

[6] Anthony Holden, *William Shakespeare: The Man Behind the Genius* (Boston: Little, Brown, 1999), p. 71.

"resoundingly" or otherwise. If anything one could deduce that the name was chosen because St. Susanna was a Catholic martyr who had given her life during an earlier persecution against the Church. It is also surely significant that the Old Testament Susanna appears in the Apocrypha, that part of the Bible explicitly rejected by the Protestants but retained by the Catholics. Far from Susanna being a "Puritan name" it could be said, with far more credibility and accuracy, that it was a politically and theologically charged Catholic name. In any event there was nothing "resoundingly Puritan" about Susanna Shakespeare herself, not least because, like her grandfather, she would later be registered as a Catholic recusant, openly defying the Puritanism of the Jacobean state.

Whatever difficulties Shakespeare was suffering because of his Catholic faith, it paled in comparison with the sufferings of his mother's family. The Ardens of Park Hall were resolutely recusant, so much so that they even maintained a private chaplain, Father Hugh Hall, disguised as a gardener, in defiance of the law that made harboring priests and hearing Mass a "treasonous" offense.[7] On October 25, 1583, Edward Arden's son-in-law, John Somerville, driven to derangement by the increasing persecution being suffered by his family, set out for London intent on killing Queen Elizabeth. He was arrested and sent to the Tower of London. Ironically this deranged regicide mission has gone down in the annals of "tom-fool Protestant history", to employ Hilaire Belloc's pejorative term for "that false official history which warps all English life",[8] as the "Somerville Plot" or the "Somerville conspiracy". There is, in fact, no evidence of any "plot" or "conspiracy" but, on the contrary, only evidence of one temporarily unbalanced man's efforts to put an end to what he perceived as the queen's intolerable intolerance. In fact, of course, his actions played right into the hands of Elizabeth's Machiavellian advisers who used the discovery of the "Somerville Plot" to arrest as many people as possible. Anyone remotely related to Somerville was in danger of arrest.

Edward Arden was arrested, as was his wife, Mary, his daughter (Somerville's wife), his sister, and his "gardener", Father Hall. On

---

[7] Three years later, in 1586, Margaret Clitherow would be cruelly put to death, in York, after being arrested for this very same "treasonous" offense of harboring a priest and hearing Mass.

[8] Letters from Belloc to Elizabeth Belloc and to Hoffman Nickerson in special collections at Georgetown and Boston Universities; quoted in Joseph Pearce, *Old Thunder: A Life of Hilaire Belloc* (London: HarperCollins, 2002), pp. 229–30.

November 18, the Tower of London diary records that Edward Arden was tortured on the rack; six days later it is reported that "Hugh Hall priest [was] also tortured on the rack".[9] Although their interrogators reported that they could find no incriminating evidence against anyone except John Somerville himself, Edward and Mary Arden, together with Somerville and Father Hall, were tried in London on December 16 and found guilty of high treason. It is indicative of such show trials that little pretense at impartiality was shown, as was illustrated by the fact that Thomas Lucy, one of the two government representatives leading the "investigation", had his brother, Timothy, on the jury. Protesting that he was dying for his faith, not for any crime, Edward Arden was executed on December 20 at Smithfield Market in London, being hanged, cut down while still alive, then disemboweled, beheaded, and quartered. His head was placed on a spike at London Bridge as a warning against other "papist traitors". Lest we should forget the full grim and grueling reality of the fate suffered by so-called "papist traitors", let's quote the historian Wood on the details of Arden's execution:

> Arden was dragged on a hurdle behind horses from Newgate through the waking city to the place of execution at Smithfield. Capital punishment in the Elizabethan state was long drawn out, savage, humiliating and very public. When sentenced you were told by the judge to prepare to be "hanged by the neck, and being alive cut down, and your privy members to be cut off, and your bowels to be taken out of your belly and there burned, you being alive". This meant they would castrate and disembowel you while you were still alive, burning your insides before your own eyes. Then your heart would be cut out and displayed to the crowd, before your body was carved up with a butcher's knife. To send a message to the people, this theatre of cruelty took place on a public stage, often in a market or meeting place, such as Tyburn, Smithfield, Cheapside or St Giles.[10]

On the night before Arden's execution, Somerville had died a violent death in Newgate Prison, though it is not clear whether he committed suicide by hanging himself or whether he had been strangled. Tellingly, the Tower diary, in recording Somerville's death, illustrates that he was not of sound mind, reinforcing the likelihood that the whole so-called "plot" was in reality the work of one deranged individual: "John Somerville,

[9] Wood, *Shakespeare*, p. 92.
[10] Ibid., p. 93.

who was hardly of sane mind, was transferred to another prison and the following night was found strangled in his prison cell whether by his own hand or by others was not established." [11] Somerville's head was placed beside Arden's on London Bridge. Mary Arden was sentenced to be hanged and burned but was subsequently pardoned by the queen, though she and her daughter were imprisoned in the Tower of London, enduring a long confinement. Father Hall was also imprisoned for a long period before being released; he was subsequently arrested at the time of the Gunpowder Plot in 1605 and was thrown into the Tower of London, where, apparently, he died.

These events were literally close to home for Shakespeare and his family, not only through their blood relations with Edward Arden but also because Somerville himself came from the village of Edstone, barely three miles from Stratford. This being so, it is entirely possible that Shakespeare knew the angry young man, not least because we know that Shakespeare, in later years, was friends with Somerville's brother. The raids on Catholic homes in the area as part of the "investigation" into the Somerville "Plot" were also "close to home". The Somervilles' house at Edstone was raided, as was Shelfield Lodge in Rowington, eight miles north of Stratford, and the home of the Grants, near Snitterfield, only two miles from Stratford. The Grants were business partners of John Shakespeare and were linked by marriage to the Somervilles. During yet another raid, at the home of the Underhills in the village of Idlicote, eight miles to the southeast of Stratford, Father Hall was arrested, after apparently eluding arrest during the initial raids at Park Hall. The Underhills were the old recusant family from whom Shakespeare would later buy his own house, New Place. It is clear, therefore, that Shakespeare was close to many of those who were caught up in the vortex of the Somerville "Plot" and must have feared for his own safety in the increasingly paranoid atmosphere now prevailing in Elizabethan England. It is also reasonable to conjecture that this might have been the time that John Shakespeare decided that it would be prudent to hide his "spiritual will" in the rafters of his house, in case his own home, in Henley Street, at which William and his wife and child were living at the time, was also raided. No doubt he was gripped with the same fear that had prompted other Catholics in Warwickshire to hide all evidence of their faith, causing Thomas Wilkes, one of the chief investigators of the "Plot" to complain to Sir Francis Walsingham, Elizabeth's spymaster,

[11] Ibid.

"that the papists in this country [i.e., Warwickshire] greatly do work upon the advantage of clearing their houses of all shows of suspicion".[12]

Further evidence of the strong connections between the recusants of Warwickshire and those of Lancashire, in the vicinity of Hoghton Tower, home until recently of William Shakeshafte, is found in official records of the interrogation of recusants during the investigation into the Somerville "Plot". In Warwick, about eight miles to the northeast of Stratford, the town clerk's book describes the interrogation of a man called Robert Chadborne, who was from Preston, barely five miles from Hoghton Tower. Under questioning, Chadborne revealed that he had not been to the Protestant church for several years:

And being asked why he would not come to the church he saith it was because his father and mother brought him up in the time of King Henry the Eighth and then there was another order. And he mindeth to serve that order and to serve the Lord God above all things.

Being asked what is in the church that he misliketh ... he praith the hearers to pardon him for he will say no more.

Being demanded whither the queen's majesty ought to be obeyed in those laws she makith ... as well in matters ecclesiastical as temporal, he answereth that first he is afraid to displease god above all things. And then afraide to displease his mighty prince.

Being demanded whither the order set down and agreed upon and commanded by the queen's majesty to be and that is now commonly used in the Church of England is according to god's institution, or as it ought to be, he answereth that it is against his conscience.

Being offered to be set at liberty upon condition that he will this night go to the church and report to the church in the time of divine service and sermons upon the Sabbath and holy days, he utterly refusith it and will not do it.[13]

Apart from further establishing connections between the recusants of Warwickshire and Lancashire, this record of an interrogation serves to illustrate the questions of conscience at the heart of the religious divisions in England during Shakespeare's time, a time in which the most profound moral dilemma ruled the hearts and lives of many Englishmen, demanding sacrifice or surrender, and forbidding compromise.

[12] Mutschmann and Wentersdorf, *Shakespeare and Catholicism*, p. 52.
[13] Wood, *Shakespeare*, p. 92.

7

LOST YEARS

In the spring of 1584 Anne became pregnant again, giving birth early in the following year to twins. They were baptized in the Stratford church on February 2, 1585, and were named Hamnet and Judith, after their Catholic neighbors Hamnet and Judith Sadler, who were presumably their godparents. Years later, in 1606, Hamnet Sadler's name would appear on the same list of Catholic recusants on which Shakespeare's daughter Susanna would appear. It is also worthy of note that Judith, like Susanna, is taken from the Apocrypha, explicitly rejected by Protestants.

The baptism of the twins represents the last documentary evidence of Shakespeare's presence in Stratford for many years. He and Anne had no further children, and it is generally assumed that Shakespeare departed in 1585 or shortly thereafter to seek his fortune in London. And this brings us to the next mystery to be solved in the quest for Shakespeare. Why did he pack his bags and leave his wife and children? Was it nothing more than a reckless, irresponsible desire to be free from familial ties and to experience the life of the city? Was he simply answering a bohemian urge to act and write? Did he sacrifice his family for art? It is possible that some of these questions could be answered in the affirmative, but our suspicions should be roused, from the outset, by the simple parochialism of these presumptions.

The motives ascribed to Shakespeare are the product of the provincialism of chronological snobbery, by which the actions of people in the past are explained, or explained away, by presuming that they had the same cultural and moral predilections as the age that is judging them. Thus Shakespeare is projected as a Byronic poet, following his Muse like a falling star that brings him at last not to Bethlehem but to Babylon; or else he is recast in the image of Wilde, torn between the stars of heaven and the gutters of Sodom (it is indeed apt that the recreating of Shakespeare in the image of Wilde was perpetrated by Wilde himself in "The Portrait of Mr W. H.", his wishful fantasy on Shakespeare's sonnets). Finally, of course, there is the present generation of critics, intent in claiming Shakespeare for their own particular agendas. For all of these critical "back projectionists", busily projecting the prejudices of their particular present into the distant past, the image of a reckless, irresponsible Shakespeare answering an artistic (or sexual) urge is attractive. When these critics imagine they see Shakespeare doing what he wants, or doing his own thing, he is really being made to do what they want, or to do their own thing (whatever "thing" that happens to be). He becomes a mere puppet, dancing to the tune of the critic. Such critics are blinded by their own provincial prejudice. They make themselves at home in the past by making the past remarkably like their own particular homes. It is for this reason, and to bring us back to our quest, that literary criticism must be answerable to the *facts* of history, not subject to the *fads* and *fashions* of modernity or postmodernity. Put simply, if you wish to know the plays at their deepest, you must know as much as possible about the person who wrote them, and in order to know the person who wrote them, you must know as much as possible about the times in which he lived. The critic must pay humble homage to history as well as to art if he is to excel in his chosen field; to paraphrase a well-known popular song lyric by the group U2, if we want to "kiss the sky" (know the truth), we have to learn how to kneel. The alternative, which is pride and prejudice, is an enemy of all forms of truth, literary or otherwise. Perhaps, indeed, it would be timely to remind ourselves that criticism is primarily a *discipline*, not an art, something of which the failed artists who end up as critics do not wish to remind themselves!

But back to Shakespeare. Did he desert his wife and children on a mere whim? Let's look at the evidence of history.

There are several parallel traditions, dating back to at least the late seventeenth century, i.e., within decades of Shakespeare's death, and emanating from at least four separate sources, that he was forced to leave Stratford due to persecution by Sir Thomas Lucy, the local magnate and anti-Catholic zealot who was appointed by Elizabeth's government to "investigate" the Somerville "Plot". The tradition states that the young Shakespeare had to escape Lucy's wrath after he was caught poaching in Lucy's deer park at Charlecote, a few miles outside Stratford. Mutschmann and Wentersdorf question the accuracy of this tradition:

> It has ... been ascertained beyond any doubt whatsoever that at the date in question, Lucy did not possess a park at Charlecote: as Smart and Fripp have amply demonstrated, the explanation given for the persecution is an absurd fabrication—absurd ... simply because the circumstances in which the deed could have been carried out were nonexistent. There is no getting away from the fact that, in the fifteen-eighties, Lucy had no deer park in which Shakespeare could possibly have poached.[1]

Before proceeding to the rest of Mutschmann and Wentersdorf's discussion of this issue, we should nonetheless insist that, logically, Shakespeare could have been caught poaching on Lucy's land even if the latter did not have a deer park. It is, therefore, not infeasible that Shakespeare was forced to leave Warwickshire because of his poaching, though we might consider that it is unlikely, especially when the other evidence is taken into account.

In order to prove their argument that the motive for Percy's persecution of Shakespeare was his religious convictions, Mutschmann and Wentersdorf quote the warrant issued following the arrest of John Somerville. This warrant, dated October 31, 1583, called for the arrest of "such as shall be in any way kin to all touched, and to search their houses". Those "touched" referred to those immediately involved, such as Somerville's wife and parents-in-law, while those who "shall be in any way kin" referred to the Ardens, which would include Mary Shakespeare, *née* Arden, and by extension her husband and her son. We should also remember that William and Anne, and their daughter, were probably living in Shakespeare's parents' house on Henley Street at this time. According to this warrant, "the Shakespeares ought to have been arrested and questioned as to their possible complicity in the alleged 'plot'; and in view of John Shakespeare's recusancy, there can be hardly a doubt that Lucy and his henchmen carried out the letter of the warrant".[2] Again, we need to temper Mutschmann and Wentersdorf's enthusiasm for their argument by insisting that the Shakespeares *might* have been arrested, not that they *ought* to have been arrested, and that there *is* an element of doubt as to whether Lucy carried out the letter of the warrant to the extent of arresting, or of searching the houses of, every member of the Arden family. Nonetheless, more temperate historians,

---

[1] H. Mutschmann and K. Wentersdorf, *Shakespeare and Catholicism* (New York: Sheed and Ward, 1952), pp. 96–97.

[2] Ibid., pp. 97–98.

such as Michael Wood, have also concluded that the Shakespeare home may have been searched as part of Lucy's "investigation".[3]

Mutschmann and Wentersdorf cite corroborative evidence for their theory in the words of Richard Davies, a Gloucestershire clergyman who was recorded at around the end of the seventeenth century as giving the following account of Shakespeare's relationship with Lucy: "Sir [Thomas] Lucy had him oft whipped and sometimes imprisoned, and at last made him fly his native country to his great advancement."[4] The reliability of this testimony is thrown into question by the unlikelihood that Lucy ever had Shakespeare whipped, let alone that he had done so often. Although Lucy was a Justice of the Peace he had no right, in law, to have someone whipped. Nonetheless, the evidence for imprisonment and persecution, coming as it does within the century that Shakespeare lived, must be taken seriously. So must the evidence of Nicholas Rowe, one of the earliest documenters of the Bard's life, and one of the most authoritative. He was the first editor of Shakespeare's work, his edition being published in 1709, and the first authoritative biographer, his biography also being published in 1709, as an introduction to his edition of the works. Rowe was one of the finest playwrights of the early eighteenth century and a poet of such merit that he was made poet laureate in 1715. It is significant that Rowe's source for the traditions, legends, and anecdotes of Shakespeare's life were collected by Thomas Betterton, the greatest Shakespearean actor of the Restoration period, who was born within twenty years of Shakespeare's death. Furthermore, Betterton collected his stories from Stratford itself, making him perhaps the most valuable source of the local oral evidence of Shakespeare's life. Here is what Rowe, presumably recounting oral evidence collected by Betterton, has to say about Lucy's persecution of Shakespeare: "[Shakespeare] was prosecuted by that gentleman [Lucy], as he thought, somewhat too severely; and in order to revenge that ill usage, he made a ballad upon him. And though this, probably the first essay of his poetry, be lost, yet it is said to have been so very bitter, that it redoubled the prosecution against him to that degree, that he was obliged to leave his business and family in Warwickshire, for some time, and shelter himself in London."[5]

---

[3] Michael Wood, *Shakespeare* (New York: Basic Books/Perseus Books Group, 2003), p. 95.
[4] Mutschmann and Wentesrsdorf, *Shakespeare and Catholicism*, p. 98.
[5] Ibid., p. 98.

It seems, therefore, from the most reliable source available, that Shakespeare was forced to leave Stratford because of an ongoing vendetta against him by Sir Thomas Lucy, the most powerful figure in the area round Stratford and Queen Elizabeth's Protestant Inquisitor following the Somerville "Plot".

But what of the poaching theory? Apart from its being contradicted by a more reliable source (Betterton), isn't it likely to be a romanticized memory of the local hero, casting him into the role of a latter-day Robin Hood, stealing from the rich to give to the poor? By the late seventeenth century, the Catholic resistance had been largely broken, and most people even in resolutely Catholic Stratford had conformed to the new religion or had lapsed into agnosticism. As memories faded, and as the years passed, the reason for Lucy's persecution of Shakespeare had become blurred. The folktales about Stratford's most celebrated son transformed him into a folk hero, a dashing and daring young man who poached from the hated Lucy. Such a theory fits with the related fact that England, by the end of the seventeenth century, had become culturally anti-Catholic to such a degree that memories of Shakespeare's Catholicism would not have been the topic of polite conversation. The real Shakespeare was already beginning to make way in the public psyche for the chimaera of the idealized and idolized Englishman, a figurehead for the nation itself. Shakespeare was becoming what the people wanted him to be. The man was being replaced by the myth.

By the middle of the eighteenth century, William Oldys, a collector of anecdotes about Shakespeare, described Lucy as "a vain, weak and vindictive magistrate".[6] Shakespeare's persecutor was now remembered as being a thoroughly bad man, purely perhaps on the evidence that he had been Shakespeare's persecutor, but few remembered the religious controversies that had made him so loathed by the largely Catholic population of Stratford.

As Shakespeare is made to "fly his native country" of Warwickshire because of the persecution of Sir Thomas Lucy we should take one last fleeting look at the woman he left behind. With Shakespeare's apparently hurried departure, we almost see the last of his wife and family, though we certainly can't presume that Shakespeare had seen the last of them. In the "lost years" that follow we know little of his movements, but we do know that he returned to Stratford regularly, if not perhaps

---

[6] Ibid., p. 99.

frequently, during the years that he was building his reputation as England's premier dramatist. We don't know how long he felt constrained to stay away from Warwickshire because of his fear of Lucy, though we know that he bought a house in Stratford three years before Lucy's death in 1600. Nonetheless, Shakespeare's marriage remains a puzzle. Why, for instance, did Anne not join her husband in London? Why did they have no more children? Why did they apparently choose to live a hundred miles apart?

Perhaps they had already separated in mind and heart before they separated physically; and yet it is also possible that the estrangement was actually *caused* by the enforced separation. Perhaps, as and when they met again, they had become strangers. Perhaps William's new life in London was not something that Anne wanted to share. To a large degree, we will never know the truth of the matter. There is, however, a beguiling piece of evidence from Shakespeare's own writing that throws some much needed light on his relationship with his wife. It is the clear reference to Anne Hathaway in sonnet 145, which constitutes a light so illuminating that the sonnet warrants quoting in full:

> Those lips that Love's own hand did make
> Breath'd forth the sound that said "I hate"
> To me that languish'd for her sake;
> But when she saw my woeful state,
> Straight in her heart did mercy come,
> Chiding that tongue that, ever sweet,
> Was us'd in giving gentle doom,
> And taught it thus anew to greet:
> "I hate" she alter'd with an end
> That follow'd it as gentle day
> Doth follow night, who like a fiend
> From heaven to hell is flown away:
>   "I hate" from hate away she threw,
>   And sav'd my life, saying "not you."

Knowing Shakespeare's predilection for puns, many critics have commented on the punning reference to his wife's maiden name in the sonnet's penultimate line. The pun is strengthened if seen phonetically as a play on the Warwickshire pronunciation of "Hathaway". Others have also suggested that the listener might also hear "Anne saved my life" at the commencement of the final line. Critical consensus seems to have rested on the assumption that this sonnet was composed for Anne during their courtship or even that it might have been read by Shakespeare as a gift to his new bride on their wedding day. If so, it can be safely labeled as his earliest surviving work. But what if the sonnet was written later, perhaps after Shakespeare had already left for London? What if it doesn't refer only to their courtship, or to their marriage, but also to some other event in their married life together? What if we were to take the pun "Anne saved my life" literally, as well as merely literarily? What if Anne *did* save her husband's life, or at least his liberty, by lying or equivocating on his behalf when Lucy's henchmen came to call? Such a reading of the sonnet reinforces the evidence that Shakespeare had to flee his home because of religious persecution and adds the enticing possibility that his wife might have "saved his life" in helping him escape. Such a reading also adds potency to the imagery of hatred, and to fiends flying from heaven to hell.

Whether such a reading of the poem is accurate or not, the fact that Shakespeare chose to include it in the volume of his sonnets, published in 1609, many years after he was forced to leave Stratford, suggests that he still loved his wife and retained a deep sense of gratitude for the time that she had "saved his life"; and it is perhaps not too wishful to suppose a sense of wistful regret that they had been constrained to spend so much of their lives apart.

And so we leave Stratford, apparently in a hurry, and enter the "lost years". So little is known of Shakespeare's life between the time he left Warwickshire, presumably in 1585 or 1586, and the time he is known to be in London in 1591 or 1592. All that we can do is make a sketch of the times in which he was living and leave the rest to our imagination, without letting it fly off on too many flights of fancy.

Hot on the heels of the so-called "Somerville Plot" came the Babington Plot, which would lead, eventually, to the execution of Mary, Queen of Scots, whom many, particularly Catholics, considered to be the true queen of England because Elizabeth, being the scion of Henry VIII's illegitimate marriage to Anne Boleyn, was herself illegitimate. Like the so-called "plot" before it, there is ample evidence to illustrate that the Babington Plot was another act of ruthlessness on the part of the Elizabethan government. Lest we be accused of bias, we'll let the non-Catholic and spotlessly secular Michael Wood explain the grim and gruesome reality behind this latest so-called "papist plot":

The plot perhaps never really existed: the government was by now adept at setting traps to snare unwary and gullible Catholics in order to bring the disaffected out into the open. They used *agents provocateurs*, men rather like Shakespeare's Iago, who pretended to be one thing but were another, and watched as their victims were led to destruction. . . .

Elizabeth asked for a new and even more horrible way to kill the plotters to ensure that they endured the maximum suffering. But she was assured that, applied with skill, hanging, drawing and quartering would satisfy her on that score. The punishments were so cruelly applied to the victims of this latest sting that, in revulsion after the first few had been butchered, the crowd spontaneously called for the hangman to let them die on the rope before he cut them down.[7]

Robert Southwell, a Jesuit priest who was destined to suffer the same gruesome method of execution several years later, provides us with contemporary evidence of the deceit employed by Elizabeth's spy network, under the sinister direction of Sir Francis Walsingham:

And as for this action of Babington, it was in truth rather a snare to entrap them than any device of their own, since it was both plotted, furthered and finished by Sir Francis Walsingham and his other complices, who laid and hatched all the particulars thereof, as they thought it would best fall out of the discredit of Catholics and cutting off the Queen of Scots.[8]

Another Jesuit, William Weston, who knew Babington personally and looked on helplessly as he saw him being lured into Walsingham's web, lamented the fate of some of those who paid the ultimate price for falling into the spymaster's trap:

One of these two young men, Thomas, was tortured in the Tower of London and died on the rack, though the heretics gave it out that he had strangled himself. The second, Jerome, was condemned to death at the same time as Anthony and the other accomplices, and was executed. Their mother was shut up in the Tower. There, after a few months, she died wasted with sorrow and with the squalor and filth of her imprisonment. If one thinks only of this present life, her end was miserable:

---

[7] Wood, *Shakespeare*, p. 101.

[8] Robert Southwell, *Humble Supplication to Her Majesty* (1591, published posthumously in 1600), pp. 17–18; quoted in William Weston, *An Autobiography from the Jesuit Underground* (New York: Farrar, Straus and Cudahy, 1955), p. 105.

but, as I see it, it was glorious: no less than a martyr's and no different from it.[9]

On July 24, 1586, in the midst of the Babington Plot but unconnected to it, Robert Dibdale was recognized as being a priest whilst walking along Tothill Street in Westminster. Dibdale, it will be remembered, was a schoolfellow of Shakespeare's at Stratford Grammar School. He was also a kinsman of Shakespeare's mother and a former neighbor of Anne Hathaway's family in Shottery. With these connections in mind, it is not only inescapable that Shakespeare would have known Dibdale personally, it is even possible that Dibdale was a guest at Shakespeare's wedding. He had been released after serving more than two years in prison in September 1582, and it seems likely that he returned home to the close-knit recusant community of Stratford before returning to the English College at Rheims in March 1583 to complete his training for the priesthood. If so, he would have been in Stratford with his family at the time of Shakespeare's wedding at the end of November 1582. Four years later, he was found guilty of being "a priest and practiser of magic" (that is, of exorcisms) and was hanged, drawn, and quartered on October 8, 1586. Once again, the butchery of the Elizabethan pogrom against Catholics was very close to home for Shakespeare and his family.

The final victim of the Babington Plot, indeed its final goal, was Mary, Queen of Scots, who was beheaded at Fotheringay on February 8, 1587, professing her Catholic faith and clothed in a red robe, the color symbolic of martyrdom in the Catholic Church. Although Shakespeare's whereabouts at this time are lost to posterity, his sympathetic feelings toward the martyred queen can perhaps be gleaned from her ghostly presence in such plays as *Julius Caesar*, *Richard II*, and *Hamlet*.

Presuming that Shakespeare had arrived in London at around this time, and presuming that he was already active in the theatre as an actor if not necessarily at this stage as a dramatist, in what sort of world would he have found himself? Although perhaps it couldn't be said that the stage was "papist", it could certainly be said that it was anti-Protestant, or at least anti-Puritan. The Puritans had carried on a war of attrition against the theatre, dubbing a newly built theatre in 1580 "the chapel of Satan".[10] Seven years later, at around the time that it is generally thought that Shakespeare arrived in London, a puritanical letter

---

[9] Weston, *Autobiography from the Jesuit Underground*, p. 104.
[10] Mutschmann and Wentersdorf, *Shakespeare and Catholicism*, p. 101.

to Sir Francis Walsingham complained that the "daily abuse of stage plays is such an offense to the godly, and so great a hindrance to the gospel, as the Papist do exceedingly rejoice at the blemish thereof, and not without cause ... When the bells toll to the lecturer [Protestant lay preacher], the trumpets sound to the stages, whereat the wicked faction of Rome laugheth for joy while the godly weep for sorrow."[11] In the summer of 1592, after Shakespeare's plays were already being performed to great acclaim, a Puritan preacher at Paul's Cross went so far as to blame the theatre for the latest outbreak of the plague: "The cause of plague is sin, if you look to it well; and the cause of sin are plays: therefore the cause of plague are plays."[12] Commenting on this sermon, Holden offers the summary verdict that "[t]o the Church, the theatres themselves were nothing less than the cause of the plague".[13] Such a judgment, simplistic to the extreme and afflicted by the stereotypes of supercilious secularism, tars all Christianity with the Puritan brush. The Church, whether we are talking about the Catholic Church or the Anglican, never believed or taught any such thing!

At some date between 1585 and 1588, at about the time of Shakespeare's appearance in England's capital, Richard Tarleton, the most famous clown on the Elizabethan stage and a leading member of Shakespeare's first acting troupe, was denounced to the authorities as a Catholic because his house on the South Bank was a meeting place for papists. Shakespeare must have known Tarleton, and, considering what we know of Shakespeare's religious persuasions, it is not unreasonable to suppose that he was one of the papists who met at Tarleton's house. Christopher Beeston, for many years a colleague of Shakespeare in the Chamberlain's company, was apparently a Catholic. His wife was listed as a recusant, as was his servant, William Allen, the latter of whom was also an actor and should not be confused with the Jesuit of the same name. William Prynne, a fanatical Puritan who made it his mission to rail against the stage, declared that "most of our present English *actors* (as I am credibly informed) [are] professed Papists".[14] Although Prynne was writing in 1633, twenty years after Shakespeare's retirement from the

---

[11] Ibid.

[12] F. P. Wilson, *The Plague in Shakespeare's London* (Oxford: Clarendon Press, 1927), p. 52.

[13] Anthony Holden, *William Shakespeare: The Man Behind the Genius* (Boston: Little, Brown, 1999), p. 105.

[14] William Prynne, *Histrio-mastix: The Players Scourge* (1633); quoted in Mutschmann and Wentersdorf, *Shakespeare and Catholicism*, p. 103.

stage, and even allowing for the fanatic's tendency to paranoid exaggeration, it is clear that Catholic sympathies and sensibilities were an integral part of theatrical life in London; and since Catholicism, by Prynne's time, was on the wane as a result of a century of draconian laws and oppression, what was true in 1633 would have been considerably more so in 1587, when Shakespeare entered the world of the thespian. Interestingly, and as an amusing aside, Prynne also railed against Shakespeare's plays in particular, complaining that they were "printed in the best Crowne paper, far better than most Bibles".[15]

Amongst the better known converts to Catholicism among Shakespeare's contemporaries were Ben Jonson, for a time, and Thomas Lodge, who went into exile in 1603, when his conversion became known, but returned in 1610, remaining a Catholic until his death in 1625. As a young man, Lodge wrote *A Defence of Poetry Music and Stage Plays* as a riposte to Stephen Gosson's attacks on the stage in *School of Abuse*. Lodge's highly popular drama *Mucedorus*, first performed in around 1589, was for a time attributed to Shakespeare, and his play *Rosalynde*, published in 1590 but performed earlier, was the inspiration for Shakespeare's *As You Like It*. Other well-known Catholic contemporaries of Shakespeare in the world of the arts included William Byrd, court composer at the Chapel Royal who would be excommunicated from the Anglican church in 1598 for his "popery", and Inigo Jones, the famous architect and stage designer.

Such evidence makes it clear "that the Elizabethan–Jacobean theatrical world was strongly Catholic in spirit. This was the sphere in which Shakespeare chose to move for the twenty-five years of his professional career in London. It was ... Catholic by tradition and by nature; and many of its leading personalities were secret if not open supporters of the old faith."[16] Whatever else had driven Shakespeare from his hearth and home in Stratford it was clearly not a desire to escape from the faith of his fathers.

---

[15] Prynne, *Histrio-mastix*; quoted in Oscar James Campbell and Edward G. Quinn, eds., *The Reader's Encyclopedia of Shakespeare* (New York: MJF Books, 1966), p. 662.

[16] Mutschmann and Wentersdorf, *Shakespeare and Catholicism*, p. 104.

8

MURDERED SPY

It is now time to turn our attention to Shakespeare's notorious contemporary Christopher Marlowe, whose sinister and sordid life during the years in which Shakespeare was establishing his early reputation would culminate, in 1593, in his murder.

Marlowe was born in Canterbury in Kent and was baptized on February 26, 1564, barely two months before Shakespeare's own baptism. His father, a shoemaker of modest means, was noted for his extreme pugnacity, and his sisters, Dorothy and Anne, had gained for themselves a reputation of considerable notoriety. Dorothy had become embroiled in a number of trade and matrimonial intrigues, whereas Anne was a "scold, common swearer and blasphemer of the name of God".[1] Although Marlowe escaped from the poverty and squalor of his dysfunctional family, through the receipt of scholarships that enabled him to go to Corpus Christi College in Cambridge, his own life would soon descend to a level of violence and venality far exceeding the worst excesses of his own kinsmen.

Even as a young man studying divinity at Cambridge, Christopher Marlowe had made some powerful friends who, as we shall see, would also become dangerous enemies. In June 1587, the university authorities were reluctant to confer on him his master's degree due to his frequent and unexplained absences, which were believed to be connected with his Catholic sympathies and perhaps with his intention of going abroad to study for the priesthood. In the end, however, the degree was conferred following an extraordinary intervention by Queen Elizabeth's privy council, the highest authority in the land except for the queen herself. The council's communication to the university authorities on July 29 is loaded with cryptic references to the secret "services" he had performed for Her Majesty's government, clearly hinting that

---

[1] William Urry, "Marlowe and Canterbury", *Times Literary Supplement* (February 13, 1964).

his absences from Cambridge were due to his spying missions against Catholics.

> Whereas it was reported that Christopher Morley [*sic*] was determined to have gone beyond the seas to Reames and there to remain, their Lordships thought good to certify that he had no such intent, but that in all his actions he had behaved himself orderly and discretely, whereby he had done Her Majesty good service, & deserved to be rewarded for his faithful dealing. Their Lordships' request was that the rumour thereof should be allayed by all possible means, and that he should be furthered in the degree he was to take this next Commencement, because it was not Her Majesty's pleasure that anyone employed, as he had been, in matters touching the benefit of his country, should be defamed by those that are ignorant in th'affairs he went about.[2]

The fact that Marlowe's name is often rendered as "Morley" in correspondence and in legal documents and was rendered as such in the inquest following his murder is itself worthy of note. It parallels the rendering of Shakespeare's name as Shakeshafte, as was certainly the case with Shakespeare's grandfather and was perhaps the case with William also, and should serve to remind us that these alternative renditions of surnames were common in Elizabethan England.

It is transparently obvious from the wording of this communication from Elizabeth's privy council that Marlowe, or "Morley", had joined Sir Francis Walsingham's spy network. The chief rumor with which Marlowe had been "defamed" was that he "was determined to have gone beyond the seas to Reames and there to remain". Rheims, in northern France, was the home of the English College at which young Englishmen trained for the priesthood. Traveling to Rheims was bad enough, indicating Catholic sympathies, whereas remaining there, as the authorities at Cambridge feared was Marlowe's desire, was far worse, indicating that he meant to become a priest. There was, however, another reason for going to Rheims, and that was to become a spy, feigning Catholicism in order to gain the trust of Catholics, but reporting back to Elizabeth's spymaster, Walsingham, any information about the movement of priests to England. The success of these spying missions can be gauged by the fact that many priests were arrested almost as soon as they arrived in the country, betrayed by the traitors in their midst. Clearly

---

[2] Quoted in Charles Nicholl, *The Reckoning: The Murder of Christopher Marlowe* (London: Vintage/Random House, 2002), p. 110.

Marlowe was such a spy. He had "done Her Majesty good service", behaving himself "discretely . . . in all his actions". He had been employed "in matters touching the benefit of his country . . . and deserved to be rewarded for his faithful dealing".

If Marlowe was a spy, and it seems inescapable that he was, it does not necessarily mean that he was a principled Protestant or even that he was particularly anti-Catholic. On the contrary, most of the government's spies were Catholics, or former Catholics, who betrayed their co-religionists for reasons of fear, blackmail, or pecuniary gain. Ironically, therefore, and paradoxically, Marlowe's becoming a spy was probably connected to his having become a Catholic first. This is certainly the judgment of his biographer, Charles Nicholl:

> He probably was—at some stage, at least—what he appeared to be: a young malcontent with fashionable papist sympathies. This would certainly figure in terms of Elizabethan spy-craft, for the turning of Catholics, through pressure or promises, was one of the government's standard policies. All of the chief anti-Catholic agents used by Walsingham . . . were themselves Catholics before they became spies. Perhaps this is the case with Marlowe too. It is a favourite maxim of those in the deception business, that the truth is the best cover of all.[3]

If, as Nicholl surmises, Marlowe was a Catholic before he became a spy, we are left with two possible scenarios. Either he became so corrupt and cynical that he could betray others without any qualms or any pangs of conscience, or else his betrayal of others, possibly leading to their torture and to their gruesome execution, led to feelings of self-loathing. In the light of the intensity of Marlowe's plays, particularly perhaps his Dr Faustus, it is not unreasonable to assume that he hated himself for his treachery. Having succumbed to the succubus of temptation, it is possible that he regretted selling his soul to the devil, but felt that there was no escape from the devil's bargain he had struck. If this is so, Dr Faustus takes on something of the quality of autobiography, reminiscent to modern readers, perhaps, of Oscar Wilde's Dorian Gray. Wilde would elude the devil's grip, being received into the Catholic Church on his deathbed; Marlowe, on the other hand, would be cut down in his prime, murdered by his fellow spies. As for the mystery surrounding his death, and the even greater mystery surrounding the

---

[3] Ibid., p. 115.

state of his soul at the hour of his death, perhaps we can posit a few intriguing questions. Was Marlowe, following the conscience that is not only palpable but positively palpitating in the moral of *Dr Faustus*, seeking to extricate himself from his own pact with the devil? Was he seeking to escape from the sordid reality of living as a spy? Was he now recoiling from having to betray his friends to his paymasters? Was there no way out? Did he know too much about the workings of Elizabeth's spy network? Did he know the names of other spies whose identities needed to remain secret? Was he killed in order that the secrets he knew went with him to the safety of the grave? Or was he, as the official story would have us believe, merely killed in a drunken brawl? As intriguing as they are, these are questions that lie beyond the bounds of our present quest.

What is pertinent to our quest, and yet remains a mystery, is the extent to which Marlowe and Shakespeare knew each other. Marlowe never mentions Shakespeare, and Shakespeare alludes to Marlowe only several years after the latter's death. And yet is it feasible that they did not know each other? Theatrical circles in London were not that large, and the two playwrights were neighbors, living in Shoreditch. They both wrote plays for Strange's Men before moving on to Pembroke's Men. Their lives were evidently moving in parallel, but is it possible that they never intersected? And if they did meet, which surely must have been likely, were they friends or enemies? And if Marlowe remained a spy, as seems to be the case, considering the violent nature of his death and the subsequent cover-up, was Shakespeare one of the Catholics upon whom he was spying?

And if there is a mystery surrounding Shakespeare's relationship with Marlowe, it is no more perplexing than that which surrounds the artistic influence that one exerted upon the other. It used to be presumed that Marlowe's influence is discernible in Shakespeare's early plays, on the assumption that Marlowe was already the most distinguished English dramatist at the time that Shakespeare is thought to have begun writing his own plays in the late 1580s. Since, however, the date of authorship of Shakespeare's earliest plays is itself a matter of dispute, it is possible that the influence could have flowed in both directions. As with so much else in the lives of both these men, the quest for Shakespeare and for Marlowe leaves many questions unanswered.

In the summer of 1592, less than a year before Marlowe's murder, he and Shakespeare had been attacked by another playwright, Robert Greene.

Writing on his deathbed, Greene composed what was effectively a last literary "confession", which would be published within weeks of his death as *Greene's Groats-worth of Witte, bought with a million of Repentance*. According to its title page, it had been "published at his dying request", and it seems that its author had more than his own "repentance" in mind as he wrote it. It was clearly also intended as a parting shot at his peers. Although addressed principally to Thomas Nashe, George Peele, and Christopher Marlowe, there was also a barbed reference to the new kid on the block, William Shakespeare.

Greene accused Marlowe of "diabolical atheism" and repented that, like Marlowe, he too had been tempted to disbelief, confessing that he "hath said, with thee (like the fool in his heart), There is no God." This accusation is followed by what appears to be a cryptic reference to Marlowe's involvement with the spy network: "Is it pestilent Machiavellian policy that thou hast studied?" The apparent connection between Machiavellianism, atheism, and Marlowe's involvement with the Machiavellian methods of the Elizabethan state parallels the argument in Jesuit pamphlets that Elizabeth's chief advisers were atheistic followers of Machiavelli. Warning Marlowe of the dangers of these "diabolical" dabblings, Greene reminds him that Machiavelli "began in craft, lived in fear and ended in despair", having "inherited the portion of Judas". There can be little doubt that "Judas", in this context, is meant to be synonymous with "Faustus", linking Marlowe, on both counts, to those who have sold their souls to the devil and have reaped their harvest in hell. One wonders, in addition, whether the reference to Judas, in relation to Marlowe, is another hint at his role as a spy betraying Catholics to the power of Caesar. Such a conclusion is supported by the fact that Greene's act of deathbed contrition was prompted, at least in part, by his reading of the *Book of Resolution* by the Jesuit Robert Persons.[4] Greene's message to Marlowe is clear enough. If he doesn't repent he will suffer the fate of Faustus and Judas, "for little knowest thou how in the end thou shalt be visited". Such a warning, given so shortly before Marlowe's violent death, carries with it not only the mark of premonition but of prophecy.

The reference to Shakespeare in Greene's *Groats-worth* is fleeting by comparison and is thrown in almost as an aside, yet it has been seized

---

[4] "Shakespeare and Religion Chronology", *Religion and the Arts*, http://www.bc.edu/publications/relarts/supplements/shakespeare/chronology.html, p. 74; published by Boston College.

upon by Shakespeare scholars as the first reference, in print, to Shakespeare as a playwright, and the first documentary evidence of any sort since the baptism of his children eight years earlier. Prompted perhaps by jealousy at the success of Shakespeare's *Henry VI* at the Rose Theatre earlier in the year, compared to the relatively poor reception, at the same theatre, of Greene's own plays,[5] Shakespeare is described as an "upstart": "An upstart Crow, beautified with our feathers, that with his *Tiger's heart wrapped in a Player's hide*, supposes he is as well able to bombast out a blank verse as the best of you: and being an absolute *Iohannes fac totum* [Jack-of-all-trades], is in his own conceit the only Shake-scene in the country."

Shakespeare is an upstart because, as a mere actor, he had shown the audacity to write plays as well as act in them. He is, furthermore, not merely a Jack-of-all-trades but a Johnny-come-lately, newly arrived on the authorial scene and already putting his rivals into the shade. The reference to the "tiger's heart" is a parody of a line in the first act of *Henry VI*, part 3 ("Oh, tiger's heart wrapp'd in a woman's hide!"), and represents the first published quotation from a Shakespeare play, albeit a misquotation. Greene's words betray a sense of snobbery toward the upstart, suggesting that Shakespeare's lack of a university education, as distinct from Peele, Nashe, Marlowe, and Greene, all of whom were Oxbridge educated, disqualified him from London's elite coterie of playwrights. Such superciliousness resurfaces in another part of the *Groatsworth* in which Greene, in the guise of "Roberto", converses with "a player" whose "voice is nothing gracious" and whose manner is rustic, but who describes himself as "a country author". Some scholars have suggested that the rustic "player" is modeled on Shakespeare, though this is disputed by others. In any event, it reinforces the suspicion that Greene looked down his nose at the playwright from Stratford who was proving such a success at the Rose Theatre.

There is a curious postscript to the publication of Greene's *Groatsworth* that may shed further light on our quest for Shakespeare. Henry Chettle, the London printer, stationer, and future dramatist who had taken charge of Greene's manuscripts after his death, received complaints from two playwrights after the *Groats-worth* was published. In his

---

[5] See Ian Wilson, *Shakespeare: The Evidence* (New York: St. Martin's Griffin, 1999), pp. 118–19, in which the author lists Philip Henslowe's share of the overall takings at the Rose Theatre for performances of Shakespeare's, Marlowe's, and Greene's plays between February and May 1592.

book, *Kind-Hart's Dream*, published in December 1592, Chettle alluded
to these complaints in the introductory "Epistle" to the work:

> About three months since died M Robert Greene, leaving many papers
> in sundry booksellers hands, among them his *Groats-worth of wit*, in which
> a letter written to divers play-makers is offensively by one or two of
> them taken ... With neither of them that take offence was I acquainted,
> and with one of them I care not if I never be [this is Marlowe, presum-
> ably].... The other, whom at that time I did not so much spare, as since
> I wish I had, for that as I have moderated the heat of living writers, and
> might have used my own discretion (especially in such a case), the author
> being dead, that I did not, I am as sorry as if the original fault had been
> my fault, because myself have seen his demeanor no less civil than he
> excellent in the quality he professes. Besides, divers of worship, have
> reported his uprightness of dealing, which argues his honest, and his
> facetious grace in writing, that approves his Art.

It has been generally presumed that Marlowe was "one of them" and
Shakespeare "the other". Since, however, neither of them is named, we
have to wonder whether either of them could have been Thomas Nashe
or George Peele, both of whom were addressed specifically by Greene.
Since Peele had a reputation for loose living, and Nashe a notoriety for
vituperation, it is thought unlikely that Chettle's eulogy to the upright-
ness, honesty, and civil demeanor of the wronged "other" could have
referred to either of these somewhat disreputable characters. If, therefore, it can be presumed that the "other" is Shakespeare, it offers us a
rare insight into his character. Ian Wilson writes that

> there is a general consensus that it is he to whom Chettle referred, not
> least because of the description of his civil demeanor and "uprightness
> of dealing" in his complaint about being libeled, which tallies with later,
> similar references to his courteous, ever-gentlemanly manner.... From
> as early as 1592, then, we are provided with a tantalizing glimpse of
> Shakespeare as he appeared to his contemporaries: gentlemanly, surpris-
> ingly well-dressed, at least on the evidence of Greene's "beautified with
> our feathers", a man of great integrity (Chettle's "honesty" and "upright-
> ness of dealing") and courtesy (his "demeanor no less civil").[6]

If this depiction of the noble Shakespeare is accurate, it helps to explain
why relatively little is known about his life. Whereas the riotous living

---

[6] I. Wilson, *Shakespeare*, p. 127.

of Marlowe or Peele ensured that their exploits were recorded for posterity, even if the gossiping source is often as disreputable as the acts
being reported, the decorous demeanor of Shakespeare seems to have
left little with which the gossips could grapple. The silence is, perhaps,
a testimony to his virtue. If this picture of Shakespeare is coupled with
the possibility that he remained a recusant Catholic who, of necessity,
kept his private life hidden from the public eye, we find ourselves with
ample explanation for the paucity of detail surrounding the known facts
of his life.

9

MARTYRED PRIEST

By the time that his plays had begun to attract the attention of Greene, Chettle, and the public at large, Shakespeare had obtained the patronage of Henry Wriothesley, third Earl of Southampton. Shakespeare is generally believed, in the early 1590s, to have written a large proportion of his sonnets for Wriothesley, and his two epic poems, *Venus and Adonis* and *The Rape of Lucrece*, were dedicated to him. This is hugely significant in our quest for a greater understanding of England's greatest poet.

Wriothesley was born on October 6, 1573, into an avowedly Catholic family and was baptized according to the rites of the Catholic Church. His father had been a defender of Mary, Queen of Scots, had been implicated in the Northern Rebellion, and had endured fines and imprisonment rather than abandon the old faith. His maternal grandfather was Lord Montague, another renowned recusant who suffered much persecution for his faith and for his defiance of anti-Catholic laws. His parents were associated with Edmund Campion during the Jesuit's missionary activity in 1580, and it is possible that, as a child, he had even seen the legendary martyr. He was, therefore, being brought up in one of the most prominent and most resolute recusant families in the whole country.

All of this changed, however, when his father died in October 1581. Young Henry, only eight years old, succeeded to the earldom and, as a minor, automatically became a royal ward under the guardianship of the queen's chief minister, Lord Burghley, the most hated and feared enemy of England's beleaguered Catholics. The child now found himself at the center of a struggle between his Catholic family, who wanted him brought up in the old faith, and his legal guardian, who wanted, at all costs, to thwart their desires. It seems that his family had employed a Catholic schoolmaster, from a well-known recusant family living near Winchester in Hampshire named Swithin Wells, who was subsequently described in a privy council warrant of 1582 as being "a dangerous Papist". Records show that he was part of the widowed Countess of Southampton's household in 1586 and 1587, indicating that he had probably been entrusted by the second earl or his executors to supervise the young earl's upbringing. Such a supposition is supported by the fact that the Catholic schoolmaster was the brother of Gilbert Wells, who was not only a close friend of the late earl but also his executor.

In order to counter these Catholic influences, Lord Burghley appointed an anti-Catholic Italian immigrant, Giovanni Florio, as a private tutor to the young Southampton. Florio was a member of Burghley and Walsingham's network of spies, having worked undercover for them previously as a "tutor" at the French Embassy in London. Burghley also sent Southampton to study at the presumably safe Protestant environment of Cambridge University from 1585 to 1589, though, as we have seen from our discussion of Marlowe, who was studying at Cambridge at the same time as Southampton, there was a considerable papist presence at the university and, indeed, "popery" was even somewhat fashionable among the students. Gaining his master's degree at the tender age of sixteen, Southampton enrolled as a student at Grays Inn, in London, to study law. It was following his arrival in London, perhaps as early as 1590, that he met Shakespeare for the first time.

In 1591, the Catholic schoolmaster Swithin Wells was denounced to the authorities for harboring priests and, in December, was executed opposite Southampton House in Holborn for having permitted Mass to be celebrated there. Although there is no documentary evidence to buttress the suspicion that the tutor-spy, Florio, was involved in the downfall of his Catholic counterpart, the fact that he boasted in his old age of his prowess in the destruction of Jesuits and papists suggests some level of involvement on his part. It was, after all, the purpose of his appointment that he should root out Catholic influences on the young Southampton, by hook or crook or rack and rope.

The question that is most relevant to our quest is whether Burghley succeeded in turning the young nobleman away from the faith of his family, or whether faith and family prevailed. Whose will triumphed in the struggle for the boy's heart and soul?

Certainly there is no denying that the young earl conformed, up to a point, to the demands of the state. There was no open recusancy, though there was ample evidence for his continued covert Catholicism. He was presented to Queen Elizabeth in 1592 and was soon regarded as one of the most popular young nobles at court. From Burghley's perspective this was all to the good. Yet the queen's chief minister did not have it all his own way. When he commanded that his young charge marry Burghley's own granddaughter, Southampton pleaded for time to decide. Having conferred with a priest, Southampton finally refused to bow to his guardian's command. Burghley was furious, and Southampton was fined the huge sum of £5000 for his obstinate disobedience. Years later it was discovered by Elizabeth's chief inquisitor and torturer, Richard Topcliffe, that Southampton's confessor and spiritual adviser was none other than the notorious and charismatic Jesuit Robert Southwell. It is clear, therefore, from the evidence of Burghley's own henchman that Southampton clung to the old faith doggedly, if largely secretly. And what does this say about Shakespeare's religious allegiance at this time? Isn't it likely that Southampton saw in Shakespeare a kindred spirit, and vice versa, and that the two men were drawn together by their shared convictions? And how did two men from such widely different backgrounds ever meet in the first place, one an aristocrat destined to be a favorite at the queen's court, the other a mere player from the provinces only recently beginning to make a name for himself as a playwright (if indeed he had written any plays by the time that they first met)? Since there seems little else that could have brought their two worlds together, isn't it possible, or perhaps likely, that they met through some secret gathering of Catholics, perhaps at a clandestine Mass celebrated by Southwell himself?

Assuming Robert Southwell was Southampton's confessor at the time that Shakespeare and Southampton first met, it brings Shakespeare into the orbit of the most famous and most feared Jesuit since Edmund Campion had challenged the authorities ten years earlier. In so doing it brings him into the very heart of the recusant underground.

Let's explore the evidence that Shakespeare may have known Robert Southwell.

Although Shakespeare and Southwell were distant cousins, their relationship, through the Ardens, is so remote that this, in itself, cannot be seen as evidence that they would have known each other. The strongest evidence springs from their mutual acquaintance with the young Earl of Southampton and the clues to be found in Southwell's writing and, less obviously, from those that can be gleaned from Shakespeare's own work.

Southwell's writing, in poetry and prose, was very widely read, even by his sworn enemies, such as Burghley, Francis Bacon, Richard Topcliffe, and even the queen herself. As for his friends in the persecuted Catholic community, his works were devoured avidly. He wrote sublimely; his prose unfolding in fluid eloquence and his poetry flying to heights that only the greatest of the metaphysical poets could match. He was not merely a priest who had somehow eluded capture since his arrival in England in 1586, but a true poet whose place in the literary canon, centuries later, is assured. When one thinks of the metaphysical poets, Robert Southwell sits comfortably in the presence of Donne, Herbert, and Crashaw. Is it any wonder, therefore, that Shakespeare, as a Catholic and as a poet, would be drawn to this particular Jesuit?

In October 1591, Southwell and eleven other Jesuits had almost been caught by Topcliffe, as they met in conclave at Baddesley Clinton, not far from Stratford where Shakespeare's family were still clinging defiantly to the old faith. A few months later, in March 1592, Shakespeare's father would be cited for recusancy and, remaining defiant, was still refusing to conform in September according to a report prepared by Shakespeare's old enemy Sir Thomas Lucy and other Justices.

While John Shakespeare was being hounded in Stratford, Robert Southwell was a secret guest of the Earl of Southampton and his widowed mother at Southampton House in the middle of London, prompting Michael Wood to wax lyrical about the dash and dare of the courageous Jesuit fugitive: "Elizabeth's Public Enemy Number One had walked the streets in broad daylight in a black velvet cloak, a saintly Scarlet Pimpernel."[1] Since Southwell also had family connections in Hampshire it is assumed by Wood, naturally enough, that he would have been a guest of the Southamptons at their estate in Titchfield, as well as at their home in London. Shakespeare could have met the famous Jesuit poet at either of these places, as indeed he could have met him at the many recusant houses in London frequented by Shakespeare's theatrical friends.

Since Southwell was, at this time, Southampton's spiritual adviser and confessor, it is not beyond the bounds of possibility that he was Shakespeare's spiritual adviser and confessor also. At any rate, it is known that Southwell knew Southampton well, and it can be seen as being entirely possible that he knew Shakespeare. This should be borne in mind as we turn our attention to the textual evidence for their friendship, or at least for their acquaintance.

---

[1] Michael Wood, *Shakespeare* (New York: Basic Books/Perseus Books Group, 2003), p. 151.

Shortly before his capture in July 1592, Southwell had been working on a manuscript of his poems and had penned three separate dedications for different sections of his work, the first being a preface addressed to the author's "Loving Cousin". Since Southwell and Shakespeare were distant cousins it has been conjectured that the preface was addressed to Shakespeare, though others have suggested that the "Cousin" in question was perhaps Southampton, since Southwell's brother and sister had each married Southampton's first cousins. Either way, the preface itself is an appeal to poets in general, or perhaps to Shakespeare in particular, to use their God-given talents in the service of the Giver of them:

> Poets, by abusing their talents, and making the follies and feignings of love the customary subject of their base endeavours, have so discredited this faculty, that a poet, a love, and liar, are by many reckoned but three words of one signification.... The devil ... hath ... possessed also most Poets with his idle fancies. For in lieu of solemn and devout matters, to which in duty they owe their abilities, they now busy themselves in expressing such passions as serve only for testimonies to what unworthy affections they have wedded their wills. And because, the best course to let them see the error of their works is to weave a new web in their own loom, I have here laid a few coarse threads together to invite some skillfuller wits to go forward in the same, or to begin some finer piece, wherein may be seen how well verse and virtue suit together.[2]

Such an exhortation to poets to wed their verse to virtue, coming as it does from a Jesuit priest, may be of little surprise perhaps and may seem to have little direct relevance to Shakespeare per se as distinct from poets in general. But if this preface is taken in conjunction with another dedication by Southwell, written presumably at around the same time and this time addressed from "The Author to the Reader", a picture begins to emerge that perhaps the Jesuit had Shakespeare specifically in mind:

> Still finest wits are 'stilling Venus's rose;
> In paynim toys the sweetest veins are spent;
> To Christian works few have their talents lent ...
> You heavenly sparks of wit shew native light,
> Cloud not with misty loves your orient clear ...

---

[2] "Shakespeare and Religion Chronology", http://www.bc.edu/publications/relarts/supplements/shakespeare/chronology.html, pp. 83–84; published by Boston College.

> Favour my wish, well-wishing works no ill;
> I move the suit the grant rests in your will.[3]

Again, there is nothing at first sight that makes this new exhortation specific to Shakespeare. From the late Renaissance onward, poets and artists had increasingly looked to pagan antiquity as the fire for their Muse and had increasingly turned their backs on the Christocentric Muse of their mediaeval forebears. Why should we conclude that such a complaint about the "finest wits" wasting their powers on "paynim toys" has anything to do with Shakespeare in particular? The clue is to be found in the first and last lines of Southwell's verse, as quoted. The line about the "finest wits" distilling "Venus's rose" has been seen as a reference to Shakespeare's poem *Venus and Adonis*, especially when coupled with the assumption of a pun on Shakespeare's name in the last line: "I move the suit the grant rests in your *will*." In other words, Southwell has made the request that the "finest wit" of the poet should be employed on something worthier than the pagan toys of Venus, but that the granting of the request rests with "Will". The fact that Southwell's "suit", in the final line, is said to rest in "*your* will" has caused some observers to surmise that this dedication is not addressed to Shakespeare directly but to Southampton as Shakespeare's patron. Either way, whether it be addressed to Shakespeare or whether it be about him, the connection remains as solid.

If this evidence raises eyebrows but still fails to convince the skeptical reader of the connection between Southwell and Shakespeare, the third dedication by Southwell should prove the *coup de grace*. It is addressed "to my worthy good cousin, Master W.S." And should the skeptic point out that Southwell must have known others with the same initials as Shakespeare, notwithstanding the significance of his being a "cousin", the connection with "poets" and the apparent punning reference to "Will", there is yet more evidence that surely puts the Shakespearian connection beyond doubt. When Southwell's poems were published shortly after he was executed as a "traitor" in 1595, the dedication was shortened so that it was addressed merely "to my worthy good cousin". The reason for the omission of the name is obvious enough. Southwell was a pariah in the eyes of the state, vilified for his "treason", and "Master W.S." would no doubt have been similarly vilified should his

---

[3] Ibid., p. 84.

identity become known. It is, therefore, significant that the name does not finally appear in an edition of Southwell's poems until an edition published in 1616, the year of Shakespeare's death! It was only then that "Master W.S.", the martyred Jesuit's "worthy good cousin", was finally beyond the reach of possible persecution.

There is further corroborating evidence of the connection between Shakespeare and Southwell in the dedicatory letter that Shakespeare wrote to Southampton for *Venus and Adonis*.

To the Right Honorable Henry Wriothesley,
Earl of Southampton, and Baron of Titchfield.

Right Honorable,
    I know not how I shall offend in dedicating my unpolished lines to your Lordship, nor how the world will censure me for choosing so strong a prop to support so weak a burden, only if your Honor seem but pleased, I account myself highly praised, and vow to take advantage of all idle hours, till I have honored you with some graver labor. But if the first heir of my invention prove deformed, I shall be sorry it had so noble a godfather: and never after ear [i.e., plough] so barren a land, for fear it yield me still so bad a harvest, I leave it to your Honorable survey, and your Honor to your heart's content which I wish may always answer your own wish, and the world's hopeful expectation.
                                    Your Honor's in all duty,
                                        William Shakespeare.

The key here, perhaps, lies in the apology for the nature of the poem and a promise to produce "some graver labor". This, of course, is exactly what Robert Southwell had urged that he do. It could perhaps be argued that the words should not be taken in this way, and that, in fact, they are merely words of self-deprecation as befits a dedicatory letter to one's patron. Perhaps this is so. And yet the timing of these various works is persuasive in support of the former possibility. Southwell was working on his poems and had written the various dedications, shortly before his arrest in July 1592. Shakespeare's poem was registered for printing on April 18, 1593, but surely it is likely that a poem of almost twelve hundred lines would have been many months in the making, especially if we assume, as we must, that Shakespeare had relatively few "idle hours" for poetry in the midst of his other commitments, not least of which was the writing of *Richard III*. Southwell may have heard from Southampton, or from Shakespeare himself, that Shakespeare had *begun* work on an epic poem on the subject of Venus and Adonis, prompting his complaint in the second dedication about the "finest wits" distilling the goddess's rose and playing with pagan toys, instead of employing their talents on more serious or "graver" Christian work. If this were so, the promise that "some graver labor" would follow must be seen as a nod of recognition between the poet and his patron in the direction of their friend, now imprisoned and destined, no doubt, for martyrdom.

The connection is strengthened further by the fact that Shakespeare's next poem, on which he was working, presumably, throughout 1593 and the early part of 1594, when Southwell was still languishing in prison, was *The Rape of Lucrece*. According to the historian and literary critic Hugh Ross Williamson,

> the atmosphere of *Lucrece* is so very different from that of *Venus and Adonis* that it is not impossible to suppose, even were there no other evidence, that Southampton had rightly read Southwell's dedication: "I move the suit; the grant rests in your Will", and that Shakespeare, moved by Southwell's dedication to him, had tried to use his talent to a worthier end and, under the form of a "fable", had written of the violation of a soul by sin. [4]

In doing so, Shakespeare may have had Southwell's own words about the power of "fables" in mind. In the preface to his *Mary Magdalen's Funeral Tears*, published in 1591, Southwell had written: "In fables are often figured moral truths and that covertly uttered to a common good which, without mask, would not find so free a passage." Although it is almost certain that Shakespeare had read this poem by Southwell, together with its preface, it is possible also that the two men had discussed the means of conveying "moral truths ... covertly", through the power of art, during their friendship prior to the priest's arrest. In any event, many critics have highlighted the similarities between Southwell's poetry and Shakespeare's. John W. Hales, in his preface to T. H. Ward's *English Poets*, comments on how curiously reminiscent Shakespeare's *The Rape of Lucrece* is to Southwell's *St Peter's Complaint*, or *Peter's Plaint*, and Christopher Devlin, in his life of Southwell, expends several pages comparing parallel passages from each of the works to highlight the similarities. He concludes with the opinion that Shakespeare's poem had been influenced directly by Southwell's: "[T]he general impression one gets—quite inde-

---

[4] Hugh Ross Williamson, *The Day Shakespeare Died* (London: Michael Joseph, 1962), p. 58.

pendently of any external evidence—is that Shakespeare pricked by Southwell's example, had tried his hand at tapping a loftier and more
metaphysical vein." [5]

There is a curious postscript to this whole discussion of Southwell's
influence on Shakespeare's early poetry. If a recent reading of the poem
is to be believed, Southwell's judgment of Shakespeare's motives for
writing *Venus and Adonis* was a little premature, especially if he ascribed
only neopagan, or more correctly merely pseudopagan, motives for distilling the flower of the goddess into verse. Richard Wilson, in "A Bloody
Question: The Politics of *Venus and Adonis*", [6] has argued that the iconog-
raphy of *Venus and Adonis* suggests that the poem is a critique of the
martyr's cause pursued by Southwell and also of the persecution of Catholics brought on by Queen Elizabeth. In its elaborate phraseology, Wilson argues, Elizabeth emerges as the predatory tyrannical Venus and
Lord Burghley as the boar who kills Adonis. If this reading is correct,
Shakespeare presumably transformed his Venus poem, which was probably written, for the most part, after Southwell's arrest, into the "graver
labor" that Southwell had himself requested. It is, in fact, Shakespeare's
tribute to Southwell. Such a conclusion is supported by the Latin epigraph that Shakespeare chose for the poem:

> *Vilia miretur vulgus: mihi flavus Apollo*
> *Pocula Castalia plena ministret aqua.*

Taken from a poem by Ovid, the lines can be seen as Shakespeare's
own positive response to Southwell's complaint that poets, "by abusing
their talents", have made "the follies and feignings of love" the subject
of "their base endeavours", so that "the devil ... hath possessed ...
most poets with his idle fancies. For in lieu of solemn and devout matters,
to which in duty they owe their abilities, they now busy themselves in
expressing such passions as serve only for testimonies to what unworthy
affections they have wedded their wills." Instead of succumbing to these
lower passions, Southwell had urged his "loving cousin" (presumably
Shakespeare) "to begin some finer piece, wherein may be seen how well
verse and virtue suit together". In responding to Southwell's challenge,
Shakespeare seems to have especially chosen an epigraph for his poem

---

[5] Christopher Devlin, *The Life of Robert Southwell, Poet and Martyr* (New York: Farrar,
Straus and Cudahy, 1956), p. 273.

[6] *Religion and the Arts* 5, no. 3 (2001): 297–316.

to serve as a personal reply to the imprisoned Jesuit and as an endorsement of his words:

> Let base conceited wits admire vile things,
> Fair Phoebus lead me to the muses' springs.[7]

During the time that Shakespeare was presumably writing *Venus and Adonis*, in the latter half of 1592, Southwell was imprisoned at the home of Elizabeth's chief torturer, Richard Topcliffe. He was repeatedly tortured in the vain hope that he could be made to betray other priests. His astounding courage in the midst of such excruciating suffering extracted a grudging tribute even from one of his sworn enemies, Robert Cecil, Lord Burghley's son, who, having witnessed Southwell being tortured, admitted to a friend: "They boast about the heroes of antiquity ... but we have a new torture which it is not possible for a man to bear. And yet I have seen Robert Southwell hanging by it, still as a tree trunk, and no one able to drag one word from his mouth." [8]

Southwell was moved from Topcliffe's house to the Gatehouse in Westminster and thence to the Tower of London, where he was tortured on a further ten occasions. On February 20, 1595, almost three years after his arrest and imprisonment, he was hanged, drawn, and quartered at Tyburn in London. Standing in the cart, beneath the gibbet and with the noose around his neck, he made the sign of the cross and recited a passage from Romans, chapter nine. When the sheriff tried to interrupt him, those in the crowd, many of whom were sympathetic to the Jesuit's plight, shouted that he should be allowed to speak. He confessed that he was a Jesuit priest and prayed for the salvation of the queen and his country. As the cart was drawn away he commended his soul to God in the same words that Christ had used from the Cross: *In manus tuas* (Into your hands, Lord, I commend my spirit). As he hung in the noose, some onlookers pushed forward and tugged at his legs to hasten his death before he could be cut down and disemboweled alive. Southwell was thirty-three years old, the same age as Christ at the time of his Crucifixion.

Was Shakespeare at this grisly scene? Did he add his voice to those doing their best to comfort the doomed Jesuit? We do not know the answers to such questions. We do know, however, that there is ample

---

[7] Marlowe's translation of Ovid's lines.
[8] Williamson, *Day Shakespeare Died*, p. 57.

evidence to suggest that Shakespeare knew Robert Southwell, and perhaps that he knew him well. It seems also that the martyred Jesuit had inspired some of Shakespeare's finest poetry. And if *Venus and Adonis* is, as Richard Wilson suggests, a cryptic fable in which Venus (Elizabeth) is a predator, and Burghley is the boar that kills Adonis (Southwell), we can see that Shakespeare did as Southwell had asked. He had composed a fable in which moral truths are figured covertly. Southwell's words would not be forgotten. In the years ahead his "cousin" would continue to use his art to convey truths, "covertly uttered to a common good which, without mask, would not find so free a passage".

10

PLAYING SAFE WITH THE QUEEN

On December 26 and 27, 1594, whilst Robert Southwell was being tortured in the Tower of London and less than two months before his execution, Shakespeare, as a member of the Lord Chamberlain's Men, was performing before the queen at her palace in Greenwich. How could a known Catholic have attained such privileged access to the inner sanctum of Elizabeth's court? Isn't this an argument against Shakespeare's Catholicism? Certainly it is often presented as such, but let's look a little closer at the evidence.

Let's begin with the most obvious facts. Shakespeare was performing as an actor in a troupe of players under the patronage of Henry Carey, who was Lord Chamberlain to the queen. It was Carey who had access to the inner sanctum, not Shakespeare. Furthermore, Shakespeare could hardly have refused to perform before the queen, having been summoned as a member of the Lord Chamberlain's Men to do so, without risking serious consequences. And, in any case, he might have considered it an honor to perform at court, regardless of his personal views toward Elizabeth. One does not consider that every celebrity who performs at the Royal Command Performance in modern England is thereby a wholehearted monarchist, nor that every celebrity who performs before the U.S. president is thereby an endorser of the president's policies.

Our devil's advocate might respond that it would have been unlikely that Shakespeare would have been part of the Lord Chamberlain's Men if he were known to be a Catholic; and, he might add, it is even more unlikely that, as a Catholic, he would have been part of a troupe invited to perform before the queen. Again, let's scrutinize the evidence a little more closely.

Discretion was generally considered the greater part of valor amongst all but the most reckless or heroic of Catholics, and there is little doubt that, if Shakespeare were a Catholic, he seems to have exhibited the height of discretion. It could be argued, therefore, that Henry Carey was oblivious of Shakespeare's Catholicism, or his Catholic sympathies, when he asked the now famous actor-playwright to join his company of players. The evidence suggests, however, that Shakespeare was not so much a "secret Catholic" whose faith was unknown to all but a chosen (Catholic) few, but that he was considered a "safe" or "tame" Catholic whose faith was known but was not considered a threat to the queen or the state. If this is the case, Shakespeare's faith would have been an open secret, one which was not discussed in public. Indeed, the rules of the *modus vivendi* between the "safe" Catholic and his potential persecutors would forbid any public expression of faith on the part of the Catholic. Forbidden to profess their faith publicly yet unprepared to conform to the new religion, such Catholics found themselves having to remain utterly silent about their faith or else, as seems to be the case with Shakespeare, they learned to walk a tightrope whereby their faith was expressed cryptically. The balance between silence and cryptic expression, which we see throughout Shakespeare's plays, demanded a subtlety and dexterity that allowed truths to emerge that would not raise the ire of the state but merely the eyebrows of the audience.

The evidence that Shakespeare might have been considered one of these "safe" Catholics is best gleaned by comparing him with other "safe" Catholics amongst his contemporaries, particularly with his patron, the Earl of Southampton, and with the great composer and gentleman of the Chapel Royal, William Byrd.

We have already looked at the evidence for Southampton's Catholicism. It is worth noting, however, that, even while he was associating with recusants, including the notorious Jesuit Robert Southwell, he was welcomed at Elizabeth's court. The difficulty for scholars is that "safe" Catholics, unlike openly defiant recusants like Southwell, can often be mistaken for conformists to the new religion. Their seeming silence seems to condemn them. Southampton is no exception. It is generally considered that he conformed after the accession of King James I to the throne. Having been imprisoned in the Tower of London for being implicated in the Essex Rebellion of 1601, he was released in 1603 following Elizabeth's death and was reported, soon afterward, to have attended an Anglican service in the king's train. This is seen to be irrefutable evidence of his conformity, and certainly suggests an element of compromise. Others following in the king's train, and therefore presumably conforming, were Henry Howard, Earl of Northampton, a well-known Catholic nobleman from a zealous Catholic family. Also in the king's train was the king's wife, Queen Anne, who was actually a convert to Catholicism. Evidently the queen felt it necessary to compromise her principles by attending Protestant services occasionally, though she obstinately refused to receive the Anglican communion, and it is clear that other Catholics did likewise, attending the services to avoid the repercussions of not doing so, but refusing to take the heretical communion. It is also clear from the foregoing that "safe" Catholics, such as Southampton, were welcomed into the court of King James, in spite of the continuing persecution of Catholicism by James himself and by his ministers. Indeed, in the case of his convert wife, Catholics were welcomed into the innermost inner sanctum of the king's presence!

The extent to which Southampton did, or did not, conform is open to question. His mother died in 1604, resolute in her faith to the last, and in January the following year, Southampton entertained the Catholic Queen Anne at Southampton House, summoning Shakespeare and his company of players to perform *Love's Labour's Lost* for her delectation. And yet such was the topsy-turvydom of Elizabethan and Jacobean politics that Southampton House was actually ransacked a few days later in the latest witch hunt against Catholics. Within days of the queen's and Shakespeare's presence, the house was searched and a vast array of incriminating Catholic literature was discovered on the premises. On January 26, 1605, it was reported that "eight or ten days since, there were above two hundred pounds' worth of Popish books taken about Southampton House and burned in St Paul's Churchyard".[1]

In the light of such evidence, Southampton's "conversion" to Anglicanism must be thrown into serious doubt. As late as 1613 he was known to be in contact with recusants and found himself at loggerheads with the authorities because of this, without ever being excluded from court. The strongest evidence for Southampton's "conversion" to Anglicanism, or, as Catholics would term it, his apostasy, would not come until 1620, when Sir Edwyn Sandys reported that he had persuaded Southampton to abandon his "Popery". This followed Southampton's election to the post of treasurer of the newly founded Virginia Company, the election to which demanded his outward conformity to Protestantism. Whether this act of "conversion", or the fact that he died whilst fighting for the Protestant king of Bohemia, King James' son-in-law, in the

---

[1] H. Mutschmann and K. Wentersdorf, *Shakespeare and Catholicism* (New York: Sheed and Ward, 1952), p. 113.

Netherlands in 1624, constitutes definitive evidence of his abandonment of the old faith has been the cause of much dispute. From the perspective of our quest for Shakespeare it is, in any case, largely irrelevant. Southampton remained a Catholic, or so it would seem, until at least 1613, about the time that Shakespeare left London and retired to Stratford, and there's no convincing evidence for his becoming an Anglican until 1620, four years after Shakespeare's death. Furthermore, the period of Shakespeare's closest involvement with Southampton, from around 1590 until 1594, coincides with the time at which Southampton is generally believed to have been a believing and practicing Catholic with connections to Robert Southwell and other outlaw priests. And, most intriguingly, Southampton's continuing dalliance with the Scarlet Lady of Rome never seems to have precluded him from the court of either Elizabeth or James, except for his imprisonment following the one act of reckless imprudence that led to his becoming embroiled in the Essex Rebellion. Southampton is a perfect example of a "safe" Catholic whose faith, though hardly secret, was tolerated, tacitly at least, for as long as it remained discreet and was seen as being unthreatening to the safety of the Monarch. The evidence, from both his life and his works, is that Shakespeare was viewed in the same way, as a "safe" Catholic, by both Elizabeth and James.

It is known that Elizabeth counted other Catholics among her favorites, and that she turned a blind eye to their popery for as long as it suited her. One notable example is Sebastian Westcote, Master of the Choristers at St. Paul's Cathedral. Under Westcote's charge, the choristers performed plays before the queen on many occasions and "contributed importantly to the development of Tudor drama".[2] As a Catholic in charge of a company of players performing before the queen, Westcote can be seen to be in a parallel situation to that in which Shakespeare found himself in December 1594. It is, therefore, interesting to note the conclusion of the historian John Harley to Westcote's seemingly anomalous position: "The success of the St Paul's actors may have contributed to Westcote's ability to escape the more severe penalties of Catholicism. Nicholas Sanders said that Westcote was willing to give up his post in the church, but was allowed to keep it because he was a favourite of Queen Elizabeth and did nothing schismatic."[3]

---

[2] John Harley, *William Byrd: Gentleman of the Royal Chapel* (Brookfield, Vt.: Ashgate Publishing, 1997), p. 17.

[3] Ibid.

The parallels between Shakespeare and his great contemporary William Byrd demonstrate, even more clearly, how "safe" Catholics could seemingly prosper in the midst of anti-Catholic persecution, even to the extent of being invited to perform at court.

William Byrd, who is generally considered to be the greatest of the Tudor composers, was a firm Catholic and yet continued to receive the favors of Queen Elizabeth. In 1572 he was appointed joint organist, with Thomas Tallis, of the Chapel Royal, under the patronage of the queen herself. Three years later, he and Tallis received an exclusive license, i.e., a state-endorsed monopoly, for the printing and sale of music. In the same year, no doubt as a mark of their gratitude for the favor that the queen had bestowed upon them, they dedicated their joint work, *Piae Cantiones*, which contained eighteen motets by Byrd and sixteen by Tallis, to Elizabeth. And yet Byrd was also persecuted as a recalcitrant Catholic and was prosecuted on several occasions as a recusant. The paradoxical nature of his position is accentuated by the fact that, as a Catholic, he composed music for the Catholic liturgy, such as his Masses for three, four, and five voices, and, in his official capacity as a composer of the Chapel Royal, he composed music for the liturgy of the state religion also. His Masses for three, four, and five voices seem to have been composed with England's beleaguered Catholics in mind, and most Byrd scholars assume that they were sung at secret Catholic Masses during Byrd's own lifetime. His beautiful motet *Ave Verum Corpus* constituted an affirmation of his belief in the Real Presence of Christ in the Eucharist at a time when it was being denied by Protestant theologians. One can easily imagine that Byrd's Catholic music would have been sung at clandestine Masses that he attended at the very time that his Anglican music was being performed in churches up and down the country. And yet Byrd lived a double life, resolutely living the life of a recusant when he was at home, but conforming to the state religion when he was at court. It is also abundantly clear that the queen not only knew of Byrd's recusancy, but that, through her ministers, she actually rescued him from the due processes of law when he and his wife were charged and brought to court. On more than one occasion court records show that the case against Byrd was abandoned "by order of the Queen's Attorney General".[4] Not only did Elizabeth intervene personally

[4] David Mateer, "William Byrd's Middlesex Recusancy", *Music and Letters* 78, no. 1 (February 1997): 1–14; Harley, *William Byrd*, p. 77.

to rescue Byrd from persecution, she even made him a gift, in 1595, of the lease of Stondon Place, in recognition of his faithful service.

The reason for the queen's tolerance of Byrd's recusancy is that, like Westcote, he had done "nothing schismatic". His loyalty to queen and country was never called into question, and it is generally believed that it was he who made the setting of the queen's poem "Look and bow down Thine ear, O Lord", which was performed during the victory celebrations at St. Paul's Cathedral following the defeat of the Spanish Armada in 1588. Elizabeth probably looked upon Byrd, and Shakespeare, in the same way she looked upon another papist favorite, Edward Somerset, the fourth Earl of Worcester, whom she described as having *"reconciled* what she thought *inconsistent, a stiff papist, to a good subject"*.[5] And yet, "loyal and circumspect as Byrd undoubtedly was, he was more intimately involved in Catholic circles, and probably knew more about Catholic intrigues, than is betrayed by the bare written records".[6] Such is the view of John Harley, and it accords with what we know of Shakespeare as much as it does with what we know of Byrd.

Other parallels between Byrd and Shakespeare can be gleaned from the evidence connecting them with the notorious Jesuits Campion and Southwell. There is evidence that Byrd may have known Campion, as there is evidence that Shakespeare knew Southwell, and it has been conjectured that Byrd might have been among the crowd who witnessed Campion's martyrdom, as it is conjectured that Shakespeare may have witnessed the martyrdom of Southwell. During Campion's execution in 1581 it is said that a spot of his blood fell on the coat of the poet Henry Walpole, who was moved by the experience to write a long poem, commencing with the line "Why do I use my paper, ink, and pen?" Byrd illustrated his sympathy with Campion by setting a part of Walpole's poem to music, and he even risked the ire of Elizabeth by publishing his setting of the poem in 1588, the very same year in which it is thought he had set the queen's poem to music. The risk that he was taking is highlighted by the fact that the poem had caused a scandal upon its original publication. The printer of it had his ears cut off, and Walpole had to flee the country. It is inconceivable that Elizabeth was unaware of Byrd's public show of sympathy for the executed Jesuit, yet she seems to have chosen to ignore her favorite's faux pas. On the

---

[5] Harley, *William Byrd*, p. 77.
[6] Ibid., p. 78.

other hand, Shakespeare's more subtle show of sympathy with Southwell in *Venus and Adonis* and *The Rape of Lucrece* was probably discreet
enough to have escaped the monarch's eye. There was, however, no
mercy shown to the poet, Henry Walpole, when he returned to England
as a Jesuit priest in 1593, having apparently converted to Catholicism as
a direct consequence of being spattered with Campion's blood. Having
been arrested only a day after his arrival in the country, after probably
being betrayed by one of Walsingham's spies, Walpole was tortured fourteen times in the space of two months, so severely that he lost the use
of his fingers, before being tried as a traitor and executed.

With a degree of circumspectness that was lacking in his setting of
Walpole's poem, Byrd showed his disgust at the treatment of the Jesuits
in his Latin motet *Deus venerunt gentes*, a setting of Psalm 78:

> *Deus, venerunt gentes in hereditatem tuam,*
> *polluerant templum sanctum tuum,*
> *posuerunt Ierusalem in pomorum custodiam;*
> *posuerunt morticinia servorum tuorum escas volatilibus coeli,*
> *carnes sanctorum tuorum bestiis terrae;*
> *effuderunt sanguinem ipsorum tanquam aquam in circuitu Ierusalem,*
> *et non erat qui sepeliret.*
> *Facti sumus opprobrium vicinis nostris,*
> *subsannatio et illusio his qui in circuitu nostro sunt.*

> [O God, the heathens are come into thy inheritance;
> they have defiled thy holy temple:
> they have made Jerusalem as a place to keep fruit.
> They have given the dead bodies of thy servants
> to be meat for fowls of the air:
> the flesh of thy saints for the beasts of the earth.
> They have poured out their blood as water,
> round about Jerusalem:
> and there was none to bury them.
> We are become a reproach to our neighbours:
> a scorn and derision to them that are round about us.]

The applicability of these words to the plight of Campion, Walpole,
and other butchered Jesuits is self-evident, especially if we remember
that parts of their dismembered bodies were nailed in the open, "to be
meat for the fowls of the air", as a warning to others.

Since Byrd was the brightest light in the musical firmament in Elizabethan England, and Shakespeare was emerging as the brightest light in the literary firmament, and since both men appear to have been Catholics, the treatment of the one by Elizabeth's ministers might be seen as a clue with regard to the treatment of the other. Could it be that Shakespeare was a favorite with the queen, as was Byrd? If so, could Shakespeare's apparent freedom, in spite of his religion, be attributable to his favored position? "Byrd's recusancy is a fact," wrote his biographer, Richard Turbet, "but so is his loyal service to Queen Elizabeth. How did he resolve these two apparently warring elements—one covert, the other overt—in his music?"[7] This question, so central to those on the quest for Byrd, is as applicable to those on the quest for Shakespeare.

Although, unlike Byrd, there is no evidence of Shakespeare ever being fined for his recusancy, we can glean yet further evidence of his own resolute Catholicism from the opening lines of his enigmatically cryptic poem "The Phoenix and the Turtle", which are generally thought to be a thinly veiled tribute to Byrd.

> Let the bird of loudest lay,
> On the sole Arabian tree,
> Herald sad and trumpet be,
> To whose sound chaste wings obey.

If the pun is accepted, Byrd is the foremost herald of the holy love between the Phoenix and the Turtle, as distinct from the enemy of their love, who is described in the following two verses as a "shriking harbinger" and as a foul precursor of the devil. Byrd is, therefore, lauded by Shakespeare as being a heavenly herald, on the side of the angels, and as an enemy of the devil and "Every fowl of tyrant wing".[8] As for Byrd himself, his "greatest music", according to D. I. Edwards, "was a lament for the tragedy overwhelming England. . . . When we hear the lamentations of Jeremiah over the desolation of Jerusalem, we . . . hear a Catholic Englishman's nostalgia for the glories of the devastated shrines of his own nation."[9] And this echoes exactly Shakespeare's lamentation, in one of his sonnets, for the "Bare ruin'd choirs [of the dissolved

---

[7] Richard Turbet, *William Byrd* (New York: Routledge, 2006), p. 322.

[8] The deep Catholic symbolism of this poem and its overarching recusant allegory have been discussed at length by several critics.

[9] "Shakespeare and Religion Chronology", http://www.bc.edu/publications/relarts/supplements/shakespeare/chronology.html, p. 69; published by Boston College.

monasteries], where late the sweet birds [monks] sang." In their art, as in their religion, the sweet Byrd and the sweeter Bard sang in harmony.

Although, as we have noted, there is no evidence that Shakespeare was ever fined for his Catholicism or that he ever appeared on any official list of recusants, as did his father and his daughter, there is a good deal of implicit evidence for his recusancy in the fact that he never attended his local Anglican church in Southwark, where he was living from 1596 until at least 1599. The historian J. Payne Collier discovered that "though the names of his fellow-actors are found in the token books, proving that they received Communion according to law in the parish of St Savior's, Southwark ... Shakespeare's name is not among them".[10] Since Collier's initial research in the 1840s many others have trawled through the Southwark parish records searching for Shakespeare's name amongst the churchgoers. He is nowhere to be found. Rather bizarrely, this has led most modern biographers of the Bard to conclude that he was (like the biographers themselves) a thoroughly modern agnostic or atheist who would have been more at home in the relativist climate of the twentieth century (with the biographers themselves), than with his "superstitious" and "bigoted" contemporaries. Such a conclusion, blinded as it is by prejudiced presumption and chronological snobbery, misses the obvious and logical point that Shakespeare remained what all the evidence suggests that he had been up until then, namely, a believing Catholic who could not bring himself, in conscience, to pass through the doors of an Anglican church. His father was definitely a recusant Catholic and so was his daughter. All the evidence suggests strongly that he had been a recusant Catholic as a youth in Stratford, and possibly in Lancashire. Confronted with such evidence, what other reasonable conclusion can one come to, when faced with Shakespeare's conspicuous absence from the parish records, than that he remained what he had been?

There is additional implicit evidence for his recusancy in the fact that Shakespeare later moved across the river to the home of Christopher Mountjoy at Cripplegate, in the city of London itself. Mountjoy, as a Huguenot, was exempt from the legal compulsion to attend Anglican services, and so were the members of his household. According to

---

[10] J. Payne Collier, *The History of English Dramatic Poetry to the Time of Shakespeare; and Annals of the Stage to the Restoration* (1846); quoted in Mutschmann and Wentersdorf, *Shakespeare and Catholicism*, p. 380.

J. J. Walsh this constitutes further evidence of Shakespeare's Catholicism: "Hugenuots ... were not required to go to the Anglican services under penalty of being fined heavily for recusancy, as were all the other families of England. It seems clear that Shakespeare by his residence with the Hugenot family could thus avoid attending the Established Church [with impunity]." This is regarded by Walsh as "significant evidence that Shakespeare, while in London, so planned his life as to avoid attendance at Anglican services".[11]

If the Huguenot connection explains why Shakespeare could have avoided being fined as a recusant following his move across the river to Cripplegate, it doesn't account for the fact that there is no sign of his being fined for his recusancy during the time that he was living south of the river in Southwark. Could it be that he was fined but that the court records are missing, like so much other evidence in our quest? Or could it be that he lived a charmed existence as a favorite of the queen who was not to be touched unless or until his Catholicism was perceived as a threat to Her Majesty? Was Shakespeare safe from prosecution and persecution as long as he was considered to be a "safe" Catholic?

Further evidence of the complex nature of life for England's Catholics, and particularly for those "safe" Catholics who served as courtiers to the queen, is to be found in a manual produced for the use of trainee priests in 1578 or 1579 that "gave guarded approval to noblemen and women who accompanied the queen to chapel to render a temporal service such as carrying books or cushions".[12] The same principle was also applied further down the social hierarchy "to exempt from censure servants and underlings who followed their masters to the parish church".[13] This laxity or licence was employed by high-ranking Catholic nobles at court, such as Lord Henry Howard, the future Earl of Northampton:

> [He] would come and continue at prayers when the Queene came, but otherwise would not endure them, seeming to perform the duty of a subject in attending on his prince [Elizabeth] at the one tyme, and at the

---

[11] J. J. Walsh, "Was Shakespeare a Catholic", *The Catholic Mind*, vol. 13 (1915); quoted in Mutschmann and Wentersdorf, *Shakespeare and Catholicism*, p. 381.

[12] Alexandra Walsham, *Church Papists: Catholicism, Conformity and Confessional Polemic in Early Modern England* (Woodbridge, Suffolk: Royal Historical Society/Boydell Press, 1993), p. 64.

[13] Ibid.

other using his conscience. He would runne out of the Queenes chamber in hir sicknes when the chaplain went to pray. Their prayer, for him, [was] like a conjuracion for a spirit.[14]

It can be seen, therefore, that not only were Catholics to be found in the queen's presence, but that both the queen and the Catholic Church turned a blind eye to the compromise and equivocation that was part and parcel of everyday life for Catholics in Elizabeth's England. All of this should be borne in mind as we endeavor to understand the context of Shakespeare's acting before the queen during the Christmas season of 1594.

[14] Ibid., p. 83.

11

RED HERRINGS AND CODPIECES

If Shakespeare appeared to be living a charmed existence, playing safe with the queen whilst playing with fire in his relationship with Catholic recusants, his relationship with the latter would leave him open to the lowest form of attack. In September 1594, as he was probably busy writing *Love's Labour's Lost* and as his patron Southampton was busy charming the queen at court, a scurrilous anonymous satire was published that portrayed him as a disreputable poet suffering from a sexually transmitted disease. Although the satire *Willobie his Avisa* was primarily an attack on Southampton, Shakespeare was dragged in for good measure. The gist of its thirty-one hundred lines is that the protagonist Willobie, or "H. W." (a scarcely concealed allusion to Henry Wriothesley, i.e., Southampton), enlists the assistance of "a familiar friend W. S." (clearly Shakespeare) in his efforts to seduce an innkeeper's daughter, who had already infected "W. S." with a sexually transmitted disease.

What, one wonders, was the motivation for such a libelous publication, produced under cover of anonymity? It is not difficult to discern, nor is it much of a challenge to discover its probable source. The powerful anti-Catholic party at Elizabeth's court, centered round the Machiavellian figure of Lord Burghley and served by a sordid spy network, would have felt horrified by Southampton's position of favor with the queen, and no doubt threatened by it. Unable to act against him directly for as long as he enjoyed Elizabeth's favor, the propagandists resorted to one of the lowest and dirtiest tricks of their trade: the anonymous dissemination of lies, calumny, and scandal. Such a supposition, or suspicion, is reinforced by the anti-Catholic tone of the satire, in which H. W. is referred to as "Italo-Hispanienses", alluding to his allegiance to the Church of Rome and also to an alleged allegiance to Spain, which, only six years after the Spanish Armada, was England's most feared and hated enemy. Clearly the satire was designed to do as much damage to Southampton's reputation as possible, and as much damage as possible to his relationship with the queen, whilst taking a sideswipe at his papist poet at the same time. It proved successful, up to a point at least. Relations between Southampton and Elizabeth cooled some-what, partly due to her growing impatience with his Catholic sympa-thies, and Southampton seems to have ceased offering Shakespeare patronage shortly thereafter.

The damage caused by *Willobie his Avisa* has extended far beyond its original target and far beyond its own time. In recent years, taking the calumnious piece of propaganda at face value, some researchers have taken this as evidence of Shakespeare's illicit relations with an innkeep-er's daughter, and even that he had contracted gonorrhoea from her! Since the source is scandalous and motivated by malice, and probably the product of the Machiavellian machinations of Burghley's campaign against England's "papists", it beggars belief that so-called serious "schol-ars" can take such claims seriously. It is the scholarship of the gossip columnist.

As if this were not ludicrous enough, other "scholars" have gone to great lengths to uncover a real "Henry Willobie", who was studying at Oxford in 1594, and have identified him with the protagonist of the satire who is described in the satire's introduction as a "young man, and scholar of very good hope". Many of these "scholars", suffering from a curious attack of Orwellian doublethink, conclude that the "H. W." in the poem is, at one and the same time, both Henry Wriothesley and this obscure Oxford student. Others have erected fabulous fantasies, mas-querading as fact, in which the obscure Henry Willobie of Oxford, for whom there is no believable evidence that either Southampton or Shakes-peare ever knew, was actually the homosexual "friend" of one or other or both of them. Putting these fantasies aside, we need look no further than Southampton for the identity of the "young man, and scholar of very good hope". He was not yet twenty-one years old when the satire was published, had until recently been studying law at Grays Inn, and, as one of the most popular new arrivals at court, was "of very good hope" of advancement. It was this "very good hope" that had led to his enemies regarding him as a dangerous papist *arriviste* and, no doubt, had prompted the anonymous attack upon his reputation.

It would seem that the obvious truth is staring any open-eyed scholar in the face. The trouble is, however, and to resort to the bawdy level of Shakespearean innuendo, the eye with which they are looking is not to be located in their face. Led by their disordered loins rather than by

their ordered reason, "queer theorists" and other gossip and gutter ori-
ented "scholars" have wasted their time, and ours, following huge red
herrings, or, perhaps, given the context, huge dead codpieces!

Given the diabolical dabblings of such "theorists" this might be a
good time to discuss, albeit at no greater length than it warrants, the
so-called "homo-eroticism" of sonnet 20, and other alleged homosexual references in Shakespeare's work.

Several critics have played with the idea that sonnet 20 suggests homosexual inclinations on Shakespeare's part, and perhaps the most notorious critic to do so was Oscar Wilde in his mischievous piece of fiction
"The Portrait of Mr W. H." To be fair to Wilde he was literally and
literarily playing with the idea, toying with a fancy or fantasy under the
guise of fiction pretending to be fact. It is Wilde at his most mischievous and least charming. It is, at any event, not to be taken seriously as
scholarship, not that this has prevented many "theorists" from taking it
very seriously indeed, including Lord Alfred Douglas,[1] Wilde's former
partner in crime, and André Gide, who described Wilde's theory as
"the only, not merely plausible, but possible interpretation of the Sonnets".[2] Other critics, such as A. L. Rowse, Ian Wilson, and Anthony
Holden have all begged to differ with Gide's dogmatic assertion, insisting that, on the contrary, sonnet 20 illustrates Shakespeare's robust assertion of his own heterosexuality.

Ian Wilson's words on this thorny "theory" are worth quoting at
length:

> Everything about [Shakespeare's] work ... conveys that he was genu-
> inely God-fearing, at a time when sodomy was a capital offence and
> religious people of all persuasions regarded it as an instant passport to
> hell. As we have already seen, he bedded and wedded an older woman
> while still in his teens, quickly having three children by her. His fellow-
> actors were likewise mostly God-fearing married men with large fami-
> lies, who ... are most unlikely to have tolerated an active homosexual in
> their midst. ... *Venus and Adonis*, the poem that Shakespeare undoubt-
> edly wrote for Southampton, is no work for sharing between gays. ...
> [It] is the full-blooded story of a highly sexed older woman's seduction

[1] See Lord Alfred Douglas, *The True History of Shakespeare's Sonnets* (Port Washington, N.Y.: Kennikat Press, 1970), pp. 14–18.

[2] Quoted in Anthony Holden, *William Shakespeare: The Man Behind the Genius* (Boston: Little, Brown, 1999), p. 269.

of a handsome young man. In line with the *Sonnets'* exhortation of their young man to marry, it is a poetic equivalent of a Titian painting, positively provoking man-woman desire.[3]

The "theorists", having soiled the sonnets, have also plagued the plays. W. H. Auden, who should have known better, suggested in 1962 that *The Merchant of Venice* made most sense if Antonio is seen as being "in love" with Bassanio. Auden's suggestion was taken up with gusto by directors and critics who have portrayed Antonio as having an unrequited homosexual attraction for Bassanio. The absurdity of such a reading of the play was addressed with incisive insight, and with admirable constraint, by the Shakespearian scholar Craig Bernthal:

> It is a measure of the critical influence of gender politics that a homosexual crush rather than close male friendship has become for many critics the most convincing explanation of Antonio's behavior throughout the play. Yet nothing in the play suggests that the bond of friendship between them needs to be sexualized to make Antonio's devotion to Bassanio credible. Certainly an Elizabethan audience, accepting biblical strictures about sex between men, would have avoided the play *en masse* had they thought Shakespeare was implying that Antonio was sexually attracted to Bassanio. *The Merchant of Venice*, however, was a very popular play, revived many times, and this is the best evidence for what Shakespeare had in mind and what his audience must have understood.[4]

Reminding his readers that in Elizabethan culture "heterosexual men stated very openly that they loved each other" without any suggestion of an erotic connotation, Bernthal elucidates what is clearly the true nature of Antonio's love for Bassanio:

> Antonio's love expresses itself not just for Bassanio, but to others whose debts he has paid or to whom he has lent money gratis. Thus, Antonio is established at the beginning of the play as a figure of one aspect of Christian love, generosity. Later in the play, when he is prepared to lay down his life for Bassanio, Antonio will become the allegorical form of love in its most perfect form, sacrifice: "I am a tainted wether of the flock, / meetest for death," he will say, as Shylock prepares to collect the pound of flesh nearest Antonio's heart. Antonio will rise to Christianity's

---

[3] Ian Wilson, *Shakespeare: The Evidence* (New York: St. Martin's Griffin, 1999), p. 146.

[4] Craig Bernthall, *The Trial of Man: Christianity and Judgment in the World of Shakespeare* (Wilmington, Del.: ISI Books, 2003), pp. 92–93.

highest ideal of love: "Greater love than this hath no man, that any man
bestoweth his life for his friend's life." [5]

By becoming "the allegorical form of love in its most perfect form,
sacrifice", Antonio is transfigured allegorically into a figure of Christ
himself, the Perfect Love who offers the Perfect Sacrifice. This is clearly
Shakespeare's deepest meaning, steeped as he must have been in Catholic doctrine and typology, and it is a meaning that takes Antonio as far
from the sex-obsessed slandering of him by modern critics as Christ is
from the scribes, Pharisees, and hypocrites of the Gospel, or as Shakespeare no doubt was from the sex-obsessed slandering of him in the
satire *Willobie his Avisa*.

A more reliable character portrait of the poet was given by William
Beeston, who as the son of Christopher Beeston, an actor in Shakespeare's company and no doubt his personal friend, is one of the most
reliable sources of the real Shakespeare that we have. Beeston told the
antiquary John Aubrey that Shakespeare was "the more to be admired,
he was not a company keeper. [He] . . . wouldn't be debauched, and if
invited to, writ [i.e., wrote] he was in pain".[6]

The abyss that separates Shakespeare from many of his modern critics
is rooted in "love" and its meaning. In Shakespeare's time love was
understood in strictly Christian terms and could encompass, to employ
the terminology used by C. S. Lewis in *The Four Loves*, "affection",
"friendship", "eros", and "charity". One could love affectionately one's
parents or one's children; one could love one's friends; one could have
the love of eros when one "falls in love" or in one's relationship with
one's spouse; and one could love in caritas, or charity, in the pure and
sacrificial love that God has for us and we are meant to have for him.
And the word "love" was employed freely in Elizabethan England whenever any of these loves were being evoked.

Ian Wilson makes this point very well in *Shakespeare: The Evidence*:

> All too seldom realized is that in Shakespeare's time the word "love" had
> not taken on its heavily sexual connotations of our own era. From the
> same decade as the *Sonnets*, Thomas Arundel wrote asking for a favour
> from Lord Burghley's son Robert Cecil, assuring him in the course of
> this "I do truly love you and therefore wish that every man should love

---

[5] Ibid., p. 92.
[6] Aubrey MS in the Bodleian Library, Oxford; cited in I. Wilson, *Shakespeare*, p. 410.

you, which love in these troublesome discontented times is sooner won by clemency ... I am wholly yours."

No one would seriously suggest that Arundel meant those words in the way they would be taken today, and innumerable similar examples can be quoted, not least family-man Ben Jonson addressing Shakespeare as "my beloved" in the First Folio.[7]

In this context, and this was the context in which Shakespeare wrote, Antonio's love for Bassanio is clearly that of friendship that matures into that of charity. It should be added that the very idea that Antonio could have had an erotic love for Bassanio would have been seen as not only perverse but impossible. Erotic love was bound up with marriage and procreation. It was, like all love, a virtue. It was not furtive but fertile. It had nothing to do with fornication or sodomy, which were vices, and to which the word "love" would be anathema. This might make uncomfortable reading for our modern critic, but it is true nonetheless. The fact is that the Elizabethans were very "politically incorrect" by today's standards, and Shakespeare, as a religiously conservative Elizabethan, was more "politically incorrect" than most of his contemporaries. To attempt to mold Shakespeare into the image of what Evelyn Waugh called "our own deplorable epoch" is not merely absurd; it disqualifies those endeavoring to do so from being taken seriously as scholars or critics. If these critics were able to empathize with the past, even if they could not bring themselves to sympathize with it, they would see and understand the works of Shakespeare as Shakespeare himself saw them. They would see them as they truly are, as the inspired work of a Catholic genius. Were they able to see the works in this way they would see, and understand, that the eroticism of the sonnets is more akin to the erotic symbolism of the Song of Songs than to anything modernity understands by the erotic, and they would begin to see that the sonnets have more to do with the psalmody of David than with the sodomy of Gomorrah.

---

[7] I. Wilson, *Shakespeare*, p. 147.

12

FRIENDS AND FAMILY

One of the great mysteries of Shakespeare's life concerns the frequency with which he returned to Stratford, and the extent to which he kept in touch with his family. If we are not careful, it becomes easy to paint Stratford out of the picture completely and to assume that Shakespeare lived in London for the whole period from the late 1580s until his return to his hometown in around 1613. It is, in fact, easy to imagine that, for the quarter of a century or so that Shakespeare was based in London, he hardly saw his family at all. There is, however, ample evidence to suggest that this was not the case.

William Beeston, the son of an actor in Shakespeare's company, and therefore one of the closest sources we have to the Bard's life, reported that Shakespeare made at least one long visit home each year, and it is likely that he made shorter visits for business dealings and special family occasions.

Tragedy struck the family in August 1596, when Hamnet Shakespeare died at the age of eleven. It is frustrating that we have no way of witnessing his father's reaction to the death and are left with no choice but to settle for the scraps of evidence to be found in the plays. We are tempted to see the boy alluded to in the character of Prince Arthur in *King John*, which was probably written before Hamnet's death, and to see him reincarnated in Macduff's son in *Macbeth* and in Prince Mamillius in *The Winter's Tale*. Such scraps are of little comfort to the investigator seeking greater insights into Shakespeare's life and character, as, no doubt, they were of no great comfort to Shakespeare himself as he wrote these boy characters into his plays.

In the same year as his son's death, Shakespeare assisted his father in an appeal for a coat of arms, which would serve as a patent of gentility, making John Shakespeare officially a "gentleman". Apart from illustrating the close familial ties between father and son, the application by John Shakespeare for such heraldic recognition and the assistance of his son in the process serve as further circumstantial evidence for their Catholicism. The historian Sir Sidney Lee emphasized the religious significance of such heraldry: "The Elizabethan puritans ... according to Guillim's *Display of Heraldrie* (1610), regarded coat-armour with abhorrence, yet John Shakespeare and his son made persistent application to the College of Arms for a grant of arms." [1]

In the following year, Shakespeare purchased New Place, one of the largest houses in Stratford, from William Underhill, who had been forced into selling the property because of the huge fines he had been compelled to pay for his Catholic recusancy. Having been one of the families singled out for persecution by Shakespeare's old enemy Sir Thomas Lucy in the wake of the so-called Somerville "conspiracy", the Underhills had suffered continual harassment for their faith and had fallen into poverty in consequence. It is, of course, certain that the Shakespeares would have known the Underhills, since both families were an integral part of the close-knit Catholic community of Stratford, and, as such, we can imagine that there was an element of neighborly benevolence in Shakespeare's purchasing of the house from his father's beleaguered and downtrodden friend. One can also imagine that Shakespeare's desire to help would have been heightened by the knowledge that William Underhill was a victim of Sir Thomas Lucy, from whom Shakespeare had himself been forced to flee around ten years earlier. Although the loathed Lucy was still alive, he was now sixty-five years old and in failing health, and, in any case, one imagines that Shakespeare's fame and popularity in London had put him beyond Lucy's faltering grasp.

In purchasing New Place, Shakespeare had bought the first home for his family, enabling his wife and two surviving children, thirteen-year-old Susanna and twelve-year-old Judith, to move out from his parents' house in Henley Street. Although Shakespeare's business and acting commitments must have kept him in London for much of the time, it is not difficult to imagine that he retreated to the relative solitude of Stratford, and to the comforts of his family, whenever the opportunity presented itself. He was now writing two plays a year, and it is entirely feasible that some of them were written, far from the maddening crowd, in his new home in Warwickshire.

---

[1] Sir Sidney Lee, *A Life of William Shakespeare*, 7th ed. (London: Smith, Elder, 1915), p. 13.

Back in London, Shakespeare found himself embroiled in a dispute between Francis Langley, a friend who owned the newly built Swan Theatre, and William Gardiner, a Justice of the Peace of singularly disreputable character "who defrauded his wife's family, his son-in-law and his stepson, oppressed his neighbors and fleeced his tenants".[2] Justice Gardiner had brought three suits of slander against Langley, accusing his adversary of stating publicly, in the spring of 1596, that he was "a false knave, a false forsworn knave, and a perjured knave". None of these suits was brought to trial, either because there was insufficient evidence to proceed or, as has been suggested, because the unsavory Gardiner had been "slandered with matter of truth".[3] Either way, Gardiner and his equally disreputable stepson, William Wayte ("a certain loose person of no reckoning or value, being wholly under the rule and commandment of the said Gardiner"),[4] seem to have decided to take the law into their own hands and to pursue the quarrel with violence, or at least with the threat thereof. Ironically, the law-abiding Langley sought protection from the courts from the illegal methods being employed by the Justice of the Peace, Gardiner. The sheriff of Surrey accordingly issued the following writ on Langley's behalf: "Be it known that Francis Langley craves sureties of the peace against William Gardiner and William Wayte for fear of death, and so forth." This required Gardiner and Wayte to promise to keep the peace, to which they would be bound for a sum of money that would be forfeit should they fail to do so.

Wayte, probably acting at Gardiner's behest, responded by petitioning the court for his own protection, securing the issue of the following writ: "Be it known that William Wayte, craves sureties of the peace against William Shakespeare, Francis Langley, Dorothy Soer, wife of John Soer, and Anne Lee, for fear of death, and so forth." Although some sources have recorded that Shakespeare was being prosecuted for physically assaulting William Wayte, this is unlikely. There is no evidence that Shakespeare shared the violent tendencies of the late Christopher Marlowe, and the fact that two of his codefendants were married women suggests that any "violence" done against Wayte or Gardiner, justified or otherwise, was executed with the tongue or with the pen, not with any other part of the anatomy or with any other implement.

---

[2] H. Mutschmann and K. Wentersdorf, *Shakespeare and Catholicism* (New York: Sheed and Ward, 1952), p. 119.
[3] Ibid.
[4] Ibid.

Nonetheless, this curious court case does give us an invaluable insight into the sort of people with whom Shakespeare was choosing to associate and, perhaps even more illuminating to our quest, the sort of people whom he chose to call his enemies.

Little is known of Francis Langley's religious persuasions, and Shakespeare's relationship with him was, presumably, principally one of business. It is interesting, however, that Anne Lee was the wife of the recusant Roger Lee, whose house had hidden many proscribed priests, and that Anne herself had been denounced in the previous year for attending Mass where she apparently helped the Jesuit, John Gerard, to hide from the authorities. Such are the people whom Shakespeare was counting amongst his friends in 1596.

Even more intriguing is the character of Shakespeare's enemy, William Gardiner. He is variously accused by his contemporaries of being "unchristian", "irreligious", "unchristianlike", "ungodly", and as "a man inclined to strange opinions". Some considered him an atheist, while others considered him a sorcerer or an alchemist. In a court case in 1588, he had been accused of "witchcraft, sorcery, keeping of two toads and holding of irreligious opinions". In the same case it had been testified against him that "Mr. Gardiner was of so devilish opinion that he thought there was no God, and that He had no government in the world, that no man [need] care how he lived [or whether he do well or ill], because he was predestined either to damnation or salvation".[5] Such evidence led Mutschmann and Wentersdorf to describe Gardiner as "one of the extreme Puritans", adding that "a more cold-blooded interpretation of the Calvinistic theory of predestination would be hard to find". This is a little unfair on the Puritans, even the most "extreme" kind, in the sense that they were certainly not "unchristian" or "irreligious", at least not according to their own lights, and would scarcely indulge in sorcery and the like. It could be said, however, that Gardiner's position, on the assumption that the charges against him were justified, represented a Puritanism of sorts, insofar as he accepted Calvinistic predestination. It should also be added, in Gardiner's defense, that this particular testimony against him would not really stand the test of any vaguely competent cross-examination in court. How credible, for instance, is a witness who claims, in the same breath, that the accused does not believe

[5] Ibid., pp. 120–21.

in God but that he believes, at the same time, that everyone is predestined to damnation or salvation?

There is, however, one belief of which Gardiner was never in danger of being accused. Nobody would ever have accused him of being a Catholic. Whether he was a Puritan, an atheist, or a sorcerer, everyone knew that he was not a papist, not least because he had earned a reputation for persecuting London's Catholic community, of which, of course, Shakespeare was now a part.

Gardiner's virulent anti-Catholicism has been preserved for posterity in a report that he sent to Elizabeth's privy council in January 1585, documenting a raid on a Catholic home in Paris Garden, the area of London south of the Thames in which the Rose Theatre was located. It warrants quoting at length, not only as a graphic illustration of the suffering of England's Catholics, but as an insight into the sort of man whom Shakespeare considered to be his enemy:

> They say that about Christmas last year they came to the house of one Hugh Katlyne, there to search for a Papist, and there they found certain suspected persons within the house. The which Hugh Katlyne would not suffer them to come in, neither to search his house, but kept the door having his weapon in his hand; and afterward they went to Serjeant Vener for a warrant, and so went to the house again, and afterward they watched the house with a strong watch, and after that, upon a new search, they came into the house, and there they found one John Worral, a notorious person of papistry, and two other of his acquaintance within. And afterward about the ninth of January, after the death of one Carter, there was burnt in Carter's house certain books of papistry for fear that they should be seen, and afterward they found divers other books of papistry, upon which they suspected Katlyne's house for; and so they went thither again to search, and found not Katlyne at home, and in searching the house they found divers suspected persons; and after that they found eight papists' books hid in sundry places in the house; and never since the aforesaid Katlyne came to his house, but stole away in the night for fear he should be taken; and the next day following there was certain pictures found in the house, and one crucifix; the which books and pictures remains in Mr. Recorder's hand.[6]

The author of this virulently anti-Catholic document was considered a "knave" by Shakespeare's friend Francis Langley, a view which was clearly

---

[6] Ibid., p. 14.

shared by Shakespeare himself, leading him to become personally involved in the dispute to the extent that he was taken to court.

Over the following months, Shakespeare would take his own revenge on both Gardiner and Wayte, writing them into *The Merry Wives of Windsor* and the second part of *Henry IV* as the characters of Justice Shallow and Slender, respectively. Both plays were first performed in 1597, so it is possible that Justice Gardiner, who died in November of that year, would have been aware that his adversary had "staged" his revenge.

Francis Langley was embroiled, albeit indirectly, in a further scandal in July 1597 when his Swan Theatre staged a satirical play called the *Isle of Dogs*, co-written by a young and unknown playwright named Ben Jonson. The target of the play's satire was Elizabeth's government, which led to Jonson being thrown into prison for three months. Jonson and Shakespeare became friends after Shakespeare had been instrumental in getting Jonson's comedy *Every Man in his Humour* accepted by the Chamberlain's Men. Shortly afterward, in September 1598, Jonson was again thrown into prison, this time for killing an adversary in a duel. During this second period in jail, he was received into the Catholic Church, remaining a Catholic for twelve years and being fined for his recusancy in 1604 and 1605, before returning to the Anglican communion in around 1610. It is, therefore, significant that England's two most celebrated dramatists were both Catholics for most of the period that they knew each other in London.

Meanwhile, back in Stratford, the grant of a coat of arms to John Shakespeare was finally confirmed in 1599, three years after his son had initially helped him begin the process. Two years later, in September 1601, he died at home in Stratford, presumably a recusant Catholic until his dying day, and now, officially, a Catholic "gentleman". He left his principal asset, the Shakespeare family home on Henley Street, to his eldest son, William. This, in itself, is significant. If John Shakespeare had remained a militant Catholic, and there's absolutely no evidence to suggest otherwise, especially as his name had appeared on the recusancy lists as recently as 1592, it is not likely that he would have left the family home in the hands of an apostate, to one whom he would have viewed as a traitor to the old faith. It should be assumed, therefore, that John Shakespeare died in the knowledge that the family home was staying in safe Catholic hands.

13

THE KING'S GOOD SERVANT

During the final years of Elizabeth's reign, Shakespeare became embroiled in a controversial play about St. Thomas More, who had been martyred for his Catholic faith on the orders of the queen's father, Henry VIII, more than sixty years earlier. As with so much else on our quest for Shakespeare, this play is shrouded in mystery. It seems to have been written initially by Anthony Munday, a playwright who had made his name as a betrayer of Catholics to the authorities. In 1578, when still a teenager, he had been sent abroad to spy on the activities of English Catholic refugees. Feigning a desire to become a priest, he had gained admittance to the English College in Rome, where he gathered material for his exposé of the College and its activities, which was published in 1582 as *The English Romayne Life*. In the previous year he had been involved in the betrayal and capture of Edmund Campion. It is, therefore, a little puzzling that Munday, more than ten years later, should choose Thomas More as his subject, and it is tempting to detect something of a change of heart on the playwright's part akin to that discernible in Marlowe's *Dr. Faustus*.

Not surprisingly, the play was blocked by Sir Edmund Tilney, Master of the Revels, who was Elizabeth's official censor. Quite simply, Thomas More was still a hot potato, more than sixty years after his death, touching a raw nerve, not only with Elizabeth, whose father had the saint's blood on his hands, but to the Elizabethan state as a whole. Thomas More had been executed by the reigning monarch for refusing to compromise his Catholic conscience on the altar of Machiavellian *realpolitik*, making him an archetype for Campion, Walpole, Southwell, and many others who had suffered a similar fate in the reign of Elizabeth. As such, any positive depiction of More could be seen as a dangerous indictment of England's present rulers.

This is all very interesting in itself, but what is particularly pertinent to our quest is the fact that Shakespeare seems to have become personally involved in the saga surrounding the play. The original manuscript of the play is still in existence and contains amendments to Munday's original text by other well-known contemporary playwrights, including Henry Chettle, Thomas Heywood, Thomas Dekker, and, most important, three pages, or 147 lines, that are generally believed to be by Shakespeare.[1] This is hugely significant because it represents the only extant handwriting by Shakespeare apart from a handful of signatures. It seems that these playwrights, representing the *illustrissimi* of Elizabethan dramatists, had all tried to patch up Munday's original work, apparently with the intention of getting it past the censorship of Sir Edmund Tilney. In Shakespeare's case, at least, we can imagine that Thomas More, as a martyr of conscience who had famously declared from the scaffold that he was dying for the faith of the Holy Catholic Church and that he was "the king's good servant, but God's first", would have been close to his heart. In any event, a closer perusal of Shakespeare's contribution to the play will illustrate his sympathy with More and, beneath the surface, the palpitating presence of the lessons to be learned by his own time from More's holy example.

The lines attributed to Shakespeare depict Thomas More's efforts to reason with a riotous mob intent on attacking recently arrived immigrants who are perceived as threatening the livelihoods of the indigenous population. His counsel of Christian charity calms the storm of rebellion. The crowd is appeased and declares, in unison, that he "says true" and that, as good Christians echoing the words of the Gospel, they should "do as we may be done by". More's words would later be resurrected by Shakespeare, resonating with those of Menenius Agrippa to the restive plebeians in *Coriolanus* and with those of Portia to the vengeful Shylock in *The Merchant of Venice*. Such words, placed in the mouth of a Catholic martyr who was beheaded by a merciless king, have particular power and resonate with the last words of another martyr, Robert Southwell, who was hanged, drawn, and quartered by a merciless queen. Southwell's last words are taken from Scripture, and it is possible that Shakespeare, who may have been present when Southwell uttered them from the scaffold, had these words in mind as he placed a commentary upon them into the mouth of More:

---

[1] For an overview of the scholarship that led to the belief that the handwriting is Shakespeare's, see Oscar James Campbell and Edward G. Quinn, eds., *The Reader's Encyclopedia of Shakespeare* (New York: MJF Books, 1966), pp. 799–800.

But thou, why judgest thou thy brother? Or thou, why dost thou despise thy brother? For we shall all stand before the judgment seat of Christ . . . Let us not, therefore, judge one another any more. But judge this rather, that you put not a stumbling-block or a scandal in your brother's way . . . Therefore let us follow after the things that are of peace, and keep the things that are of edification, one towards another.[2]

Perhaps this connection between Southwell and Shakespeare's More is a trifle tenuous, and it is certainly not crucial or even very important to our quest, but it is interesting that most scholars believe that Shakespeare was working on his addition to Munday's play in around 1595, the year of Southwell's execution. It is entirely feasible, therefore, that the shadow of the recent martyr was on Shakespeare's mind as he wrote about Southwell's famous forerunner.

Even more intriguing than the 147 lines believed to be in Shakespeare's own hand are the twenty-one lines later in the play, written in the hand of an anonymous scribe but ascribed by critical consensus to Shakespeare. These are the words that Shakespeare puts in the mouth of Sir Thomas More, immediately after his appointment as the new Lord Chancellor, as he contemplates the responsibilities of his political office:

> It is in heaven that I am thus and thus,
> And that which we profanely term our fortunes
> Is the provision of the power above,
> Fitted and shap'd just to that strength of nature
> Which we are born [withal]. Good God, good God
> That I from such an humble bench of birth
> Should step, as 'twere up to my country's head
> And give the law out there. I in my father's life
> To take prerogative and tithe of knees
> From elder kinsmen, and him bind by my place
> To give the smooth and dexter way to me
> That owe it him by nature. Sure these things
> Not physick'd by respect might turn our blood
> To much corruption. But, More, the more thou hast
> Either of honor, office, wealth, and calling,

---

[2] These lines from Romans, chapter 14, were recited by Robert Southwell from the scaffold on the day of his execution.

Which might accite thee to embrace and hug them,
The more do thou in serpents' natures think them,
Fear their gay skins with thought of their sharp state,
And let this be thy maxime: to be great
Is, when the thread of hazard is once spun,
A bottom great wound up, greatly undone.

According to Fernando de Mello Moser, a scholar of both More and Shakespeare, this soliloquy represents

a perfectly clear presentation of the awareness of two planes of existence: that of the provision of the power above, which we profanely call fortunes, and that of human vanities, wearing gay serpent skins but, like serpents, only too likely to bite mortally, through the temptation of worldly advantage turning these into an end in themselves, and thereby ultimately destroying the victim on both planes of existence at the same time.... Thomas More had chosen to fall—at one level, certainly, for the sake of the higher one.[3]

Interestingly Moser also connects the underlying philosophy of this soliloquy with both the mediaeval past and the Baroque future, stressing the Catholicism inherent in both: "As I see it, the speech presents an example of the ... subordination of the Wheel of Fortune, in the religious sphere, to the workings of Providence: an achievement of the late medieval tradition which reappears, modified, in the Jesuit drama of the Baroque Age."[4]

In essence, we see much of Shakespeare's own (Catholic) philosophy encapsulated within these few lines. Reality is to be understood in the profundity of providence not in the profanity of worldly fortune. So axiomatic is this understanding of reality that it is the motive force and the leitmotif of much of his work. On the one hand we have the heroes and heroines of his plays, pursuing virtue and embracing suffering, and on the other we have the machiavels, pursuing self-interest and inflicting suffering on others. This being so, it is difficult indeed to read the plays without being reminded of the likes of Thomas More and Robert Southwell, on the one hand, and Henry VIII and Elizabeth on the other.

---

[3] Fernando de Mello Moser, *Dilecta Britannia: Estudos de Cultura Inglesa* (Lisbon, Portugal: Serviço de Educação e Bolsas/Fundação Calouste Gulbenkian, 2004), pp. 150–51.
[4] Ibid., p. 150.

Further evidence of Shakespeare's admiration for More is discernible in Shakespeare's sonnet 23, in which we see the same pun on More's name that he used in his addition to Munday's play:

> As an unperfect actor on the stage,
> Who with his fear is put besides his part,
> Or some fierce thing replete with too much rage,
> Whose strength's abundance weakens his own heart;
> So I for fear of trust forget to say
> The perfect ceremony of love's right,
> And in mine own love's strength seem to decay,
> O'ercharged with burden of mine own love's might:
> O let my books be then the eloquence,
> And dumb presagers of my speaking breast,
> Who plead for love, and look for recompense,
> More than that love which more hath more expressed.
> O learn to read what silent love hath writ,
> To hear with eyes belongs to love's fine wit.

If the middle "more" in the twelfth line of the sonnet is capitalized *(More than that love which More hath more expressed)*, the sonnet is transfigured into a moving tribute to the saint, in which Shakespeare contrasts his own "unperfect" love, weakened by "fear" and "rage", with the holy love "which [M]ore hath more expressed". There is also a sublime allusion to the Mass as "The perfect ceremony of love's right", reinforced by the pun on "right/rite", and illustrating a deep theological understanding of the Mass as the "perfect ceremony" that re-presents Christ's death for sinners as "love's right" and "love's rite". Unlocking this beguiling sonnet still further we see that the poet laments that he is not present at this "perfect ceremony" as often as he should be because of "fear of trust", perhaps a reference to the spies who were present at these secret Masses intent on reporting the names of "papists" and on betraying the priests to the authorities. Since he does not have the heroic self-sacrificial love, even unto death, of a Thomas More (or a Robert Southwell), the poet desires that his "books" be his "eloquence", the "dumb presagers of my speaking breast". The final two lines are surely addressed to both the poet himself and to his reader, beseeching the latter to "learn to read" in his plays what the poet's love, silent through fear, dare not speak openly. Since they will not *hear* the poet speak his mind openly, his readers must *see* what he means in his plays, hearing with their eyes and using their own "love's fine wit" to discern his deeper meaning.

> O learn to read what silent love hath writ,
> To hear with eyes belongs to love's fine wit.

Bearing in mind Shakespeare's evident devotion to Thomas More it is no surprise that he was persuaded to intervene in an effort to get Munday's play past the censor who had written "Perform this at your peril" in the margin beside the speech in which More addresses the rioters. It is, therefore, reasonable to conclude that Shakespeare had been asked specifically to make this particular part of the play more acceptable. Apart from the call for mercy and for Christian charity, the main thrust of More's discourse to the mob in Shakespeare's addition to the play is the fact that authority, under God, is vested with the monarch and does not reside with the mob, which, therefore, has no right to take the law into its own hands. Clearly Shakespeare had the queen's censor in mind as he wrote these words, hoping that the call for law and order, at a time when anti-immigrant feelings were again running high in London, would sway Sir Edmund Tilney to permit the play to be performed. It would, however, be a gross error to believe that Shakespeare's support for the monarchy indicated that he subscribed to the Protestantism of Henry VIII or Elizabeth. On the contrary, Shakespeare's words, placed in the mouth of More, represented the Catholic position on the role of the monarchy, as distinct from the early anti-monarchist murmurings of the Puritans. In 1642 the whole issue of the monarchy would boil over into bloody civil war with the Puritans, under Cromwell, defeating the Monarchists, under Charles I. The Puritans would execute the king and establish a short-lived "Commonwealth" or Republic. It is important to realize that England's Catholics fought on the side of the Protestant king against his Puritan enemies. The Catholic position in Shakespeare's time was no different. Catholics were in favor of the monarchy but hoped for the conversion of the monarch. Shakespeare, as a Catholic, would have echoed the last words of More that he was the king's (or queen's) good servant, but God's first.

In spite of the best efforts of Shakespeare and the other playwrights to make the play acceptable, Tilney refused to lift the ban on its performance. It would be a further four hundred years, during the reign of another Elizabeth, before Munday's *Sir Thomas More* would finally be performed. When the Royal Shakespeare Company staged the play at the new Globe Theatre in the summer of 2004, Shakespeare and More were at last united in art as they had always been in creed. The Bard who, in Jonson's memorable tribute, "was not of an age, but for all time" had finally been allowed to pay homage to the saint who, in the title of Robert Bolt's memorable play, was "a man for all seasons".

Queen Elizabeth died in March 1603, much to the relief of England's Catholics, after a reign of forty-four bloody years. The fact that Shakespeare shared the relief of his co-religionists is discernible not so much from what he said on the occasion of the queen's death but from what he failed to say. The playwright Henry Chettle, challenging Shakespeare to write a eulogy to the deceased Elizabeth, lamented that England's foremost poet had failed to pay her tribute. In his own eulogy to the queen, *Englande's Mourning Garment*, Chettle, calling Shakespeare by the fanciful name of "Melicert", urged him to add his voice to the chorus of praise:

> Nor doth the silver tongued *Melicert*,
> Drop from his honied muse one sable teare
> To mourne her death that graced his desert,
> And to his laies opend her Royall eare.
>   Shepherd, remember our *Elizabeth*,
>   And sing her Rape, done by that *Tarquin*, Death.

If Chettle was awaiting "Melicert's" response he would have found the silence deafening. Shakespeare apparently had no intention of shedding a solitary tear for Elizabeth, sable or otherwise, nor had he any intention of calling upon his "honied muse" to mourn her death. As the apparent allegory of his poems *Venus and Adonis* and *The Rape of Lucrece* had already testified, albeit somewhat cryptically, he viewed Elizabeth not as the victim of violence but as the predatory perpetrator of it. It was not of her rape by death that he desired to sing but of the rape of England and the death of the martyrs.

The fact that Shakespeare seems to have shared the general feeling of euphoria experienced by the Catholics of England after the death of Bloody Bess can be seen by the products of his "honied muse" in the months that followed. The plays that are believed to have been written in the period immediately after the death of the queen and the accession to the throne of her successor, James I, are the appropriately titled *All's Well That Ends Well* and the most overtly Catholic of all his plays, *Measure for Measure*. It's almost as though a huge weight had been lifted from his overburdened Muse and that he felt finally able to express himself more freely without fear of censorship or retribution. If the evidence of these plays is to be believed, Shakespeare shared the hope of all Catholics that the new king would herald a new dawn of tolerance toward Catholicism.

King James was the only son of Mary Stuart, Queen of Scots, who had been the hope of many Catholics until she was executed on the orders of Elizabeth in 1587. Unlike his mother, James was not a Catholic, having been raised as a Protestant, but he had hinted heavily that he would introduce the principle of religious toleration should he become king. At first it appeared that the new king was as good as his word. In the first year of his reign it was decreed that fines and other penalties would no longer be imposed for recusancy, and it is surely no coincidence that this newfound sense of liberty permeates the two plays that Shakespeare is believed to have written at this time.

With the onerous pecuniary burden removed, thousands of conforming or closet Catholics stayed away from Anglican services and sought once again to practice their faith fully and openly. "It was at once apparent", wrote Mutschmann and Wentersdorf, "that Elizabeth's policy of extermination had not achieved its purpose, and that Catholicism still constituted a formidable power in most parts of the country." [5]

Predictably, the Protestants in Parliament, fearing a resurgent and resurrected Catholicism, immediately began to put pressure on the king to reintroduce penal measures against the "papists". In February 1604 James yielded to the intense pressure being placed on him and once more banished all Catholic priests from the country. In the following month, however, he read a proclamation to the Puritan-dominated Parliament declaring his intention to examine the anti-Catholic laws of his predecessor with a view to amending them. Although he sought to placate Parliament with a promise that the reestablishment of Catholicism in England would not be tolerated, he remarked nonetheless that he would like to see an end to the persecution of the Catholic laity, especially the aged and the young. The king's words were welcomed by all but the most militant Catholics, whereas they were greeted with great suspicion and displeasure by most Protestants. Rumors began to circulate that the king was a secret papist, fueled by the fact that his

---

[5] H. Mutschmann and K. Wentersdorf, *Shakespeare and Catholicism* (New York: Sheed and Ward, 1952), pp. 27–28.

wife was a convert to Catholicism. Even if such rumors were untrue, Catholics gained succour from the fact that the queen was a Catholic. After all, if the king was prepared to tolerate the Catholicism of his own spouse, surely he would tolerate it amongst the rest of his subjects. Such were the hopes of the Catholics and the fears of the Protestants.

Parliament flexed its anti-Catholic muscles in implied defiance of the king's wishes, and in July 1604 a bill was passed that confirmed all the Elizabethan statutes against recusants. Furthermore the authorities renewed their persecution of Catholics with renewed vigor. The short-lived joy of the Catholics was plunged into the abyss of despair, their hopes dashed by the knowledge that James's promises were worthless in the face of Parliamentary defiance. Many Catholics had held on to their faith grimly, in the knowledge that the aging queen could not live forever and in the hope that things would be better under James. Now they were faced with the dark and stark reality that there was to be no respite under the new king. For some, this was the final straw. Realizing that there was no immediate prospect of religious liberty, many succumbed at last to the state religion, conforming reluctantly; others were tempted to violence as a last desperate effort to restore the faith of their fathers. Whereas the former group had surrendered, the latter group became the unwitting tools of the new generation of spymasters. With regard to the latter, scholars such as Antonia Fraser, Hugh Ross Williamson, and others have shown that the angry Catholics who became involved in the infamous Gunpowder Plot of 1605, such as Robert Catesby and Guy Fawkes, were the dupes of the Machiavellian machinations of Sir Robert Cecil, son of the infamous Lord Burghley, and his network of spies. The plot may not have been instigated by Cecil, but there seems ample evidence to suggest that he knew about it well in advance and, through the deployment of his spies, manipulated events in order to ensure that the plot failed in its aim of killing the king and his ministers but succeeded in increasing the persecution of Catholics in its wake. The failed plot certainly served as a veritable coup for the virulent anti-Catholic party in James's government, under the leadership of Cecil, who bayed for the blood of all treacherous Catholics.

There is no evidence that Shakespeare sympathized with the violent idealism of the plotters, and it is likely that he shared the abhorrence that most Catholics felt toward such extremism. Yet, as a Catholic, he would have shared the sense of desolation that descended on all England's Catholics at the renewal of the persecution, following as it did so soon

after the initial exhilaration of the queen's death and the king's accession. His hopes, and the hopes of his co-religionists, were seemingly
lying in irreparable tatters.

Although, as usual, there is a frustrating lack of direct documentary
evidence to elucidate Shakespeare's reaction to the new wave of persecution, we have, as ever, the implicit evidence to be discovered in his
plays. Whereas the plays written during the period following the king's
succession demonstrated a sense of freedom and hopefulness, the plays
written after the renewal of the persecution, *Othello*, *King Lear*, and
Macbeth, are amongst his darkest. It is the apparent morbidity of plays
such as these that led Chesterton to describe Shakespeare as being "delirious".[6] In truth, the plays were no more delirious than the times in
which the playwright lived, times in which an Edmund or Iago lurked
with Machiavellian menace in the corridors of power, and times where
faith itself was not only feverish but often times deadly. They were
times that were encapsulated in the closing lines of *King Lear*, Shakespeare's most delirious play:

> The weight of this sad time we must obey,
> Speak what we feel, not what we ought to say.
> The oldest hath borne most: we that are young
> Shall never see so much, nor live so long.

Shakespeare would never be a "traitor" to his king, like Robert Catesby
or Guy Fawkes, but would bear the burden of the sad times in which
he lived in sullen obedience. Like Cordelia, he would love in silence,
not saying what he ought to say except in his plays, and even then only
cryptically. His was not the path of violence or of martyrdom, except
the martyrdom of silence, but of patience and obedience. He would
remain obedient to his king, his country, his faith, and his conscience,
saying, through the medium of his plays, with Sir Thomas More, and
with Cordelia, that he was the king's good servant, but God's first.

---

[6] G. K. Chesterton, *Chaucer* (New York: Farrar and Rinehart, 1932), p. x.

14

LAST YEARS

As with the Somerville "Plot", Shakespeare found himself uncomfortably connected to some of the leading players in the Gunpowder Plot. Robert Catesby, Francis Tresham, and Thomas, Robert, and John Winter were all from prominent recusant families in Warwickshire and, furthermore, were all distantly related to Shakespeare on his mother's side. Much of their plotting had been done at Clopton House, just outside Stratford, and, in consequence, the house was raided on November 6, 1605. A large quantity of "Romanist Relics" were seized during the raid, and one of John Shakespeare's friends and neighbors, George Badger, was implicated: "Here is a cloakbag stayed by the Bailiff of Stratford, which came from Northbrooke to be delivered to one Badger here. It is full of copes, vestments, crosses, crucifixes, chalices and other massing relics. The party that brought them has been sent to gaol." [1] As for Shakespeare's relatives, Catesby was killed whilst resisting capture, whereas the others were hanged.

The aftermath of the Gunpowder Plot and its destructive impact on England's Catholics was summed up succinctly by Mutschmann and Wentersdorf:

> The effect of the so-called Gunpowder Plot on the situation of the English Catholics was, as might be expected, disastrous. The conspiracy, the work of a few extremists, was associated with the Catholics as a body. It was useless for the moderate, compromising majority to protest their innocence of any complicity and their detestation of such methods. The king had been struck in his weakest spot—his fear for his personal safety had proved itself justified, and from 1606 onwards he was an uncompromising opponent of religious toleration. [2]

---

[1] H. Mutschmann and K. Wentersdorf, *Shakespeare and Catholicism* (New York: Sheed and Ward, 1952), p. 68.

[2] Ibid., pp. 29–30.

The penal laws against Catholics were once again enforced with the utmost severity, and new oppressive laws were passed to apply even more pressure on obstinate "papists". A fine of £100 was imposed on any Catholic who failed to have his child baptized by a Protestant minister within a month of its birth. Similar fines were levied on those who sought to marry without presenting themselves to a Protestant minister to be married according to the rites of the Church of England. It should also be noted that there was a cynical as well as a doctrinal or political motive for these anti-Catholic laws. Quite simply, the fines collected from England's Catholics had become a valuable source of revenue for the government. In 1612 alone the huge sum of £371,060 was extorted from recusants.[3] Through this calculated policy of extortion, the Protestant Ascendancy in England enriched itself with Catholic money, while, at the same time, ruining the Catholic aristocracy. It could be said, therefore, that the first phase of the Protestant Reformation in England, under Henry VIII, had been motivated in large part by the pillaging of land belonging to the Catholic religious orders, whereas the second phase was motivated, in part, by the pillaging of the Catholic laity. Pecuniary gain more than doctrinal differences was at the darkened heart of the English Reformation.

As a result of these ruinous laws, the number of openly defiant Catholics decreased steadily during King James's reign. Many Catholics began reluctantly to attend the Anglican services as the only way of avoiding financial ruin or imprisonment. After more than seventy years of largely unmitigated persecution the resolve of many of England's Catholics was at last beginning to weaken. It is, therefore, interesting to note that members of Shakespeare's own family were still resolutely defiant. In May 1606 Shakespeare's daughter Susanna was on a list of recusants brought before Stratford's church court. This fact, which was not discovered until as recently as 1964, is hugely significant.[4] It shows that Catholicism had lived on in the family, being passed from one generation to the next, and adds to the body of evidence suggesting that Shakespeare had himself remained a Catholic throughout his life.

---

[3] Ibid., p. 30.

[4] Kent County Archives Office, Maidstone, Kent: Sackville MSS, ref. U269 Q22, pp. 37 and 39. The contents of this newly discovered document amongst the papers of the Sackville family at Knole was first discussed by H. A. Hanley in his article "Shakespeare's Family in Stratford Records", published in the *Times Literary Supplement* on May 21, 1964.

Susanna Shakespeare, who was now twenty-three years old, was among the younger generation of Stratford recusants, yet many others on the list were of Shakespeare's own generation or of the generation of his parents. Those listed included old friends and neighbors, such as the Cawdreys, the Reynoldses, and the Wheelers, all of whom, like John Shakespeare, were former aldermen and high bailiffs of Stratford as well as being, and evidently remaining, avowed Catholics. Also on the list were Shakespeare's friends Hamnet and Judith Sadler, who had been the godparents of his twins. Such were the people with whom Shakespeare presumably spent his time on his visits to Stratford.

In September 1608, Mary Shakespeare, the poet's mother, died. Although we know little of her final years, there is a suggestion of Shakespeare's deep devotion to her in the play he seems to have written around the time of her death. *Coriolanus*, with its repeated references to "mother", "my mother", and "good mother", has been viewed by several critics as reflective of Shakespeare's feelings toward his own mother. There is even, perhaps, a cryptic reference to his mother's sacrificial Catholic faith, and a self-critical reference to his own "safe" Catholicism, in the famous scene in which Volumnia, Coriolanus's mother, beseeches him not to attack Rome, accusing him of being a traitor to his own family should he proceed to do so. The accusation is heightened by the fact that Coriolanus's wife and child are also present when she accuses him of treachery. Faced with the rebuke of all three generations of his family, Coriolanus repents of his willingness to attack Rome and yet laments that his failure to do so might prove costly, even deadly:

> O my mother, mother! O!
> You have won a happy victory to Rome;
> But, for your son,—believe it, O, believe it,
> Most dangerously you have with him prevail'd,
> If not most mortal to him.[5]

Faced with our knowledge of the dangerous times in which Shakespeare lived, it is difficult to read such lines without the palpitating presence of peril presenting itself to us. Torn between personal success and private passion, and between worldly reward and the faith of his family, the poet had to balance his vocation with his conscience. Admired by

[5] *Coriolanus,*5.3.185–89.

the great who had received their worldly reward, but attracted to the good whose only reward, if the faith of his fathers was true, was in the world to come, he walked the tightrope between convenience and conviction. The tension so evident in his plays is the tension of this tightrope, a tension that is necessary in order for the poet to keep his balance. If the tension slackened, even for an instant, he was in danger of tumbling into the jaws of the king's condemnation, with the temporal punishment that went with it, or of tumbling into the jaws of that other abyss that awaits those who incur the condemnation of the other King, with the eternal punishment that is its consequence. Such was the dilemma that Shakespeare, as a Catholic on the fringes of King James's court, faced with each and every play he wrote.

The fact that many of the Puritans in Parliament considered the theatre to be a dangerous disseminator of papist ideas can be gleaned from a sermon by the Puritan preacher William Crashaw, delivered at St. Paul's Cross in London in 1608: "The ungodly plays and interludes so rife in this nation: what are they but a bastard of Babylon [a derogatory synonym for Rome in puritanical Biblespeak], a daughter of error and confusion; a hellish device—the devil's own recreation to mock at holy things—by him delivered to the heathen and by them to the Papists, and from them to us?"[6] Apart from its relevance to our quest, this attack on "papist plays" by the puritanical Crashaw is noteworthy as being one of the pithiest putdowns of Western culture ever made. In one terse, bombastic sentence, the entire legacy of the West is dismissed as being a contagious disease, passed from the devil to the "heathen" Greeks and Romans, and then to the "Papist" Catholics until finally, via Shakespeare and his fellow playwrights, it had contaminated modern England. Two years later, in February 1610, Crashaw was again equating Shakespeare and his ilk to the devil in a sermon he preached to the Lord Governor of Virginia. On this occasion he fulminated that the greatest threat to the newly founded colony was to be found in Catholicism, culture, and other satanic manifestations: "We confess this action hath three great enemies: but who be they? even the Devil, Papists, and Players."[7] Ironically, William Crashaw's son, Richard, one of the greatest of the metaphysical poets, would become a Catholic and would die in lonely exile in Italy in 1649.

---

[6] Mutschmann and Wentersdorf, *Shakespeare and Catholicism*, p. 102.
[7] Ibid.

Responding to these puritanical attacks upon plays and players, Phillip Rosseter, a Catholic actor and lessee of the Whitefriars Theatre, retorted in December 1610 "that a man might learn more good at one of their plays or interludes than at twenty of our roguish sermons".[8]

Not surprisingly, Catholics preferred the plays of Shakespeare to the "roguish sermons" of the Puritans. In 1610 Sir John Yorke, of Gowthwaite Hall in Nidderdale in Yorkshire, was convicted for entertaining a group of players who performed anti-Protestant plays at his own and at other recusant houses.[9] Intriguingly, *King Lear* and *Pericles* were among the plays performed at these secret recusant gatherings, indicating that recusant audiences readily deduced the cryptic Catholic meaning of the plays, and suggesting also that Shakespeare's faith, however discreetly practiced, was known to his fellow Catholics.

Further evidence of the disdain with which the Puritans held the theatre in general, and Shakespeare in particular, emerged in the *History of Great Britain* by the Protestant historian John Speed, published in 1611. Discussing the Lollard leader, Sir John Oldcastle, who had suffered during the reign of Henry V and who was considered a proto-Protestant and as the "morning star of the Reformation",[10] Speed was at pains to discredit attacks upon his reputation by papists and playwrights. Complaining that the Jesuit Robert Persons had described Oldcastle as "a ruffian, a robber and a rebel", Speed riposted by suggesting that Persons was a liar, along with "his poet", Shakespeare: "And his [Persons's] authority, taken from the stage-players, is more befitting the pen of his slanderous report than the credit of the judicious, being only grounded from this Papist [Persons] and his poet [Shakespeare], of like

---

[8] Ibid.

[9] Peter Milward, *The Catholicism of Shakespeare's Plays* (Southampton: Saint Austin Press, 1997), p. 137; Milward's source was a paper given at the "Lancastrian Shakespeare" conference at Lancaster University in 1999 by Professor Masahiro Takanaka, of the Renaissance Institute at Tokyo's Sophia University. (Peter Milward to Joseph Pearce, e-mail correspondence, March 28, 2007.) Masahiro Takenaka, "The Cholmeley Players and the Performance of *King Lear* in Yorkshire", *Renaissance Bulletin* (2001). See also: C.J. Sisson, "Shakespeare's Quartos as Prompt Copies, with Some Account of Cholmeley's Players and a New Shakespeare Allusion", *Review of English Studies* (1942); Hugh Aveling, *Catholic Recusants of the West Riding of Yorkshire* (London: Leeds Philosophical & Literary Society, 1963); C.W. Brody, "Players of Interludes in North Yorkshire in the Early Seventeenth Century" (York: North Yorkshire County Record Office Publications, 1976); John L. Murphy, *Darkness and Devils: Exorcism and King Lear* (Athens, Ohio: Ohio University Press, 1984).

[10] From John Foxe's *Book of Martyrs*; quoted in Milward, *Catholicism of Shakespeare's Plays*, p. 103.

conscience for lies, the one ever feigning and the other ever falsifying the truth." [11]

This astonishing attack upon Shakespeare, calling him a falsifier of the truth and a sidekick of the Jesuits, demonstrates the general suspicion with which he was held by the Puritans. The specific connection between Persons and Shakespeare, upon which Speed was grounding his attack, is to be found in Persons's account *Of Three Conversions of England*, published in 1603, and its connection with Shakespeare's *Henry IV*, part I. Persons's work was effectively a piece of revisionist history in which he refutes John Foxe's Protestant version of England's religious history. In his discussion of Oldcastle, Persons dismisses him as "a ruffian knight, as all England knoweth, and commonly brought in by comedians on their stages". This is seen by most scholars as an allusion to Shakespeare's depiction of Oldcastle, under the tactful alias of Sir John Falstaff, whom Prince Hal addresses as "that father ruffian, that vanity in years". [12] The fact that Falstaff is Shakespeare's alias for Oldcastle has been generally accepted by scholars ever since the connection between Oldcastle and Falstaff was made by James O. Halliwell-Phillips in 1841. [13] The connection is not only deduced from Oldcastle's appearance in *The Famous Victories of Henry the Fifth*, which is generally thought to be Shakespeare's source play, but also from Shakespeare's punning reference to Falstaff, by Prince Hal, as "my old lad of the castle", in the play's second scene.

Persons's "ruffian knight" is clearly a reference to the "father ruffian" in Shakespeare's play and shows, equally clearly, that Shakespeare shared the Jesuit's view of Oldcastle, as a heretic and a rogue, not Foxe's and Speed's view that he was a hero and a martyr. It is, therefore, of little wonder that Speed attacks Persons and Shakespeare as feigners and falsifiers of the truth, the former "feigning" the truth in his history of England and the latter "falsifying" it in his history plays. Nor is it any wonder that he should seek to shackle them together as "this Papist and his poet", endeavoring to tar Shakespeare with the Jesuit brush.

Unlike Shakespeare, who was presumably aware of Speed's attack upon him, Robert Persons would never know of this latest controversy caused

---

[11] From John Speed, *History of Great Britain*; quoted in Ian Wilson, *Shakespeare: The Evidence* (New York: St. Martin's Griffin, 1999), p. 228.

[12] Act 2, scene 4.

[13] See James O. Halliwell-Phillips, *An essay on the character of Falstaff and Shakesperiana* (1841).

by his writings. He died the previous year, after thirty years of pamphleteering on behalf of the Catholic cause from the sanctuary of the continent, to which he had fled in 1580. Commenting on Persons's legacy, John Donne, who had come from a staunchly Catholic family, blamed the Jesuit, rather than the government, for the sufferings of England's Catholics. Persons's rhetoric had, according to Donne, "occasioned more afflictions, and drawn more of that [Catholic] blood ... than all our Acts of Parliament have done". Referring to his own family's suffering, Donne pointed the finger of blame at the Jesuits for provoking the persecution and, even more incredibly, seemed to be suggesting that he and his family were the real martyrs, not Jesuits such as Campion and Southwell, who had been hanged, drawn, and quartered for their faith: "I have beene ever kept awake in a meditation of Martyrdome, by being derived from such a stocke and race, as, I believe, no family ... hath endured and suffered more in their persons and fortunes, for obeying the Teachers of Romane Doctrine, than it hath done."[14] Writing in 1610, the year of Persons's death, Donne's words were typical of the sort of doublethink being practiced by many apostatizing Catholics who were seeking justification for their conformity to the religious demands of the Jacobean state.

In the same year in which Donne's equivocating words were written, a Royal Proclamation "for the due execution of all former laws against recusants" ushered in a new wave of persecution against Catholics, tempting other recusants to follow in Donne's apostatizing footsteps. Amongst those who did so was Shakespeare's friend Ben Jonson, who formally rejoined the Anglican church after the years of recusancy that had followed his earlier conversion, perhaps under Shakespeare's influence, to Catholicism. But what of Shakespeare himself? Did he succumb to this new trend of capitulation? Did he follow Donne's example, surrendering the faith of his fathers and accepting, however reluctantly, the new religion? Was he, like so many of his co-religionists, tiring of the tempest of religious persecution? Was he willing to surrender his principles and beliefs in order to gain the worldly peace that could only come with conformity to the dictates of the Jacobean state? These questions, so crucial to our quest, are answered by the last act that Shakespeare

---

[14] See John Donne, *Pseudo-Martyr* (Montreal: McGill-Queen's University Press, 1993); cited in the "Shakespeare and Religion Chronology", http://www.bc.edu/publications/relarts/supplements/shakespeare/chronology.html, published by Boston College.

performed in London before retiring, once and for all, to the sanctuary of Stratford.

Although some authorities believe that Shakespeare may have retired to Stratford as early as 1610, perhaps in the wake of the latest wave of persecution, his last major legal transaction in London would not take place until March 1613, when he purchased the Blackfriars Gatehouse. At first glance, the purchase of a property in London might seem to be of no particular interest to our quest. Clearly it was not bought for the poet himself to live in. He had already shaken the London dust from his feet and had retired to New Place, the large house in Stratford he had purchased for his family from recusant friends back in 1597. Why, then, did he buy it? Most academics, failing to dig any deeper than the surface, have unquestionably accepted the most obvious answer. "It was, apparently, an investment pure and simple", wrote Samuel Schoenbaum, a view shared by A. L. Rowse, who concluded that "the gatehouse was no more than an investment".[15] If, however, we dig a little deeper we are confronted with a number of problematic questions. If Shakespeare was interested in purchasing property purely as an investment, why did he not do so earlier? By the time that he bought the Gatehouse he had been living in London for a quarter of a century, seemingly content to rent accommodation for the whole time. There is no record of Shakespeare buying any other property in London, whereas there is evidence to show that he lived in rented accommodation. Isn't it odd that he should suddenly decide to invest in property after seemingly showing no previous interest in doing so? At the very least, these questions should prompt the diligent investigator to search for other motives. Let's do so.

An investigation into the history of the Blackfriars Gatehouse reveals that it was "a notorious center of Catholic activities".[16] As its name would indicate, it had originally belonged to the Dominican Order and had been the lodging of the Prior until the dissolution of the monasteries. During the reign of Mary the mansion was in the possession of Thomas Thirlby, the Catholic bishop of Ely, who sold it to his cousin William Blackwell, the town clerk of London. At the latter's death in 1569, the Gatehouse was inherited by his widow, Mary, née Campion,

[15] Samuel Schoenbaum, *William Shakespeare: A Documentary Life* (Oxford: Oxford University Press, 1975), p. 223; A. L. Rowse, *William Shakespeare: A Biography* (New York: Harper and Row, 1963), p. 445.
[16] Mutschmann and Wentersdorf, *Shakespeare and Catholicism*, p. 136.

who was related to Edmund Campion, the Jesuit martyr. The papist sympathies of Mary Blackwell are suggested by the fact that the Catholic Bishop of Ely was allowed to lodge at her house until his death in 1570. Further evidence of these sympathies can be seen from the fact that Mary Bannister, the sister of another Jesuit martyr, Robert Southwell, was a tenant at the Gatehouse for a time, and from the fact that Katherine Carus, a kinswoman of the Lancashire Hoghtons and the widow of a defiantly recusant judge, had died there "in all her pride and popery".[17]

In 1585 Mary Blackwell was accused of recusancy, and, in the following year, a government informer reported his suspicions that the house had become a center for secret Catholic activity: "Now there dwells in it one that is a very unconformable man to her Majesty's proceedings. It has sundry backdoors and bye-ways, and many secret vaults and corners. It has been in time past suspected, and searched for papists, but no good done for want of knowledge of the backdoors and bye-ways of the dark corners."[18] This description, awash with suggestions that the house concealed several priests' holes,[19] clearly establishes the Gatehouse as a hub of recusant activity by the mid-1580s, around the time Shakespeare first arrived in London. Is it possible that Shakespeare was part of these clandestine gatherings upon his arrival in London and that he continued to frequent such gatherings throughout the remainder of his time in the city? Was it here that he attended Mass?

In 1590 the Gatehouse passed into the possession of Mathias Bacon, Mary Blackwell's grandson, who leased it to a Catholic, John Fortescue, whose father, Sir Anthony Fortescue, had been implicated in a conspiracy against Elizabeth in 1562, and whose mother was related to Cardinal Pole. John Fortescue married Ellen, the daughter of Ralph Henslowe, a Catholic recusant from Hampshire who was a kinsman of the Earl of Southampton. In 1591, two priests, Anthony Tyrrell and John Ballard, reported that they had delivered "such stuff as we brought from Rome" to John and Ellen Fortescue, and in the same year it was

[17] Richard Wilson, *Secret Shakespeare: Studies in Theatre, Religion, and Resistance* (Manchester: Manchester University Press, 2004), p. 260.
[18] T. Wright, ed., *Queen Elizabeth and Her Times: A Series of Original Letters*, 2 vols. (London: 1838), 2: 249; cited in Mutschmann and Wentersdorf, *Shakespeare and Catholicism*, p. 137.
[19] Priests' holes were secret hiding places concealed with architectural ingenuity in many recusant households. These can still be seen in many of England's surviving Tudor houses.

recorded that "Fennell the priest does use to come very much to Mr John Fortescue's house".[20] In 1598, acting on a report that the Gatehouse was a hive of recusant activity that had "many places of secret conveyance in it" and "secret passages towards the water", i.e., toward the river Thames, from whence priests could make their getaway, the authorities raided the house. John Fortescue was absent during the search, but his wife and daughters were interrogated, admitting that they were recusants, but refusing to confess that they had hidden priests in the house.

John Fortescue, writing to the Earl of Essex about the raid on his house, was at pains to avoid incriminating himself: "I crave no favor either of her Majesty or of any peer within this realm, if any unnatural or disloyal act can be proved against me, either in harboring, maintaining or abetting either priest or Jesuit, and forbidden by her highness' laws. And ... if I have retained my conscience at all, her Majesty has been no loser by it, nor myself, God knows, any great gainer."[21] These words have always been considered a "denial" by Fortescue that he had harbored priests, an error that is even made by normally astute observers of the evidence, such as Mutschmann and Wentersdorf. In reality, however, his words do not constitute a denial at all. A closer reading of what Fortescue is actually saying illustrates a perfect example of the Jesuitical art of equivocation, in which one avoids incriminating oneself without ever resorting to the sin of lying. He does not deny harboring priests, which would have been a lie, but states that he craves "no favor", i.e., mercy, from the queen or her ministers if the charge "can be proved" against him. He concludes by stating that he has retained his conscience and that, in so doing, he has not harmed the queen. On one level he is referring to his recusancy, which does not constitute a threat to the queen, but, on the contrary, has harmed him, through persecution, whilst leaving her unscathed. Perhaps, on a deeper level, he is saying that doing God's will, through the following of his conscience, should be seen as harming nobody. In any event, his words do not constitute a denial but an equivocation.

Fortescue's equivocation, as opposed to his denial, should be borne in mind in relation to the account by the Jesuit Oswald Greenway, who states in his autobiography that he had paid a surreptitious visit to the

---

[20] Mutschmann and Wentersdorf, *Shakespeare and Catholicism*, p. 137.
[21] Ibid., p. 138.

Gatehouse on the day after the raid, being informed that there had been priests in the house during the search but that their hiding places had not been discovered.

Fortescue, his wife, and their two daughters were all imprisoned after the raid, but seem to have recommenced their recusant activity following their release. In 1605, the Jesuit John Gerard asked Ellen Fortescue, in her husband's absence, if he could use the Gatehouse as a "safe-house", in which Catesby, Percy, Winter, and other "gunpowder plotters" could meet in secret. Wisely and prudently, she declined to admit the conspirators, claiming that she did not approve of Catesby. Her prudence on this occasion probably saved her life, and the lives of her family. A few months later, after the plot had been discovered, Father Gerard, now the most wanted man in England, appeared in desperation at the Gatehouse, wearing a wig and false beard as a disguise, and asking for shelter, stating that he did not know where else to hide. "Full of sadness" (*plenus dolore*), John Fortescue replied: "Have you no one to ruin but me and my family?"[22] Unlike many of his Jesuit *confreres*, Father Gerard managed to escape the clutches of his pursuers, slipping out of the country in disguise. Shortly afterward, John Fortescue also went into exile, harried out of his home and his country by the incessant persecution.

Little is known of the history of the Gatehouse in the few years from the time that the Fortescues went into exile and the time that Shakespeare purchased it from its latest owner, Henry Walker, but as late as 1610 it was reported in Naples that it was the base for Jesuits plotting to "send the King an embroidered doublet and hose, which are poisoned and will be death to the wearer".[23] As much as such a statement can be dismissed as the product of the idle fantasies of embittered exiles or anti-Catholic spies, it is apparent nonetheless that Shakespeare had chosen to purchase one of the most notorious Catholic houses in the whole of London. This in itself is curious enough, but it is not by any means the end of the story.

Shakespeare chose to lease the Gatehouse to John Robinson, son of a gentleman of the same name who was an active Catholic. It was

[22] From original documents in the archives of St. Cuthbert's College in Ushaw, Co Durham; cited in E. K. Chambers, *William Shakespeare: A Study of Facts and Problems*, 2 vols. (Oxford: Clarendon Press, 1930), 2:167–68.

[23] John Morris, *The Troubles of Our Catholic Forefathers*, 3 vols. (London: Burns and Oates, 1972), 1:144.

reported, in 1599, that John Robinson senior had sheltered the priest Richard Dudley in his home. He had two sons, Edward and John, the former of whom entered the English College at Rome and became a priest, the latter of whom became Shakespeare's tenant. It is clear, therefore, that Shakespeare knew that in leasing the Gatehouse to John Robinson he was leaving it in the possession of a recusant Catholic. In consequence, and as Ian Wilson surmised in *Shakespeare: The Evidence*, Robinson was "not so much Shakespeare's tenant in the Gatehouse, as his appointed guardian of one of London's best places of refuge for Catholic priests".[24] Furthermore, John Robinson was not merely a tenant, but was quite obviously a valued friend. He visited Shakespeare in Stratford during the poet's retirement and was seemingly the only one of the Bard's London friends who was present during his final illness, signing his will as a witness.

Should further proof be needed that Shakespeare had purchased the Gatehouse in the knowledge that it was being used to shelter Catholic priests, an intriguing postscript should help to dispel any remaining doubts on the subject. On October 26, 1623, at three o'clock in the afternoon, a clandestine congregation of Catholics, about three hundred in number, were assembled in a secret upper garret "over the Gatehouse" for what was presumably their regular Sunday Mass. It was perhaps a larger congregation than usual, crowded into the secret upper room for a Mass celebrated by the Jesuit Father Drury. Suddenly a main beam of the floor collapsed under the weight, killing more than ninety people. It was only through this disaster that the secret "church", which had perhaps been used for many years, was discovered by the authorities.[25]

Although Shakespeare had been dead for six years at the time of this tragedy, it serves nonetheless as the final piece of a jigsaw that enables us better to assemble the missing pieces on the basis of common sense and probability. Here are the facts. The Blackfriars Gatehouse had been a hub for recusant activity in London since at least 1586, and probably earlier. When Shakespeare purchased it he must have known of its reputation, and he chose to lease it to an active Catholic whose brother had presented himself to the English College at Rome to study for the priesthood in 1613, the very year in which Shakespeare bought the

---

[24] I. Wilson, *Shakespeare*, p. 397.
[25] A full account of this tragedy is given in Henry Foley, S.J., *Records of the English Province of the Society of Jesus*, 7 vols. (London: Burns and Oates, 1877), 1:77–98.

property. The fact that John Robinson continued to lease the property until after Shakespeare's death suggests strongly that it continued to be used for clandestine Catholic activity, including the celebration of the Mass, during the years that Shakespeare owned it. Such a possibility is strengthened still further by the fact that the Gatehouse was still being used as a base for secret Masses after his death.

Having assembled these pieces together, let's try to place Shakespeare himself in the picture. Is it not only possible but, given the evidence, perhaps even probable that Shakespeare had attended Mass in the secret upper garret over the Gatehouse? Given that the Gatehouse had presumably been used for these Masses since at least the mid-1580s, when Shakespeare first arrived in London, isn't it likely that he had attended Mass there on many occasions during the twenty-five years or so that he was in London? If this is so, isn't it likely that Shakespeare bought the property, for the huge sum of £140, more than twice the sum he paid for New Place in Stratford, because he wanted to safeguard its future as a home for London's persecuted Catholics? Did he perhaps buy it as a *spiritual* investment, more than as merely a financial investment, in the knowledge that, as the benefactor, he would be prayed for at the Masses to be held there? Did he perhaps stipulate his desire that this should be so?

If so, and surely this is the most likely explanation for Shakespeare's final act in London, he would have been echoing in his actions the words of Prospero in the final words of the final act of the last play he wrote:

> And my ending is despair,
> Unless I be reliev'd by prayer,
> Which pierces so, that it assaults
> Mercy itself, and frees all faults.
>   As you from crimes would pardon'd be,
>   Let your indulgence set me free.[26]

Desiring the prayers of the Catholic faithful in the hidden recesses of the Gatehouse, as he had desired the prayers of the audiences who watched his final play, Shakespeare disappeared into the sunset of his own life, returning to his home and family. At long last, after the tempest of his life, he hoped to rest in peace.

---

[26] Although there are later plays attributed to a collaboration between Shakespeare and John Fletcher, *The Tempest* is the last play that is solely Shakespeare's.

15

"HE DIED A PAPIST"

Very little is known of Shakespeare's retirement in Stratford. It is, however, intriguing that one of the few surviving pieces of evidence of this final period of his life connects him with the notorious Somerville family, who had given their name to the alleged "plot" of 1583. It seems that one of Shakespeare's closest friends in his final years was Sir William Somerville, who resided in Edstone, about four miles to the north of Stratford. Sir William was the brother of John Somerville, who had died in mysterious circumstances in prison while awaiting execution for apparently plotting to kill Queen Elizabeth.

In 1818 a member of the Somerville family wrote to the Shakespeare scholar James Boswell, son of the celebrated biographer of Samuel Johnson, of Sir William's friendship with Shakespeare: "Mr. [William] Somerville of Edstone, near Stratford-upon-Avon ... lived in habits of intimacy with Shakespeare, particularly after his retirement from the stage, and had his portrait painted, which, as you will perceive, was richly set and carefully preserved by his descendants."[1] This portrait, which is still extant, is by the famous miniaturist Nicholas Hilliard and is one of the most famous portraits, or alleged portraits, of the Bard. Although scholars readily accept that the painting is indeed by Hilliard, many have cast doubt on whether it is actually a portrait of Shakespeare. The principal doubt arises from the fact that the man depicted is markedly different from most other portraits. Since, however, most scholars cast equal doubt on all the other portraits there is something of a *non sequitur* in this argument against its authenticity! Either way, and whether or not the portrait is genuine or otherwise, there seems no reason to doubt that Shakespeare and Sir William Somerville were friends, especially when the Somerville family's evidence harmonizes so well with what we know of the poet's other Catholic friends.

[1] James Boswell, *Variorum Shakespeare* (1821), cited in H. Mutschmann and K. Wentersdorf, *Shakespeare and Catholicism* (New York: Sheed and Ward, 1952), p. 168.

Sir William Somerville died in 1616, and in the same year, appropriately enough on St. George's Day, his fifty-second birthday, Shakespeare also died.

Happily for those on the quest for the poet, a great deal of light is shed on the mystery surrounding his life in the evidence he left at his death.

The fact that "he died a papist", as was recorded by an Anglican clergyman, Richard Davies, more than seventy years later, is suggested by the evidence of Shakespeare's will. The reference in the will to the Blackfriars Gatehouse, "wherein one John Robinson dwelleth scituat", is interesting because the same John Robinson was also a signatory of the will itself. Even secularist misreaders of Shakespeare's life, such as Peter Ackroyd, admit that Robinson's Catholic affiliations "are really not in doubt" [2], and, this being so, it is intriguing, to say the least, that he emerges, at the last, as apparently the closest of Shakespeare's London friends. He is the only one of his city friends who is known to have attended New Place in the poet's final illness, the only one to be a signatory of the will, and he is, at the same time, the friend who is most closely and unmistakably connected to the Catholic underground in London.

As for the beneficiaries of the will, it is surely noteworthy that Shakespeare bequeathed his property to his daughter Susanna not to his other daughter, Judith, especially since Susanna, like her father, appears to have remained a staunch Catholic. Not only was she listed as a recusant as recently as 1606, but the words of her own epitaph suggest strongly that she adhered to the faith of her fathers right up until the time of her death in 1649, by which time England had fallen into the hands of a puritan republic:

> Witty above her sex, but that's not all,
> Wise to salvation was good Mistress Hall,
> Something of Shakespeare was in that, but this
> Wholly of him with whom she's now in bliss.
> Then, Passenger, hast ne'er a tear,
>   To weep with her that wept with all;
> That wept, yet set herself to cheer
>   Them up with comforts cordial.
> Her love shall live, her mercy spread,
>   When thou hast ne'er a tear to shed.

[2] Peter Ackroyd, *Shakespeare: The Biography* (New York: Nan A. Talese/Doubleday, 2005), p. 497.

The intimation that Susanna, like her father, was "wise to salvation" could be seen as a veiled reference to the illegal faith that they shared, and, through which, they hoped to be reunited "in bliss". The second half is awash with pseudo-Shakespearean allusions to the valley of tears, with echoes of the *Salve Regina*, lamenting the times in which she and her father had been constrained to live.

Those of Shakespeare's friends who were beneficiaries of his will included his old friend Hamnet Sadler, who was godfather to Shakespeare's twins and who was, like Susanna, listed as a recusant in 1606. Another beneficiary was Thomas Combe, a staunch and defiant Catholic who would be listed as a recusant five years later, in 1621, and again, twenty-five years later, in 1640–1641. The Catholic brothers John and Anthony Nash, longstanding friends of the poet, were also left money in the will.

Thomas Russell, another neighbor, was not only a beneficiary of the will, but was appointed by Shakespeare as an "overseer" whose responsibility was to superintend the execution of the will itself. Such a responsibility obviously indicates that Russell was a good and trusted friend. What sort of man was Russell, that he might have earned so much trust from the dying Shakespeare? According to the Shakespeare scholar, Leslie Hotson, he is "best ... judged by his friends, Tobie Matthew, Endymion Porter and William Shakespeare".[3] Tobie Matthew, the son of the Anglican Archbishop of York, became a Catholic in 1606 and went on to become a renowned Jesuit scholar. Endymion Porter was raised by his Catholic relatives in Spain and married a Catholic who was known to be a "busy convert-maker".[4]

William Reynolds, another beneficiary of Shakespeare's will, was sent to Warwick Jail for his recusancy in the autumn of 1613, languishing there with Shakespeare's old Henley Street neighbor George Badger. On October 2, 1613, Badger wrote to the chief clerk of Stratford, revealing that another Stratford Catholic, William Slaughter, who had been named with John Shakespeare on the recusancy list of 1592, had appeared at the jail "to release William Reynolds of Stratford" on security. This episode is of particular interest because it shows that some of Shakespeare's dearest friends in Stratford, with whom he had remained on the closest terms during the final years of his life, were being imprisoned

---

[3] Cited in Mutschmann and Wentersdorf, *Shakespeare and Catholicism*, p. 167.
[4] Ibid.

for their Catholic faith. It is also tempting to conjecture, though of course it cannot be proved, that William Reynolds had actually been bailed out with Shakespeare's money, with William Slaughter merely acting as an agent. The circumstantial evidence at least makes such an apparently fanciful supposition a possibility. We know that Shakespeare, as the owner of the second largest house in Stratford, was one of the wealthiest people in the neighborhood; we know that he had already put his money where his faith was in the purchasing of the Blackfriars Gatehouse only six months earlier; and we know that William Reynolds was one of his closest friends, being one of a mere handful of associates who were listed in his will. Such a supposition may indeed be fanciful, but it is also eminently plausible.

Apart from the curious proliferation of Catholics who are mentioned in Shakespeare's will, it is intriguing that some of his closest relatives are omitted altogether. Take, for instance, his brother-in-law, Bartholomew Hathaway, who was living with his large family only two miles from New Place. Why was he left out of the will? E. K. Chambers, one of the most reputable Shakespeare scholars of the twentieth century who is not noted for coming to rash conclusions, wrote that "possibly the explanation is in a difference of religion. Bartholomew's will is Protestant, and both he and his son Richard, who was a baker in Stratford, were churchwardens".[5]

Since Shakespeare's will was signed on March 25, 1616, less than a month before his death, it is safe to presume, as Richard Davies reported, that "he dyed a papist". It is also safe to presume, though of course it can't be proved, that he received the last rites of the Church from a Catholic priest as he lay on his deathbed. Shakespeare was well connected with the Catholic recusant underground so he must have known priests who could minister to him in extremis. He was also well connected with local Catholics, as his will amply demonstrates, so he would have known people who knew how to gain access to a priest locally. We should also remember that his friend John Robinson, who visited him during his final illness, had a brother who was a priest. If, therefore, it is safe to assume that there was a priest present, it is nonetheless no surprise that no contemporary record survives to confirm it. The persecution of Catholics was continuing with the utmost brutality, with four priests being executed in the very year of Shakespeare's death, leading

[5] Cited ibid., p. 195.

Father Bowden to the obvious conclusion that "the ministrations of a priest in Shakespeare's case would have been carefully concealed at the time, and even later would have been divulged only with caution, for similar executions continued to take place until 1681".[6]

Perhaps it was the cautious divulgence, by one of those present, of the ministrations of a priest at Shakespeare's death, which was the source of Richard Davies' assertion that England's greatest poet had "dyed a papist". This was certainly the view of Michael Wood:

> Davies had no reason to lie, and plenty of reasons to know. He is not a primary source, but it would be incredible if such a story should have surfaced had the poet been a conforming Protestant. What the story means, of course, is another matter entirely. All we can say is that Davies had heard that the poet received the last rites from a priest according to the Catholic faith.[7]

Even Peter Ackroyd was forced to concede that Davies was "a zealous Anglican [who] would not have passed on this report with any great pleasure". As a zealous proselytizer for the relativist and secularist (mis)-reading of Shakespeare's life and work, Ackroyd himself passed on this report without any great pleasure and sought immediately to explain it by explaining it away:

> It can be taken to mean that Shakespeare was given the sacrament of extreme unction at the time of his death. But this may have been at the instigation, or even the insistence, of his recusant family. He may have been too weak and too sick to comprehend the matter. Yet it is also sometimes the case that lapsed or quondam Catholics will, in extremis, embrace the possibility of redemption.[8]

It is difficult to read these words without detecting a superciliousness between the lines. Shakespeare was, of course, far too smart and modern to have embraced the faith of his fathers, so he must have been either bullied into allowing a priest on the scene or perhaps was simply too senile to know what was going on. The worst-case scenario, as far as Ackroyd is concerned, is that Shakespeare may have betrayed his modern/postmodern principles at the last moment, succumbing, at the last, to superstition, though, of course, only through fear of death, not

---

[6] Richard Simpson, *The Religion of Shakespeare* (London: Burns and Oates, 1899), p. 109.
[7] Michael Wood, *Shakespeare* (New York: Basic Books/Perseus Books Group, 2003), p. 340.
[8] Ackroyd, *Shakespeare*, p. 473.

through faith in the Resurrection. Immediately after this grudging acceptance that Shakespeare may possibly have betrayed his "enlightened"
philosophy on his deathbed, Ackroyd exorcises the horrific possibility
by insisting that his tragedies are set in "worlds with no god" and that
Shakespeare himself "professed no particular faith" but that he was "above
faith".[9] Such a conclusion flies in the face of a veritable mountain of
evidence, as discernible in the facts of Shakespeare's own life and in the
clear Christian morality of his plays.

Shakespeare was buried on April 25, 1616, two days after his death,
in the chancel of Holy Trinity, the local Anglican parish church. This
has caused many researchers to conclude erroneously that he must have
died as a conforming member of the Church of England. Such a conclusion is readily refuted by the fact that the churchyard of Holy Trinity is full of the graves of those who are known to have died Catholic,
including many of Stratford's most notorious recusants. "That Shakespeare was buried in Stratford Parish Church, as both his father and his
mother were, is no more argument against his recusancy than against
theirs", wrote Hugh Ross Williamson.[10] Shakespeare is buried in an
Anglican church for the same reason that he was married in an Anglican church, and for the same reason that his children were baptized in
an Anglican church. Put bluntly, Catholics had little choice but to acqui-
esce in the matter of births, marriages, and deaths, as the historian Alexandra Walsham explained:

> The taint of illegitimacy blighted infants whose baptisms were not offi-
> cially registered, and serious legal difficulties over the settlement of estates
> could follow clandestine marriages contracted by [Catholic priest] mis-
> sioners. Bribing the parson to fiddle the books and double ceremonies
> were not uncommon.... Desire to be interred in consecrated ground
> also compelled many to acquiesce in Protestant burial rites or conduct
> their own nocturnal funerals in the churchyard.[11]

Hugh Ross Williamson records that recusant Catholics accomplished a
burial in ground newly consecrated by a priest by having two shrouds

---

[9] Ibid., p. 474.

[10] Hugh Ross Williamson, *The Day Shakespeare Died* (London: Michael Joseph, 1962),
p. 113.

[11] Alexandra Walsham, *Church Papists: Catholicism, Conformity and Confessional Polemic in
Early Modern England* (Woodbridge, Suffolk: Royal Historical Society/Boydell Press, 1993),
p. 85.

in the coffin. "In the second shroud was laid some earth properly consecrated by a Catholic priest and on this the corpse, already shrouded,
was laid and in it wrapped." [12] If this were the case with Shakespeare it
might help explain the enigmatic epitaph on his tomb:

> Good Frend for Jesus sake forbeare,
> To dig the dust enclosed heare:
> Blest be ye man that spares these stones,
> And curst be he that moves my bones.

With astonishing incongruity, Anthony Holden concluded his own
biography of Shakespeare by assuming that if the poet had written his
own epitaph it was "the first time in all his miraculous writings" that
"this lapsed Catholic, humanist non-believer managed ... to mention
the name of Jesus without (quite) taking it in vain".[13] There seems
little point in wasting breath or ink in refuting such nonsense, not least
because the proliferation of evidence of Shakespeare's enduring Catholicism is itself all the refutation that is necessary. It does beggar belief,
however, that writers as accomplished as Ackroyd and Holden can write
full-length biographies of Shakespeare without seeing the Catholic truth
that is literally and literarily staring them in the face.

A more reliable scholar of Shakespeare's life is Hugh Ross Williamson, who perceived the biographical and textual evidence that pointed
to the poet's Catholicism. His brief summary of this evidence is so
incisive and succinct that it is worth quoting at length:

> At this point, it may be convenient to recapitulate briefly the evidence
> on which the claim for Shakespeare's Catholicism rests. There are, in his
> life, some certainties, some probabilities and some possibilities. It is cer-
> tain that both his parents were open Catholics who suffered on account
> of their faith, so that the probability is that ... he was brought up as any
> other child would be in a devout Catholic home. If he went to school at
> five, it is certain that his first schoolmaster was a Catholic. It is also
> certain that from the age of seven to eleven he was taught by a Catholic
> who eventually became a priest and that among his schoolfellows was
> one who became both priest and martyr. If he remained at school till he
> was fifteen, his last master was a Catholic, whose younger brother was
> also a martyr. It is certain that he was married by a Catholic priest.

---

[12] Williamson, *Day Shakespeare Died*, p. 113.
[13] Anthony Holden, *William Shakespeare: The Man Behind the Genius* (Boston: Little, Brown,
1999), p. 328.

It is certain that, by reason of the Shakespeares' relationship with the great Catholic "cousinage" in the Midlands ... he was affected by the Somerville plot and possibly on account of it left Stratford. It is certain that the object of his literary attack, Sir Thomas Lucy, was the chief persecutor of Catholics in Stratford. It is possible that Lucy ordered his imprisonment.

It is certain that his patron, Southampton, was a Catholic. It is probable that the martyr and poet, Robert Southwell, dedicated a volume of his religious poems to Shakespeare and it is possible that this influenced *The Rape of Lucrece*.

In London we have no record, from the parish "token" books, that Shakespeare ever attended an Anglican service, though the signatures of his friends and associates are there. On the other hand we know that at some period he went to lodge in a family diplomatically immune from the penalties of non-attendance at church. We have no record, among his poems, of any mourning poem for Elizabeth I or praise of James I, such as his contemporaries profusely indulged in; this may be because no Catholic was likely to celebrate a persecuting monarch. His plays, however they are regarded, afford evidence of his understanding of Catholicism and, when considered carefully in their setting, suggest sympathy with it. It is possible that he owned a copy of Hall's *Chronicle* which he annotated in the Catholic sense: in any case, his bias in the historical plays is Catholic. It is certain that he was said to have "died a Papist" by an early writer and he was mentioned for his Papistry by Speed during his own lifetime. We know that he bought, towards the end of his life, a notorious centre of Catholic activity in London and installed in it a known and practising Catholic, who also witnessed his will.

What does all this amount to? Obviously there is not the same kind of "proof" that Shakespeare was a Catholic as there is that Cardinal Newman was a Catholic. But there is sufficient evidence on which to base a verdict.[14]

Williamson proceeds to a humorous anecdotal example given by the Shakespeare scholar R. W. Chambers, as a means of weighing the evidence for Shakespeare's Catholicism:

A Jew, obviously in a state of some distress, was met by his Rabbi, who enquired the cause. "I was called as a witness," was the reply, "and I was fined £10." "No, no, Abe. You mean you were called as a defendant and fined £10." "No, I was called as a witness; and the Judge said: 'What

14 Williamson, *Day Shakespeare Died*, pp. 114–16.

is your name?' And I said (as you know) 'Abraham Isaac Jacob Solomon.' And the Judge said: 'Are you a Jew?' And I said, 'Now don't be a silly ass.' And I was fined £10."

Yet no one of these names is conclusive. Think of Abraham Lincoln, Izaak Walton, Jacob Tonson, Solomon Grundy. But most of us would agree that the *combination* suggests Jewish origin with sufficient certainty to render the retort upon the Judge eminently justifiable.[15]

Chambers' anecdote is singularly apt. With Shakespeare's life and work as our reliable witnesses, it is as certain that William Shakespeare is a Catholic as it is that Abraham Isaac Jacob Solomon is a Jew. It is equally certain that many of those who sit in judgment on Shakespeare's life, blithely ignoring the preponderance of evidence pointing to his Catholicism, are incorrigible asses warranting rebuke.

And so we come to the conclusion of our quest, discovering that Shakespeare had died as he had lived, as a resolute Catholic. And we can say with confidence that if this cannot be proved with mathematical certainty, it can at least be considered to be proven beyond all reasonable doubt. This is sufficient to convict him of his Catholic convictions in the eyes of any right-minded jury in the venerable court of common sense. It is only because we live in an age of uncommon nonsense that Shakespeare remains misunderstood and misconstrued by the "silly asses" of academe. There is, however, no real cause for concern. Shakespeare will outlive the asses as he will outlive the deplorable zeitgeist that they serve. Intellectual fads and fashions are always coming and going, but, as C. S. Lewis reminds us, they are mostly going. Shakespeare, on the other hand, and as Ben Jonson reminds us, "was not of an age but for all time".

[15] Ibid., p. 116.

PREFATORY NOTE TO THE APPENDICES

Having ascertained, beyond any reasonable doubt, that Shakespeare had retained his strong Catholic convictions throughout his life, it becomes imperative that we discover how to read his works from the perspective of his Catholicism. Quite simply, the discovery that Shakespeare was a Catholic forces us to revisit his work with fresh and unprejudiced eyes. In appendix A, "The Challenge of Shakespeare", the critical method required to read the plays, sonnets, and poems correctly is outlined. In appendix B, "*King Lear*: Finding the Comedy in the Tragedy", this method is employed to illustrate how one of Shakespeare's greatest plays comes to life in the light of the Catholic life of the playwright.

APPENDIX A

THE CHALLENGE OF SHAKESPEARE

But let your reason serve
To make the truth appear, where it seems hid.

—Isabella (*Measure for Measure*, 5.1.65)

At the start of a new millennium, and almost four hundred years after his death, William Shakespeare continues to shake the shallow presumptions of his critics. He challenges them to question their own prejudices, to put aside contemporary fads and fashions, and to penetrate the perennial truth of the permanent things presented in his plays. Sadly, in an age characterized by superciliousness, few critics rise to the challenge. Some critics even deny that there is a challenge. Harold Bloom, criticizing G. K. Chesterton for suggesting that Shakespeare was a Catholic dramatist, asserts that "we cannot know, by reading Shakespeare and seeing him played, whether he had any extrapoetic beliefs or disbeliefs ... by reading Shakespeare, I can gather that he did not like lawyers, preferred drinking to eating, and evidently lusted after both genders".[1] It is perhaps a sorry reflection of the state of modern literary criticism that this woeful lack of penetration not only gains credence in academic circles but actually gains disciples.

Let's peruse Bloom's critique a little more closely. Apart from his apparent inability to glean any meaning, intended by Shakespeare, from any of the plays—political, philosophical, moral, or religious—beyond the indulgence of the lower appetites, his use of the phrase "extrapoetic beliefs or disbeliefs" is curious. Is he really suggesting that poesis is possible in a vacuum, that poets create in the absence of belief in anything? If they believe in nothing, why are they inspired to say anything?

[1] Harold Bloom, *Shakespeare: The Invention of the Human* (New York: Riverhead, 1998), pp. 7–8.

If they believe in nothing, how *can* they say anything? If they believe in nothing, why do they have anything to say? *Pace* Bloom, poesis, like thought itself, is rooted in belief and is impossible without it. Shakespeare had to believe in something or else he would have written nothing.

At the heart of much modern criticism, as practiced by a plethora of postmodern parvenus, is an irritation with the power of the author. If one is constrained to listen to the author one cannot do one's own thing with the text. One must bow before a higher authority, the authorial authority. In an age that hates authority this is perceived as a limitation of the freedom of the reader to do what he wants with the text. Yet, as Edmund Burke reminds us, liberty must be limited in order to be possessed; and as Oscar Wilde warns us (and he should know), anarchy is freedom's own Judas. Taking liberties with liberty leads to anarchy, and anarchy, in reality, is the rule of the most ruthless and the enslavement of everyone else. We have laws against rape and murder to ensure that we are not at the mercy of rapists and murderers. This might be obvious to most sensible people, but not, apparently, to the intellectual libertines in literature departments in many of today's colleges and universities. There is, alas, no law against the rape and murder of literary texts.

Even when postmoderns accept the existence of meaning, and many don't, they believe that the reader has as much "right" to interpret the meaning of a work as does the author. This is tragic, not for the work of literature itself, which retains its value regardless of the ways in which it is abused, but for the reader who is depriving himself of the full depth and beauty of the work he is reading and studying. In this respect it might be said that there are two types of readers: those who do things to books and those who allow books to do things to them.[2] One approach is rooted in pride, and its illegitimate offspring, superciliousness and arrogance; the other in humility, and its fruitful progeny, wisdom and discernment. The former is self-deceptive, the latter receptive. Most modern criticism falls into the former category. If one believes that one knows as much as the author or has as much "right" to interpret the meaning of the text, or if one dismisses the intention of the author as being irrelevant, one will be squeezing the work into the narrow confines of one's own prejudiced presumptions, doing things with the work to make it fit into one's own limited *weltanschauung*. If, on the other

---

[2] For a more detailed discussion of this approach to critical reading, see C. S. Lewis, *An Experiment in Criticism* (Cambridge: Cambridge University Press, 1961).

hand, one accepts that the author knows more than the reader about his own work, one will be able to grow and to stretch oneself in the beautiful space that the genius of the author creates. After reading a book in such a *receptive* way, allowing it to do things to us, we will find that we have grown into someone wiser than we had been before we read it. All of this presumes, of course, that the work in question has literary merit and is worth reading.

The whole issue of the relationship between an author and his work, and by extension the importance of this relationship to the reader's understanding of the work, was summed up succinctly by J. R. R. Tolkien, who wrote that "only one's guardian Angel, or indeed God Himself, could unravel the real relationship between personal facts and an author's works. Not the author himself (though he knows more than any investigator), and certainly not so-called 'psychologists'." [3] In these few words we are given the tools to form a true appraisal of the role and limitations of literary criticism. Let's look closer at what he is saying.

One does not need to share Tolkien's Christian faith in order to recognize, or agree with, his insistence on the transcendent nature of the creative process and its products. Even an atheist such as Percy Bysshe Shelley recognized the quasi-mystical forces at work in the creative process, forces that transcend the conscious will of the author (or artist, or musical composer, etc.). In his essay "A Defense of Poetry", Shelley wrote:

> Poetry is not like reasoning, a power to be exerted according to the determination of the will. A man cannot say, "I will compose poetry." The greatest poet even cannot say it; for the mind in creation is as a fading coal which some invisible influence, like an inconstant wind, awakens to transitory brightness; this power arises from within, like the colour of a flower which fades and changes as it is developed, and the conscious portions of our natures are unprophetic either of its approach or its departure. Could this influence be durable in its original purity and force, it is impossible to predict the greatness of the results; but when composition begins, inspiration is already on the decline, and the most glorious poetry that has ever been communicated to the world is probably a feeble shadow of the original conceptions of the poet.[4]

[3] Humphrey Carpenter, ed., *The Letters of J. R. R. Tolkien* (London: George Allen and Unwin, 1981), p. 288.

[4] Perch Bysshe Shelley, *A Defense of Poetry* (Boston: Ginn and Company, 1891), p. 39.

The insistence by Tolkien and Shelley of the transcendent nature of the creative process is crucial to a true understanding of literature and literary criticism. It is, however, the crucial *misunderstanding* of this transcendence that has led to much of the error in modern criticism. The modern misapprehension springs from the assumption that the transcendence negates the validity, and therefore the relevance, of the author's *intention*. Since the author's intention is subject to the mystical power of creativity we need not take the intention seriously. Furthermore, if the author's intention is relatively worthless, so, ultimately, is the author himself, leaving us only with the text. The problem is that this line of reasoning arises from a misunderstanding of what Tolkien and Shelley are actually saying. Shelley insists that "the most glorious poetry ... is probably a feeble shadow of the original conceptions of the poet". In other words, the poet is the original conceiver of the poem, and the poem a pale shadow of the poet's conception. The poem is derived from, and dependent on, the poet. It follows, therefore, that we will better understand the conception, i.e., the poem, if we better understand the conceiver, i.e., the poet. T. S. Eliot in "The Hollow Men" echoes Shelley:

> Between the conception
> And the creation ...
> Falls the Shadow ...
>
> Between the potency
> And the existence ...
> Falls the Shadow.

For Eliot, who was on the path to Christianity when he wrote "The Hollow Men", the fall of the Shadow was the shadow of the Fall, but, for the atheist poet and the Christian poet alike, there is a shared understanding that the *existence* of the work cannot be separated from the *potency* that resides in the *personhood* of the poet. It is for this reason that Tolkien insists that the author "knows more than any investigator", even if the author himself cannot grasp the transcendent mystery at the heart of creativity. If for "investigator" we read "critic", it can be seen that Tolkien, Shelley, and Eliot are insisting that we must understand the solidity of the author and his beliefs before we listen to the opinions and beliefs of the "hollow men". Even if we accept, as we should, that a great work of literature will have a profundity of meaning beyond the conscious design of the author, we still need to see the transcendent beauty through the prism of the *personhood* of the author. If we fail to discipline ourselves to follow this critical modus operandi we will see literature through the blurred focus of our own inadequate vision, or through the inadequate vision of a critic. Such an approach does not negate the necessity of employing our own judgment, or of giving consideration to the judgment of critics, but it insists that we should subject our judgment, and that of the critics, to the authorial authority of the person from whom, or through whom, the work was given life. This is the literary litmus test. Any literary criticism that fails to take this test, or fails to pass this test, is unworthy of the name.

Let's take some practical examples to illustrate the crucial connection between an author and his work. Tolkien could not have written *The Lord of the Flies* any more than William Golding could have written *The Lord of the Rings*; Shelley could not, and would not, have written Christian allegorical poems such as Coleridge's "The Rime of the Ancient Mariner" or Wordsworth's "Resolution and Independence"; Hopkins's "The Wreck of the Deutschland" could not have *existed* without the *potency* of the poet's deep Christian faith and his grounding in scholastic philosophy; et cetera, et cetera. Surely this is obvious. Surely it requires a mere modicum of common sense to see the truth that one must see the work, first and foremost, through the eyes of the author, as far as this is possible.

As a further aside, it is perhaps illuminating to compare the study of literature with the study of history. If we insist on studying history through the prejudices and presumptions of our own day we will succeed only in misinterpreting the motives and purpose of historical actions. If we do not know what people believed we will not understand why they behaved and acted as they did. We will not understand what really happened. Our prejudice or our ignorance will have made us blind. In order to understand history we must understand enough to empathize with, even if we don't sympathize with, the protagonists of the period being studied. And what is true of history is equally true of literature. We must know what the author believed in order to know what he is saying and doing in his work. We must empathize with, even if we don't sympathize with, the author's beliefs. Failure to understand the author's beliefs will lead to a failure to understand the work. Our prejudice or our ignorance will have made us blind.

There was a peripatetic purpose behind this lengthy digression from our Shakespearian topic. It is this. Once we accept that the author-work nexus is axiomatic to a true understanding of literature, it becomes clear that the more we know about Shakespeare the more we will understand his work.

Do the plays reflect Shakespeare's beliefs? Of course they do. As already illustrated, all artistic work is an expression of the artist's beliefs, consciously or subconsciously. If this is the case, a deeper awareness of the playwright's beliefs will yield a deeper understanding of the plays. For this reason, the debate over Shakespeare's religious beliefs is sending shockwaves through literature departments around the world. In *Shakespeare and the Culture of Christianity in Early Modern England*, Dennis Taylor, professor of English at Boston College, discusses the way in which the work of historians was impacting upon the work of Shakespearian criticism.

> In or about 1985, the landscape of Shakespeare and religion studies began to change. In that year, Ernst Honigmann and Gary Taylor, representing mainline Shakespeare criticism, argued for the continuing influence of Shakespeare's Catholic background on his plays. Since 1985, there has been a flood of criticism reconsidering Shakespeare's relation to his Catholic contexts.... What we have seen since 1985 is the widespread acceptance of the importance of Shakespeare's Catholic background on both his mother's and his father's side, so much so that Honigman and Taylor's 1985 work—and Peter Milward's *Shakespeare's Religious Background* (1973)— are now routinely cited, with various qualifications, in standard editions and biographies of Shakespeare.[5]

If Shakespeare was a Catholic, or was greatly influenced by the Catholicism of his parents and the persecution that surrounded the practice of Catholicism in his day, it forces us to reread the plays in an entirely new light. The more that historical evidence comes to light, the less able are the doyens of postmodernity to do what they like with the plays. In the past, the lack of knowledge of the personhood of Shakespeare has enabled critics to treat him as a *tabula rasa* upon which they can write their own prejudiced agenda. For the proponents of "queer theory" he becomes conveniently homosexual; for secular fundamentalists he is a proto-secularist, ahead of his time; for "post-Christian" agnostics he becomes a prophet of postmodernity. It was all so easy when Shakespeare was a myth, but now that he is emerging as a man, a living person with real

---

[5] Dennis Taylor and David N. Beauregard, eds., *Shakespeare and the Culture of Christianity in Early Modern England* (New York: Fordham University Press, 2003), p. 24.

beliefs, the distortion becomes more difficult. For "postmodern" Shakespeare scholars the emergence of tangible evidence for the Catholic Shakespeare is not only a challenge but a threat. If he was a recusant Catholic, or a Church papist, or merely a reluctant conformist who retained significant sympathy with the "old faith", he becomes irritatingly antimodern. He would have believed that the practice of homosexuality was a sin, or that the secular state should be subject to the teachings of the Church, or that the religious conformity of the mediaeval past was superior to the post-Reformation fragmentation of Christian belief. From the perspective of the modernist and postmodernist, Shakespeare emerges as an unenlightened and recalcitrant reactionary. From the perspective of tradition-oriented scholars, the evident clarity of moral vision that they had always perceived in the plays becomes more explicable and more clearly defined.

As for Harold Bloom's criticism of Chesterton for writing that Shakespeare was a Catholic dramatist, or his singularly curious assertion that none of Shakespeare's beliefs are discernible in his work, it is gratifying to see that the ghost of Shakespeare, like the ghost of Hamlet's father, has returned to haunt him. In a paradoxical twist worthy of a Chestertonian epigram or a Shakespearian plot, the ghost of the author has exorcised the critic.

APPENDIX B

KING LEAR—FINDING THE COMEDY
IN THE TRAGEDY

The story of King Lear did not originate with Shakespeare. It had been told by Geoffrey of Monmouth in the twelfth century and reemerged in book 2 of Edmund Spenser's *Faerie Queene*, published in 1590, and also in Sir Philip Sidney's *Arcadia*, first published in 1590 and republished in a more complete edition in 1598. Although, no doubt, Shakespeare was aware of these versions of the story it is likely that his principal sources were the *Chronicles* of Holinshed, published in 1577, and, perhaps most influential of all, a dramatized version of the story, entitled *The True Chronicle History of King Leir and His Three Daughters*. This play, possibly written by George Peele, had been in the repertoire of the Queen's Men since the 1580s, though it wasn't published until late in 1605, around the time that Shakespeare is thought to have started work on his own version of the story.

It seems inescapable that Shakespeare would have known the earlier dramatized version and may even have acted in it. It is, however, a rather frivolous, whimsical work, climaxed with a happy ending, and is very different from the play that Shakespeare would write. Michael Wood, in his biography of Shakespeare, has us imagine him browsing in John Wright's shop near London's Newgate Market in the autumn of 1605:

> There, in a freshly inked pile of quartos on the flap board of the shop, lay his old favourite, now available for the first time in print: "The True Chronicle History of King Leir and his three daughters ... As it hath been divers and sundry times lately acted". Given his long fascination with the tale, Shakespeare could not have resisted it.[1]

In fact, *pace* Wood, there is no evidence that the earlier "Leir" was ever a "favourite", and Shakespeare's decision to write a new version of the

---

[1] Michael Wood, *Shakespeare* (New York: Basic Books/Perseus Books Group, 2003), p. 274.

play as soon as he became aware of a published edition of the earlier version suggests that he was initially inspired by a desire to write something very different. It might not have been so much "fascination" with the earlier play as provocation by it. Peter Milward, in *Shakespeare's Meta-drama: Othello and King Lear*, writes that the earlier play had been "savagely torn to pieces and ... thoroughly rewritten" by Shakespeare, expurgating its "clearly Protestant, anti-Papist bias". Milward concludes that Shakespeare "was, no doubt, put off by the protestant bias of the old play, just as he had already undertaken in his play of *King John* to modify a similar bias in *The Troublesome Reign of King John*".[2]

Milward unearths further fascinating evidence to suggest a possible source for Shakespeare's inspiration for the writing of *Lear*. In 1603 Sir Brian Annesley, a knight at the court of Queen Elizabeth, died, leaving behind three daughters. Prior to his death, the two elder daughters had tried to have him certified as insane in order to profit from his estate. They were prevented in their efforts by his youngest daughter, Cordelia, who had a monument erected to her parents "against the ungrateful nature of oblivious time". Cordelia Annesley became the second wife of Sir William Harvey, almost certainly an acquaintance of Shakespeare, and it is possible that it was from Sir William that Shakespeare learned of this curious parallel to the story of Lear and his daughters. Further evidence that this might be the case is suggested by the fact that there is no mention of Lear's madness in the original tale, and also from the fact that Shakespeare uses the spelling "Cordelia" for Lear's youngest daughter, whereas it is rendered as "Cordella" in the earlier version of the play.

Regardless of the source of his inspiration for writing a new version of the story, or his motivation for doing so, it would clearly be woefully inadequate to limit our discussion of the play to the likely seeds from which it grew without paying due attention to the abundant fruits of Shakespeare's own inimitable imagination. *King Lear*, possibly his greatest work, surpasses and transcends in literary quality and philosophical depth all the earlier versions of the story. The play is, in fact, not one story but two. It interweaves the story of Lear and his daughters with the parallel story of Gloucester and his sons, the latter of which is probably derived from "The Tale of the Blind King of Paphlagonia" in

---

[2] Peter Milward, S.J., *Shakespeare's Meta-drama: Othello and King Lear* (Tokyo: The Renaissance Institute, 2003), p. 104.

Sidney's *Arcadia*, in such a way that we cannot truly speak of plot and subplot, but only of co-plots woven together with majestic skill.

The co-plots parallel each other on the literal level. Lear is betrayed by the deception of his self-serving daughters, Regan and Goneril; Gloucester by the deception of his illegitimate son, Edmund. Cordelia, the loyal and faithful daughter of Lear, suffers the hardships of exile because of her father's blind arrogance; Edgar, the loyal and legitimate son of Gloucester, suffers the hardships of exile through his father's blind ignorance. Lear and Gloucester lose everything in the worldly sense but, in the process, gain the wisdom they were lacking. The overarching and most obvious moral theme resonates with the Christian paradox that one must lose one's life in order to gain it, or with the words of Christ that there is no greater love than to lay down one's life for one's friends. Lear and Gloucester embody the truth of the former, Cordelia and Edgar (and Kent) the truth of the latter.

Apart from this overarching moral dimension that should be obvious to all, there is another dimension to Shakespeare's work, rooted in the politics of his day but relevant to the politics of all ages. This dimension, arising from the creative interaction of Shakespeare's Catholic sensibilities with an environment hostile to Catholicism, is discovered in what Peter Milward calls the *meta-drama* of the plays or what Clare Asquith has referred to as the *shadowplays* within the plays.

At this juncture, and before we proceed to look for the meta-dramatic elements in *Lear*, it is necessary to understand the nature of the Catholic dimension in the play. In essence, Shakespeare seems less concerned with the doctrinal differences between Protestants and Catholics than with the persecution of nonconformist believers at the hands of the secular state. In Shakespeare's time, under the reign of Elizabeth and James, Catholics were the victims of Anglican conformists far more than they were the victims of relatively powerless Protestant nonconformists. The Church of England was neither Catholic nor Protestant but was an uneasy amalgam of both. From its very inception at the behest of Henry VIII, the Church of England was rooted in compromise between its "catholic" and "protestant" members. The former belonged to the so-called "high" church, the latter to the so-called "low" church. Although such differences were tolerated within the state-church, there was no tolerance for nonconformists who refused to join the Anglican communion. It is for this reason that Shakespeare's Catholicism manifests itself in *King Lear* as a dialectic against secularism and the secularist state more than as a dialogue with Protestantism. It is not sectarian but antisecularist. The meta-drama is not played out as Catholics versus Protestants, but as Christian orthodoxy versus secular fundamentalism. The dynamism of the underlying dialectic, and therefore of the dialogue, is centered on the tension between Christian conscience and self-serving, cynical secularism. Whereas the heroes and heroines of Shakespearian drama are informed by an orthodox Christian understanding of virtue, the villains are normally Machiavellian practitioners of secular *real-politik*, and not Christian "heretics". In this sense, and paradoxically perhaps, the Catholic meta-drama represents one of the most "modern" aspects of Shakespearian drama in terms of its applicability to the contemporary world.

In *King Lear* the meta-drama is present from the very first scene when the king promises political power to those who "love us most". Lear, symbolic of the state, demands all. There can be no room for other loves. Immediately his self-serving daughters, Goneril and Regan, outdo each other in sycophantic promises of absolute allegiance. It is left to Cordelia, the youngest daughter, to "Love, and be silent". She loves her father but cannot "heave [her] heart into [her] mouth", uttering platitudes to curry favor beyond that which her conscience dictates is decorous. Unlike the feigned or affected affection of her sisters, her love is "more ponderous than [her] tongue"; it is genuine and will not debase itself with falsehood or flattery. She will love the king "according to [her] bond, no more nor less". She cannot offer the king (or state) any allegiance beyond that which her conscience dictates is appropriate morally. The parallels with the position that Catholics found themselves in during the reign of Henry VIII, and in Shakespeare's time under Elizabeth and James, is patently obvious. When Henry VIII declared himself supreme head of the Church of England, effectively making religion subject to the state, his subjects were forced to choose between conforming to his wishes, and thereby gaining his favor, or defying his will and incurring his wrath. Only the most courageous chose conscience before concupiscence; most chose to please the king and ignore their consciences. There are always more Gonerils and Regans than there are Cordelias.

The meta-dramatic element is made even more apparent in Cordelia's justification for her refusal to kowtow:

> Good my Lord,
> You have begot me, bred me, loved me. I

Return those duties back as are right fit,
Obey you, love you, and most honor you.
Why have my sisters husbands, if they say
They love you all? Haply, when I shall wed,
That lord whose hand must take my plight shall carry
Half my love with him, half my care and duty.
Sure I shall never marry like my sisters,
To love my father all. (1.1.97-106)

On the literal level Cordelia proclaims that her future husband has rights over her love that she is not at liberty, in conscience, to dispense with, even to her father. On a deeper level Shakespeare may have been employing marriage as a metaphor for the relationship of the individual believer with Christ. Catholic ecclesiology is rooted in the belief, itself rooted in Scripture, that Christ is the Bridegroom and the Church his Bride. Cordelia's "husband" is Christ, and she is not at liberty to render unto Caesar that which belongs to Christ. The allegory and its applicability are clear. Catholics are not permitted, in conscience, to offer all their love to their father or mother, or to their king or country. They can only love as Cordelia loves, according to their bond. Our parents and our country have begotten us, bred us, loved us, and we should "return those duties back as are right fit" in obedience, love, and honor. This is "right fit", but it goes beyond our bond, beyond the bounds of a good conscience, to obey, love, and honor father or mother, king or country, as gods. The worship of our parents or the worship of the state is a mark of disordered love that presages evil.

"But goes thy heart with this?" asks Lear, following Cordelia's sagacious discourse. "Ay, my good lord", she replies. "So young, and so untender?" says Lear. "So young, my Lord, and true", says Cordelia. The exchange is tellingly poignant. Cordelia is not merely being true to her heart, her conscience (and her God), she is being true to Lear. He is wrong, and she is right to tell him so. It is for his good as much as it is for hers. It is no wonder that it has been suggested that the very name of Cordelia is a punning reference to *Coeur de Lear* (Lear's Heart) with echoes of *Coeur de Lion* (Lion Heart). Cordelia has the heart of a lion, and she is the heart of Lear. When Lear loses Cordelia he loses his heart and his way.

Apart from the obvious parallels with the secular politics of Elizabethan and Jacobean England, with its persecution of Catholics and other "nonconformist" dissidents, the other major meta-dramatic element revolves around the nature and meaning of "wisdom". It is often said that the Fool can be seen as the personification of Lear's conscience, the voice of (self)criticism that informs Lear of the folly of his actions and the seriousness of the predicament in which his folly has left him. This, however, is only half the story—and the less important half. The more important half of the story only begins once the Fool disappears without trace. It is only once Edgar takes his place as "Fool" that the deeper wisdom is revealed.

Why does the Fool disappear? Why does a character who has played such an important and integral part in the play, declaiming many of its best and wittiest lines, suddenly disappear into thin air, having declared, as an apparent riposte to Lear, that "I'll go to bed at noon"? Superficially it might appear that this is a formal *faux pas* on Shakespeare's part. If lesser playwrights allow characters to disappear, leaving apparent loose ends, without so much as a "by your leave", it would be seen as a fatal flaw in their literary abilities. Are we to assume, therefore, that the Fool's disappearance is evidence of a flaw in Shakespeare's literary abilities? Although we might be tempted to make such an assumption, we do so at our peril. Only the most arrogant literary critics would presume to know more about the art of playwriting than the world's greatest playwright. It is, therefore, much safer to assume that Shakespeare had some deeper meaning in mind for the Fool's sudden and unannounced departure. Let's explore further.

As already stated, it is often assumed that the Fool serves as the king's conscience. As a "fool", a character devoid of discernible family connections and without roots or destiny beyond his function within the drama, he is ideally suited for employment as a personified abstraction conveying allegorical significance. "But where's my Fool?" asks Lear. "I have not seen him this two days." We know therefore that the Fool (*Lear's conscience*) was significantly absent when Lear made the rash decision to hand his kingdom to Goneril and Regan (*who may be said, within the context of this allegorical reading, to represent false love or secular ambition*), whilst banishing Cordelia (*representing true, self-sacrificial love and perhaps also, as Lear's "heart", Lear's own capacity to love truly and self-sacrificially*). Equally significant is the knight's response to Lear's complaint about the Fool's absence: "Since my young lady's going into France, sir, the Fool hath much pined away." Cordelia's banishment has led to the pining away of Lear's conscience. It can be deduced, therefore, on a psychological level, that his injustice toward Cordelia has left him feeling guilty and that the witticisms of the Fool represent the incessant nagging of the king's conscience.

The Fool first enters the play in person as Lear receives the first of the snubs from his disloyal "loving" daughters, via Oswald, Goneril's steward. As Lear begins to perceive that he might have been foolish in handing over power to his two unworthy daughters whilst banishing the worthy one, the Fool emerges for the first time to rebuke him for the foolishness of his action. When Lear threatens him with "the whip" for daring to speak so candidly, the Fool responds with words of salient and sapient indignation: "Truth's a dog must to kennel; he must be whipped out, when Lady the Brach may stand by th' fire and stink." Such words must have resonated powerfully amongst those members of Shakespeare's audience who feared being persecuted by the secular powers (*Lady the Brach*) for adhering to religious truths that had been made illegal. The adherents of Truth were suffering, literally left out in the cold, whilst those whose inequities stank to high heaven could warm themselves by the fire (before ultimately being cast into it!).

"Dost thou call me fool, boy?" Lear asks in response to the Fool's nagging witticisms/criticisms. "All thy other titles thou hast given away; that thou wast born with", replies the Fool. Literally the Fool is indeed calling the king a fool, and a fool he is; yet, since "foolishness" is being used as a metaphor for "conscience" and the wisdom it serves, the Fool is also saying that Lear is left with nothing but his conscience. All the other titles, all the other worldly accretions with which he had been robed, have been removed; he is left naked except for his "foolish" conscience, a metaphysical nakedness which is itself a foreshadowing of Lear's physical nakedness in the pivotal scene in act 3.

It is, however, a common mistake to assume that the words of the Fool encompass and encapsulate the wisdom that Shakespeare wishes to convey in the play, whereas, in fact, and on the contrary, he shows that the wisdom of the Fool is insufficient. It is itself naked. Conscience can only be informed by the "wisdom" it serves, and the "wisdom" of the Fool is very much a worldly wisdom. It understands politics; it understands *real-politik*; it is Machiavellian, albeit in an apparently benign way (unlike the "wisdom" of Edmund, who epitomizes Machiavellianism at its most base and ugly). "Thou hadst little wit in thy bald crown when thou gav'st thy golden one away." This is the limit and the summit, the crowning moment, of the Fool's wisdom. The king is foolish, in the eyes of the Fool, for losing his kingdom, for losing his power, for exchanging the comforts of his crown for the discomforts of his crown-lessness. The Fool would not understand the wisdom of Kent, speaking from the discomfort and humiliation of the stocks, into which he has been placed for defying the secular power, that "Nothing almost sees miracles but misery". This, for the Fool, would be folly. Yet this is, for Shakespeare, as for Kent, the beginning of wisdom. The deepest insights in *King Lear* come from those who come to wisdom through suffering, who perceive, furthermore, that the *acceptance* of suffering is the beginning of wisdom. For the Fool, who seems to believe that wisdom is connected with the pursuit of comfort, or the elimination of suffering, such words would be foolish.

Shakespeare's intention in showing the necessity of suffering to the attainment of wisdom is made manifest in his juxtaposition of Kent's words of wisdom with those of Edgar. The second scene of act 2 ends with Kent's proclamation that "Nothing almost sees miracles but misery"; scene 3 has Edgar, now an outlaw forced to adopt the guise of madness as Poor Tom, proclaiming that "Edgar I nothing am." Edgar is "nothing" in his "misery" and is fit to see miracles, or fit to be the means by which others may see them. He will "with presented naked-ness outface the winds and persecutions of the sky" and, in his own nakedness, will inspire Lear to do likewise.

Edgar, disguised as Poor Tom (a "madman"), becomes the voice of sanity and wisdom in the second half of the play, in much the same way that the Fool is the voice of sanity and wisdom in the first half. The difference is that Poor Tom's wisdom is spiritual, unlike the world-liness of the Fool, and, indeed, is avowedly Christian. The Fool greets Poor Tom's arrival with fear: "Come not in here, Nuncle, here's a spirit. Help me, help me!" And again, the Fool repeats: "A spirit, a spirit. He says his name's Poor Tom." Edgar enters, reciting a line from a ballad about the Franciscans (*Through the sharp hawthorn blows the cold wind*), and bemoaning how the devil, "the foul fiend", had led him "through fire and through flame". The Franciscan connection is apposite and surely not accidental since St. Francis was known as the *jongleur de Dieu*, God's juggler, or a "fool for Christ" who famously stripped himself naked in public and, "with presented nakedness", wit-nessed to his "houseless poverty". Edgar, as Poor Tom, plays the Fran-ciscan part to perfection and begins to eclipse the Fool as the voice of sanity and to replace him in the role as Lear's conscience. Compare, for instance, the pragmatic worldliness of the Fool's "wisdom" with

Poor Tom's allusion to the Ten Commandments followed by his can-
did confession of sin:

Fool: This cold night will turn us all to fools and madmen.

Edgar: Take heed o' th' foul fiend; obey thy parents; keep thy word's
justice; swear not; commit not with man's sworn spouse; set not thy
sweet heart on proud array. Tom's a cold.

Lear: What hast thou been?

Edgar: A servingman, proud in heart and mind; that curled my hair, wore
gloves in my cap; served the lust of my mistress' heart, and did the act of
darkness with her; swore as many oaths as I spake words, and broke
them in the sweet face of heaven. One that slept in the contriving of
lust, and waked to do it. Wine loved I deeply, dice dearly; and in woman
out-paramoured the Turk. False of heart, light of ear, bloody of hand;
hog in sloth, fox in stealth, wolf in greediness, dog in madness, lion in
prey. Let not the creaking of shoes nor the rustling of silks betray thy
poor heart to woman. Keep thy foot out of brothels, thy hand out of
plackets, thy pen from lenders' books, and defy the foul fiend. Still through
the hawthorn blows the cold wind. (3.4.79-100)

"Tom's a cold". Sanity, seen as madness by the worldly, is out in the
cold, confessing its sins, and gaining wisdom through suffering. (Meanwhile, insanity, "Lady the Brach", is in the warmth of Gloucester's castle, standing by the fire in the stench of its own iniquity, corrupted by
the pursuit of comfort.) Tom repeats the refrain from the Franciscan
ballad, and Lear, pricked with the hawthorn of conscience more than
by the cold wind, emulates Poor Tom's example, and the example of
St. Francis, by tearing off his clothes and proclaiming "off, off, you
lendings!" This is the pivotal moment of the play, the point on which
the drama turns, the moment when Lear finally goes "mad". It is the
"madness" of religious conversion. His conscience is baptized, and the
Fool makes way for Edgar. From this moment the Fool fades from view
(so much so that his disappearance is hardly noticed), and Edgar emerges
in his place as Lear's *Christian* conscience. "The Prince of Darkness is a
gentleman", Poor Tom proclaims; and, when Lear asks him, "What is
your study?" he answers: "How to prevent the fiend, and to kill vermin." To Lear's unbaptized conscience, these words would have appeared
foolish. He would have seen the poverty-stricken surface of the tramp
and not the depths of his wisdom; he would have perceived that the

vermin were fleas or lice, not sins and vice. Now, however, he refers to Poor Tom as "this philosopher" or as this "learnèd Theban", the latter reminiscent of the famous Teiresias, the blind seer of Greek legend whose eyeless vision is far better than those with eyes to see. The parallel with Poor Tom, who sees more in the "blindness" of his "madness" than the world sees in its "sanity", and who in his poverty is richer than kings, is clear enough.

Once one perceives the importance and profundity of Edgar's role and purpose, one begins to see that even his "nonsense" makes sense, albeit in the coded way in which a riddle makes sense. Take, for instance, the words with which Edgar brings this pivotal scene to a close:

> Child Rowland to the dark tower came;
> His word was still, "Fie, foh, and fum,
> I smell the blood of a British man." (3.4.185-87)

Rowland, the nephew of Charlemagne, the Holy Roman emperor, and the hero of the mediaeval classic *The Song of Roland*, is a symbol of Christian resistance to the infidels; he is also a symbol of Christian martyrdom. The juxtaposition of Roland with the nursery tale of Jack the Giant-Killer is intriguing. This nursery tale, a great favorite of G. K. Chesterton, who perceived it as a perennial reminder of the struggle of the righteous underdog against the encroachments of iniquitous power, appears to be an allusion to the play's own inner struggle between the Machiavellian giants of infidel iniquity and the righteous underdogs, stripped of power but gaining thereby in faith and wisdom. As with *The Song of Roland*, Shakespeare's *Lear* recounts the struggle between the Christian underdog and the infidel hordes; and, as with Jack the Giant-Killer, it is a struggle between the Giant Might of the State and the plight of powerless dissidents. The recitation of the Giant's ominous chant, "Fie, foh, and fum, I smell the blood of a British man", seems to evoke the martyrdom of Catholics in Shakespeare's own time at the hands of the Giant power of the state, and conjures the shadow of the looming presence of the play's own malicious giants, Goneril, Regan, and Edmund, who crave for the blood of their powerless enemies.

The use of the crime of "treason" as the justification for the persecution, and execution, of Catholics in Elizabethan and Jacobean England is evoked in the use of the charge of treason by Cornwall and Regan against the innocent Gloucester. The word "traitor" is employed no fewer than four times by Cornwall and Regan in the space of only eighteen lines, a repetition that must have resonated potently with the highly charged politics of Shakespeare's England.

Edgar's words at the beginning of act 4, coming immediately after the horrific punishment carried out by Cornwall and Regan against the "traitor" Gloucester (Edgar's father), and immediately before he sees him in his pitiable blinded state, are particularly powerful and singularly apt:

> Yet better thus, and known to be contemned,
> Than still contemned and flattered. To be worst,
> The lowest and most dejected thing of fortune,
> Stands still in esperance, lives not in fear:
> The lamentable change is from the best,
> The worst returns to laughter. (4.1.1-6)

It is "better" to be "known to be contemned" (by the state), Edgar insists, "than still contemned [by God] and flattered". The one whose conscience is clean "stands still in esperance [hope]" (of salvation) and "lives not in fear" (of final damnation). The words about the "lamentable change" being "from the best" whilst the "worst returns to laughter" reminds us of *The Consolation of Philosophy* by Boethius, as do the words of Kent from the "misery" of the stocks: "Fortune, good night; / Smile once more, turn thy wheel."

The arrival of Gloucester allows Shakespeare to play with the axiomatic paradoxes at the heart of the play: the blind seer, the wise fool, and the sane madman. "I stumbled when I saw", says Gloucester, alluding to his "blindness" (when he still had his sight) in believing the treachery of Edmund and in condemning the innocent Edgar. "Bad is the trade that must play fool to sorrow", says Edgar, possibly a coded allusion to Shakespeare's own position as a "closet dissident" daring only to speak out against the injustices of the time in the meta-dramatic language of blind men, madmen, and fools. "'Tis the times' plague, when madmen lead the blind", says Gloucester, employing the paradox with the double-edged sharpness of the *double entendre* and with the implicit meta-dramatic indictment of the *status quo* in Jacobean England. Seeing more clearly now that he is blind, Gloucester speaks disdainfully of "the superfluous and lust-dieted man" who "will not see because he does not feel". Physical blindness is as nothing compared to the metaphysical blindness of those who succumb to the comfortable numbness of secular ambition and the materialism it serves.

The same axiomatic paradox prevails in the following scene in which Albany becomes Goneril's "fool". "My fool usurps my body", says Goneril, expressing her contempt for her husband. As ever, however, the "fool" in *Lear* is more than it seems. Though, no doubt, Goneril is referring to her husband, it is Edmund who is "usurping" her body. We have just learned of Goneril's adulterous relationship with him, or at least her adulterous intentions toward him. In this sense, Shakespeare is saying that Goneril, being a fool, sees her husband as a fool, whereas, in fact, Edmund is the fool, morally speaking, through his lack of virtue. One might even say that Goneril's own lustful passion, her sin, is the "fool" that usurps her body. Legitimacy, in the Christian understanding of marriage, is the love, conjugal and otherwise, between husband and wife; illegitimacy is lust and adultery, both of which can be said to usurp the legitimate bounds of marriage. In this context, Edmund's own illegitimacy seems to accentuate the deeper meanings of "foolishness" being presented to us.

If Albany is Goneril's "fool" we should not be surprised that he fulfills the same function as Lear's Fool and Lear's "madman", Edgar. Throughout the scene he is the conveyer of wisdom, though Goneril, unlike Lear, is not disposed to listen to the promptings of her "conscience". "O Goneril!" Albany exclaims upon entering the scene, immediately after Goneril has proclaimed him her "fool":

> You are not worth the dust which the rude wind
> Blows in your face. I fear your disposition:
> That nature which contemns its origin
> Cannot be bordered certain in itself;
> She that herself will sliver and disbranch
> From her material sap, perforce must wither
> And come to deadly use. (4.2.30-36)

On the literal level of the drama, the virtuous Albany is warning his wife that her sinfulness and her evil disposition will have evil consequences; on the deeper level of the meta-drama it is difficult to avoid the conclusion that Shakespeare, the Catholic or at least the Catholic sympathizer, is referring to the Anglican church, and its anomalous position, when he speaks of the "nature which contemns its origin cannot be bordered certain in itself" (that which breaks with tradition will not have the authority to define doctrine) and "will sliver and disbranch from her material sap" (will become separated from the living tradition and sacramental life of the Church), and thus "perforce must wither and come to deadly use". Albany's words echo the "prophecy" of the Fool in act 3:

> When priests are more in word than matter;
> When brewers mar their malt with water;
> When nobles are their tailors' tutors,
> No heretics burned, but wenches' suitors ...
> Then shall the realm of Albion
> Come to great confusion. (3.3.81-84, 92-93)

On the most obvious level, the reference to priests being "more in word than matter" alludes to hypocritical clergy failing to practice what they preach. Shakespeare may, however, have had more in mind than a merely Chaucerian condemnation of bad clergy. By Shakespeare's time, the speculation of many Catholics toward Anglicanism was such that it was commonly believed that the Anglican clergy was not validly ordained, and that, therefore, they were priests "more in word than matter".[3]

Goneril responds to her husband's reproach with contempt, telling him that "the text is foolish" upon which his sermon is based. Albany replies that "wisdom and goodness to the vile seem vile: Filths savor but themselves." The riposte is incisive. Goneril considers Albany's Christian approach to virtue "foolish" because her lack of virtue makes her blind to "wisdom and goodness". Albany is a "fool" to the eyes of the blind. Goneril's contempt for Christianity is made manifest when she calls her husband a "milk-livered man" who "bear'st a cheek for blows", indicating her disdain for anyone who "turns the other cheek". She, like Edmund, her partner in adultery, is a disciple of Machiavelli, not Christ.

The denouement begins in earnest when Edgar heals his father of his suicidal despair. "Why I do trifle thus with his despair is done to cure it." "Thy life's a miracle", Edgar tells Gloucester after the latter's failed "suicide" attempt, adding that the "fiend" (despair) has parted from him. Gloucester's recovery of hope is connected to his embrace and acceptance of suffering:

---

[3] The invalidity of Anglican clergy was not formally promulgated by the Catholic Church until *Apostolicae Curae* in the reign of Pope Leo XIII (1878–1903) but because of the changes to the consecration of bishops in the Edwardian Ordinal, during the short reign of King Edward VI (1547–1553), speculation had already begun with regard to the validity, or otherwise, of Anglican Orders.

> henceforth I'll bear
> Affliction till it do cry out itself
> "Enough, enough," and die. (4.6.75-77)

"Bear free and patient thoughts", counsels Edgar, reminding Gloucester that true freedom is connected to patience, particularly patience
under crosses, patience in the face of adversity and suffering. He who
loses such patience, loses his freedom and becomes a slave to his appetites, a slave to sin.

As Edgar utters these words of perennial wisdom to his father, King
Lear enters "fantastically dressed in wild flowers". It is now that Shakespeare's genius really excels. Lear, the epitome of "madness", emerges as
a figure of Christ, the epitome of sanity. "No, they cannot touch me
for coining", Lear proclaims, "I am the King himself." This is the first
clue to the figurative appearance of Christ, though it becomes more
obvious later. Lear is not a counterfeit king; he is "the King himself",
the True King from whom all other kings derive their authority. Edgar
alludes to the Christ connection immediately by heralding Lear's appearance with the exclamation "O thou side-piercing sight!" a phrase that
encapsulates both the tragedy and the comedy of Lear's "madness". His
flower-clad appearance is side-piercingly comic, yet Edgar's words also
remind us of the piercing of Christ's side after his death on the Cross.
No doubt, to the eyes of the blind, the sight of the "King of the Jews"
wearing a crown of thorns would have been side-piercingly comic. Lear
declares that he is "cut to th' brains", referring to a presumably imag-
inary head wound and also to his "madness". His words remind us of
the crown of thorns piercing the head of Christ. Lear's purgatorially
purified imagination is now fit to receive the stigmata, the very wounds
of Christ, echoing the Franciscan "madness" of Edgar (St. Francis having famously received the stigmata). Immediately afterward we are given
an even clearer indication of the juxtaposition of Lear's suffering with
the suffering of Christ:

> *Lear:* No seconds? all myself?
> Why, this would make a man a man of salt,
> To use his eyes for garden water-pots,
> Ay, and laying autumn's dust.
> *Gentleman:* Good sir—
> *Lear:* I will die bravely, like a smug bridegroom.
>   What!

> I will be jovial: come, come; I am a king;
> Masters, know you that? (4.6.196-203)

The imagery in these few lines is awash with references to the Agony in the Garden. "No seconds? all myself?" alludes to the fact that Christ is left alone in his Agony. Having beseeched his disciples, his "seconds", to stay awake, they had fallen asleep. This weakness on the part of his closest companions "would make a man a man of salt, To use his eyes for garden water-pots". The tears of salt water fall to the ground, watering the Garden. Ultimately Christ's Passion and subsequent Resurrection ("Then there's life in 't'", says Lear at the end of this Passion-coded discourse) would water "autumn's dust", the dust of the Fall. He "will die bravely" on the following day, "like a smug bridegroom". Christ, of course, referred to himself, through his parables, as the Bridegroom, and he is, of course, "a king", though many denied his Kingship and were scandalized by it: "I am a king; Masters, know you that?" The faithful know it; the infidels do not.

Why, one wonders, is Shakespeare so intent on equating Lear with Christ? He is indicating that, having shown contrition and having taken up his own cross, Lear has mystically united himself with the Suffering of Christ. In so doing, Christ's very Presence will be mystically united with the one who takes up his cross and follows him. Lear is one with Christ.

The profundities now come thick and fast. "Nature's above art in that respect", proclaims Lear, an allusion to the popular Renaissance debate concerning the relative importance of nature ("gift", talent, or inspiration) and art (training). In insisting on the primacy of God-given talent and inspiration over artfulness or cunning, Lear is really encapsulating the inherent dynamic of the whole play. On one side are the "sheep" who come to an acceptance of God's grace, and the virtue that is its fruit (Lear, Cordelia, Edgar, Kent, Gloucester, Albany); on the other are the "goats" who refuse God's grace and rely on their own artfulness and cunning (Goneril, Regan, Edmund, Cornwall).

Lear now swaps roles with Edgar, espousing seemingly delirious "reason in madness", or, rather, reason in riddles. In the sense that Edgar was a figurative representation of Lear's Christian conscience, Lear *becomes* Edgar as soon as he becomes one with his conscience. Referring to the words of flattery of Goneril and Regan, he remarks with humility that "they told me I was everything; 'tis a lie, I am not ague-proof." When Gloucester asks to kiss his hand, he responds: "Let me wipe it first; it smells of mortality." Cured of his pride, he denounces the harlotry of his daughters with the same shrill sanity that had characterized Edgar's earlier denunciation of the "fiend":

> Behold yond simp'ring dame,
> Whose face between her forks presages snow,
> That minces virtue and does shake the head
> To hear of pleasure's name.
> The fitchew, nor the soilèd horse, goes to 't
> With a more riotous appetite.
> Down from the waist they are Centaurs,
> Though women all above:
> But to the girdle do the gods inherit,
> Beneath is all the fiend's.
> There's hell, there's darkness, there is the
>   sulphurous pit,
> Burning, scalding, stench, consumption; fie, fie, fie!
>   (4.6.120-31)

Having gained the "madness" of humility, Lear is now ready to be reunited with Cordelia.

"Ripeness is all", Edgar reminds his father, and Lear is now ripe enough in wisdom and virtue to meet the daughter he had wronged and beg forgiveness, just as Gloucester had ripened through suffering to be reconciled with the son he had wronged. Having been reunited with his heart (*coeur de Lear*), the king is now ready to suffer whatever fortune throws at him. Even the prospect of prison is desirable if it means being united with Cordelia.

> Come, let's away to prison:
> We two alone will sing like birds i' th' cage:
> When thou dost ask me blessing, I'll kneel down
> And ask of thee forgiveness: so we'll live,
> And pray, and sing, and tell old tales, and laugh
> At gilded butterflies, and hear poor rogues
> Talk of court news; and we'll talk with them too,
> Who loses and who wins, who's in, who's out;
> And take upon's the mystery of things,
> As if we were God's spies: and we'll wear out,
> In a walled prison, packs and sects of great ones
> That ebb and flow by th' moon. (5.3.8-19)

Lear gets his desire instantly, as Edmund orders them to be taken to prison. His response is one of joy: "Upon such sacrifices, my Cordelia, / The gods themselves throw incense." It is difficult to read these lines of Lear without the ghostly presence of martyred Catholics coming to mind. As we have seen, there is circumstantial evidence to suggest that the young Shakespeare had known the Jesuit martyr Edmund Campion, and even stronger evidence to suggest that he had known Robert Southwell, the Jesuit poet and martyr who had ministered secretly to London's beleaguered Catholics in the early 1590s. The Jesuits were "traitors" in the eyes of Elizabethan and Jacobean law but were "God's spies" in the eyes of England's Catholics. If caught they were imprisoned and tortured before being publicly executed. Since it seems likely that Shakespeare had known Southwell, and since it is even possible that he might have been amongst the large crowd who witnessed Southwell being executed, the words of Lear resonate with potent poignancy: "Upon such sacrifices . . . the gods themselves throw incense." Within this context the repetition of the word "traitor" four times in only eighteen lines by Regan and Cornwall during their inter-rogation of Gloucester has perhaps an added significance. It is also significant perhaps that Edmund declares himself a disciple of the new secular creed of Machiavelli almost immediately after these words of Lear are spoken. "[K]now thou this, that men / Are as the time is", he declares, implicitly deriding the "madness" of Lear's faith-driven words in favor of relativism and self-serving *real-politik*. Lear had himself criticized the Machiavellian worldliness of Edmund and his ilk in his stated desire that he and Cordelia, from the sanity and sanctity of their prison cell, should "laugh at gilded butterflies", those elaborately attired courtiers fluttering over nothing but fads and fashions, "and hear poor rogues talk of court news", in the knowledge that they as "God's spies" will outlast, even in "a walled prison", the "packs and sects of great ones" that "ebb and flow by th' moon". Fashions come and go, Lear seems to be saying, but the Truth remains. He also seems to be implying, through his reference to the moon, that it is Edmund and the play's other "gilded butterflies" and "poor rogues" who are the real lunatics, trading the promise of virtue's eternal reward for life's transient pleasures, trading sanity for the madness of Machiavelli.

Lear's "reason in madness" culminates in the enigma of his last words, uttered over the dead body of Cordelia.

> Do you see this? Look on her. Look, her lips,
> Look there, look there. (5.3.312-13}

His last vision, moments before his death, is that of Cordelia risen from the dead. He dies, therefore, deliriously happy.

Perhaps G. K. Chesterton had *King Lear* in mind when he dubbed Shakespeare "delirious" in comparing him to Chaucer:

> Chaucer was a poet who came at the end of the medieval age and order ... the final fruit and inheritor of that order ... he was much more sane and cheerful and normal than most of the later writers. He was less delirious than Shakespeare, less harsh than Milton, less fanatical than Bunyan, less embittered than Swift.[4]

The fact is that Chaucer could condemn the corruption of his own day through the perspective of a Christian faith that he knew all his compatriots shared. Shakespeare lived at a time of philosophical and theological fragmentation in which the mediaeval age and order had been broken. He could not condemn the corruption of his age through the perspective of the Christian faith that he shared with Chaucer because the faith of Chaucer was now outlawed. Like Cordelia he had little option but to "love, and be silent". Shakespeare's delirium was the delirium of Lear, the delirium of Edgar. It was "reason in madness". Indeed one cannot avoid hearing the delirium of Shakespeare in the words of Edgar as he enunciates the final words of this finest of plays.

> The weight of this sad time we must obey,
> Speak what we feel, not what we ought to say.
> The oldest hath borne most: we that are young
> Shall never see so much, nor live so long. (5.3.325-28)

In Edgar's words we hear a lament for contemporary England, and a lament, perhaps, for Shakespeare's own recently deceased father, who had been persecuted for his Catholic faith. We hear also a lament for the loss of Catholic England and the rise of the modernism of Machiavelli. We hear a swansong for Chaucer's England. Yet there remains hope, a hope that is enshrined in the play's happy ending. "All friends shall taste the wages of their virtue", says Albany, "and all foes the cup

---

[4] G. K. Chesterton, *Chaucer* (London: Faber & Faber, 1932), p. 12.

of their deservings." Justice is done. Edmund, Goneril, Regan, and Cornwall are dead. Cordelia and Lear are also dead, but there is an inkling in Lear's final vision that the lips of Cordelia, and those of Lear himself, are about to "taste the wages of their virtue". And, of course, there is sublime hope in the fact that the kingdom is left in the hands of Edgar, whose baptized Christian conscience had restored Lear to his sanity. It is the meekness of Edgar that inherits the earth, not the Machiavellian madness of Edmund or the more benign secularism of the Fool. As with the climax to all good comedies, all's well that ends well.

It is indeed ironic, and paradoxically perplexing, that this most delirious of Shakespeare's plays is usually considered a tragedy, even though, for those who see with the eyes of Lear, or Edgar, or Cordelia, it has a happy ending. Perhaps the real tragedy is that so many of those who read Shakespeare do not possess the eyes of Lear, Edgar, and Cordelia. In the infernal and purgatorial sufferings of life it is all too easy to lose sight of the promise of Paradise. If we succumb to this self-inflicted, self-centered blindness we will see only a tragedy where we should see a Divine Comedy.

SELECTED BIBLIOGRAPHY

Ackroyd, Peter. *Shakespeare: The Biography.* New York: Nan A. Talese/ Doubleday, 2005.

Alvis, John E., and Thomas G. West, eds. *Shakespeare as Political Thinker.* Wilmington, Del.: ISI Books, 2000.

Asquith, Clare. *Shadowplay: The Hidden Beliefs and Coded Politics of William Shakespeare.* New York: Public Affairs/Perseus Books Group, 2005.

Bernthall, Craig. *The Trial of Man: Christianity and Judgment in the World of Shakespeare.* Wilmington, Del.: ISI Books, 2003.

Bloom, Harold. *Shakespeare: The Invention of the Human.* New York: Riverhead, 1998.

Boaden, James. *On the Sonnets of Shakespeare: Identifying the Person to Whom They Are Addressed; and Elucidating Several Points in the Poet's History.* London: Thomas Rodd, 1837.

Campbell, Oscar James, and Edward G. Quinn, eds. *The Reader's Encyclopedia of Shakespeare.* New York: MJF Books, 1966.

Caraman, Philip, S.J. *Henry Garnet 1555–1606 and the Gunpowder Plot.* London: Longmans, Green, 1964.

Carpenter, Humphrey, ed. *The Letters of J. R. R. Tolkien.* London: George Allen and Unwin, 1981.

Chambers, E. K. *William Shakespeare: A Study of Facts and Problems.* 2 vols. Oxford: Clarendon Press, 1930.

Chesterton, G. K. *Chaucer.* New York: Farrar and Reinhart, 1932. *Chaucer* (1932); republished in *G. K. Chesterton: The Collected Works*, vol. 18, San Francisco: Ignatius Press, 1991.

Clark, Cumberland. *Shakespeare and the Supernatural.* London: Williams and Norgate, 1931.

Connelly, Roland. *The Eighty-Five Martyrs.* Great Wakering, Essex: McCrimmon Publishing, 1987.

——— *No Greater Love: The Martyrs of the Middlesbrough Diocese.* Great Wakering, Essex: McCrimmon Publishing, 1987.

Coursen, Herbert R. *Christian Ritual and the World of Shakespeare's Trag-edies*. Lewisburg, Penn.: Bucknell University Press/Associated University Presses, 1976.

De Groot, John Henry. *The Shakespeares and "The Old Faith"*. Fraser, Mich.: Real-View Books, 1995; originally published in 1946.

Devlin, Christopher. *The Life of Robert Southwell, Poet and Martyr*. New York: Farrar, Straus and Cudahy, 1956.

Donne, John. *Pseudo-Martyr*. Montreal: McGill-Queen's University Press, 1993.

Douglas, Lord Alfred. *The True History of Shakespeare's Sonnets*. Port Washington, N.Y.: Kennikat Press, 1970.

Duffy, Eamon. *The Stripping of the Altars: Traditional Religion in England 1400–1580*. New Haven/London: Yale University Press, 1992.

Elton, Charles I. *William Shakespeare: His Family and Friends*. New York: E.P. Dutton, 1904.

Enos, Carol Curt. *Shakespeare and the Catholic Religion*. Pittsburgh: Dorrance Publishing, 2000.

Fendt, Gene. *Is Hamlet a Religious Drama? An Essay on a Question in Kierkegaard*. Milwaukee: Marquette University Press, 1998.

Fields, Bertram. *Players: The Mysterious Identity of William Shakespeare*. New York: Regan Books/HarperCollins, 2005.

Foley, Henry, S.J. *Records of the English Province of the Society of Jesus*. 7 vols. London: Burns and Oates, 1877.

Fraser, Antonia. *The Gunpowder Plot: Terror and Faith in 1605*. London: Weidenfeld and Nicholson, 1996.

Fripp, Edgar Innes. *Shakespeare: Man and Artist*. London: Oxford University Press, 1938.

Greenblatt, Stephen. *Will in the World: How Shakespeare Became Shakespeare*. New York: W.W. Norton, 2004.

Hadfield, Andrew. *Shakespeare and Renaissance Politics*. London: Arden Shakespeare/Thomson Learning, 2004.

Harley, John. *William Byrd: Gentleman of the Royal Chapel*. Brookfield, Vt.: Ashgate Publishing, 1997.

Holden, Anthony. *William Shakespeare: The Man Behind the Genius*. Boston: Little, Brown, 1999.

Honigmann, E. A. J. *Shakespeare: The "Lost Years"*. Totowa, N.J.: Barnes and Noble Books, 1986.

Kerman, Joseph. *The Masses and Motets of William Byrd*. Berkeley: University of California Press, 1981.

────── *Write All These Down: Essays on Music*. Berkeley: University of California Press, 1994.

Kilroy, Gerard. Aldershot, Hampshire: *Edmund Campion: Memory and Transcription*. Ashgate, 2000.

Lee, Sir Sidney. *A Life of William Shakespeare*. 7th ed. London: Smith, Elder, 1915.

Leithart, Peter J. *Brightest Heaven of Invention: A Christian Guide to Six Shakespeare Plays*. Moscow, Idaho: Canon Press, 1996.

Lewis, B. Roland. *The Shakespeare Documents: Facsimiles, Transliterations, Translations, & Commentary*. Stanford: Stanford University Press, 1940.

Lewis, C. S. *Selected Literary Essays*. Cambridge: Cambridge University Press, 1969.

Longworth, Clara. *Shakespeare Rediscovered*. New York: Charles Scribner's Sons, 1938.

Machiavelli, Niccolò. *The Prince*. Holmes, Penn.: Folio Society, 1970.

Marx, Steven. *Shakespeare and the Bible*. Oxford: Oxford University Press, 2000.

Mathew, David. *Catholicism in England 1535–1935*. London: Catholic Book Club, 1936.

Milward, Peter, S.J. *The Catholicism of Shakespeare's Plays*. Southampton: Saint Austin Press, 1997.

────── *Jacobean Shakespeare*. Naples, Fla.: Sapientia Press, 2007.

────── *The Plays and Exercises: A Hidden Source of Shakespeare's Inspiration?* Tokyo: Renaissance Institute/Sophia University, 2002.

────── *Shakespeare the Papist*. Naples, Fla.: Sapientia Press, 2005.

────── *Shakespeare's Meta-Drama: Hamlet and Macbeth*. Tokyo: Renaissance Institute/Sophia University, 2003.

────── *Shakespeare's Meta-Drama: Othello and King Lear*. Tokyo: Renaissance Institute/Sophia University, 2003.

———— *Shakespeare's Religious Background.* Bloomington: Indiana University Press, 1973.

Morris, John. *The Troubles of Our Catholic Forefathers.* 3 vols. London: Burns and Oates, 1972.

Moser, Fernando de Mello. *Dilecta Britannia: Estudos de Cultura Inglesa.* Lisbon, Portugal: Serviço de Educação e Bolsas/Fundação Calouste Gulbenkian, 2004.

Mutschmann, H., and K. Wentersdorf. *Shakespeare and Catholicism.* New York: Sheed and Ward, 1952.

Nicholl, Charles. *The Reckoning: The Murder of Christopher Marlowe.* London: Vintage/Random House, 2002.

Pesce, Dolores, ed. *Hearing the Motet.* Oxford: Oxford University Press, 1997.

Richmond, Velma Bourgeois. *Shakespeare, Catholicism, and Romance.* New York: Continuum International, 2000.

Riggs, David. *The World of Christopher Marlowe.* London: Faber and Faber, 2005.

Rowse, A. L. *William Shakespeare: A Biography.* New York: Harper and Row, 1963.

Santayana, George. *Interpretations of Poetry and Religion.* New York: Charles Scribner's Sons, 1922.

Schaar, Claes. *Elizabethan Sonnet Themes and the Dating of Shakespeare's Sonnets.* Lund, Sweden: C.W.K. Gleerup/Ejnar Munksgaard, 1962.

Schoenbaum, Samuel. *William Shakespeare: A Documentary Life.* Oxford: Oxford University Press, 1975.

Simpson, Richard. *Edmund Campion: A Biography.* Edinburgh: Williams and Norgate, 1867.

———— *The Religion of Shaksepeare.* London: Burns and Oates, 1899. Reprint, New York: AMS Press, 1974.

Smith, Stephen W., and Travis Curtwright, eds. *Shakespeare's Last Plays: Essays in Literature and Politics.* Lanham, Md.: Lexington Books, 2002.

Sobran, Joseph. *Alias Shakespeare: Solving the Greatest Literary Mystery of All Time.* New York: Free Press, 1997.

Southern, A. C. *Elizabethan Recusant Prose 1559–1582.* London: Sands, 1950.

Stopes, Charlotte. *Shakespeare's Warwickshire Contemporaries*. Stratford: Shakespeare Head, 1908.

Taylor, Dennis, and David N. Beauregard, eds. *Shakespeare and the Culture of Christianity in Early Modern England*. New York: Fordham University Press, 2003.

Turbet, Richard. *William Byrd*. New York: Routledge, 2006.

Walsham, Alexandra. *Church Papists: Catholicism, Conformity and Confessional Polemic in Early Modern England*. Woodbridge, Suffolk: Royal Historical Society/Boydell Press, 1993.

Waugh, Evelyn. *Edmund Campion: Jesuit and Martyr in the Reign of Queen Elizabeth*. London: Longmans, Green/Whitefriars Press, 1935.

Weston, William. *An Autobiography from the Jesuit Underground*. New York: Farrar, Straus and Cudahy, 1955.

Williamson, Hugh Ross. *The Gunpowder Plot*. Long Prairie, Minn.: Neumann Press, 1996.

——— *The Day Shakespeare Died*. London: Michael Joseph, 1962.

Wilson, Ian. *Shakespeare: The Evidence*. New York: St. Martin's Griffin, 1999.

Wilson, Richard. *Secret Shakespeare: Studies in Theatre, Religion, and Resistance*. Manchester: Manchester University Press, 2004.

Wood, Michael. *Shakespeare*. New York: Basic Books/Perseus Books Group, 2003.

INDEX

Ackroyd, Peter, 18–19, 47, 165, 168–70
Acton, John, 61
actors and acting. *See* the stage, under S
Aesop's Fables, 60
Agazzari, Alphonsus, 37
agnosticism or atheism of Shakespeare, allegations of, 18–19, 126, 168–69, 179
Allen, William (actor), 97
Allen, William (Jesuit), 37, 53
All's Well That Ends Well, 22n22, 147
Anglican Church, 183–84, 193
Anne (queen to James I), 120, 149
Annesley, Cordelia, 182
Annesley, Sir Brian, 182
anti-Stratfordians, 24–29
antisecularism of *King Lear*, 183–84
Apocrypha, names of Susanna and Judith Shakespeare drawn from, 84, 88
Apologye (More), 61
apostatizing Catholics, 152, 157–58
Apostolicae Curae, 193n3
Aquaviva, Claude, 59
Aquinas, Thomas, 13, 21, 22
Arcadia (Sidney), 181, 182–83
Arden, Alice (aunt), 43
Arden, Edward, 43–44, 73, 74, 84–86
Arden, Margaret (aunt), 43
Arden, Mary (grandmother), 84–86
Arden, Mary (mother), 42–44, 53–54, 69, 90, 153
Arden, Robert (grandfather), 42
Arden, Simon, 46
Arden family, 42–44, 53–54, 69, 84–87
aristocratic theories of Shakespearean authorship, 25–27
Arnold, Matthew, 17–18
As You Like It, 65, 98
Aspinall, Alexander, 71

Asquith, Clare, 64–65
atheism or agnosticism of Shakespeare, allegations of, 18–19, 126, 168–69, 179
Aubrey, John, 67, 133
Auden, W. H., 132
Audley, John, 51
authorialist approach to literary criticism, 9–10, 17–18, 174–80
authorship of Shakespeare's plays, theories regarding, 24–29
Ave Verum Corpus (Byrd), 122

Babington Plot, 94–96
Bacon, Francis, 24–26, 29, 109
Bacon, Mathias, 159
Baconians, 24–26, 29
Badger, George, 49, 151, 166
Ballard, John, 159
Bannister, Mary, 159
baptism
   of Edmund Shakespeare (brother), 79–80
   of Hamnet and Judith Shakespeare (son and daughter), 47, 88
   of Marlowe, 99
   of Shakespeare, 55–57
   of Susanna Shakespeare (daughter), 83–84
Bearman, Robert, 77
Becket, Thomas, 34
Beeston, Christopher, 67, 71, 97, 133
Beeston, William, 67, 133, 135
Belloc, Hilaire, 20
Bernthal, Craig, 132–33
Betterton, Thomas, 91–92
birth of Shakespeare, 13, 55–57
Blackfriars Gatehouse, 158–63, 165, 167
Blackwell, Mary Campion, 158–59
Blackwell, William, 158